CATALOG COPY That *SIZZLES*

CATALOG
COPY
That *SIZZLES*

All the Hints, Tips, and Tricks of the Trade
You'll Ever Need to Write Copy That Sells

Herschell Gordon Lewis

NTC Business Books
NTC/Contemporary Publishing Group

Library of Congress Cataloging-in-Publication Data

Lewis, Herschell Gordon, 1926–
    Catalog copy that sizzles : all the hints, tips, and tricks of the
trade you'll ever need to write copy that sells / Herschell Gordon
Lewis.
        p.   cm. — (—Sizzles)
     ISBN 0-8442-2447-2
    1. Commercial catalogs.   I. Title.   II. Series.
HF5862.L49   1999
659.13'3—dc21
                                     99-26318
                                       CIP

Some of the material in this book was previously published in *How to Write
Powerful Catalog Copy.*

Cover design by Scott Rattray
Cover and interior illustration copyright © Barton Stabler/Artville, LLC.
Interior design by City Desktop Productions, Inc.

Published by NTC Business Books
A division of NTC/Contemporary Publishing Group, Inc.
4255 West Touhy Avenue, Lincolnwood (Chicago), Illinois 60712-1975 U.S.A.
Printed in the United States of America
International Standard Book Number: 0-8442-2447-2

99 00 01 02 03 04 05 HP 19 18 17 16 15 14 13 12 11 10 9 8 7 6 5 4 3 2 1

Contents

Preface

We all have heard these standard boilerplate comments about what we do:

- "A copywriter is a copywriter, right?"
- "Rules for catalog copywriting don't differ from rules for space ads or mail-order packages, do they? I mean, if you can write one you can write another, can't you?"
- "Changing copy for a catalog on the World Wide Web isn't necessary. It's the same merchandise and it's the same bunch of customers."
- "A catalog copywriter who can write about plastic pipe should be able to write about women's fashions, don't you think?"

One of those statements is true: the last one.

It's true because catalog copywriting is a combination of a special discipline (one I wish all copywriters had) and the ability to jump from one item to another without having to re-dress for radical surgery.

Somebody is leafing through your catalog. Here's a picture. It grabs attention.

Now what?

The page-flipper has become a live prospect. It's your turn. The cosmic moment—whether the metamorphosis becomes complete, page-flipper to live prospect to actual buyer—is in your hands . . . or rather, at your fingertips because those fingertips are on the keyboard.

Are those fingertips trained salespeople or dull salesclerks? Do they just describe or do they start the salivary glands churning? Effective copywriting isn't an accident.

Somebody has landed on your website. Your home page makes a promise and has logical links to other pages.

Now what?

The surfer or casual visitor has become a live prospect. It's your turn. The cosmic moment—whether the metamorphosis becomes complete, surfer to live prospect to actual buyer—is in your hands . . . or rather, at your fingertips because those fingertips are on the keyboard. And your visitor's fingertips are on the mouse, ready to click. Click in? Or click out?

Are the words from your fingertips powerful enough to control the fingertips of your visitor? Effective copywriting isn't an accident.

In fact, the decision as to what kind of copy you're writing is not only deliberate, it's cosmic. In this book I identify fourteen kinds of catalog copywriting. Your choice has a profound effect on response, and response is, after all, the ultimate way to keep score.

If you think fourteen represents a lot of stylistic differences, consider: these are the major kinds. A complete list might be twice as long . . . or endless.

We're in the twenty-first century. The old Sears & Roebuck catalog, as huge a fountainhead as it was, is history . . . ancient history, at that. In this century, with specialization followed by *hyper*specialization redefining both our craft and our target readers, the professional copywriter who moves from job to job may have to relearn the copy approach with each new job. Already, high-fashion copy, copy aimed at young people, computer and electronics copy, and many areas of business-to-business copy use a jargon all their own. The Internet has supplied an astounding pile of terms that say to outsiders, "You're an outsider."

In this madhouse, we need some beacons shining into the murk, guiding copy into a response-pulling haven.

I'm counting on this book being one of those beacons. That's because the new rules of catalog writing, superimposed on timeless rules, transcend any aberration of style. A professional catalog copywriter *can* write for *The Sharper Image* one month, *Bloomingdale's* the next, *Warehouse.com* the next, and *Marcus Dental International* the next.

That writer may need a list of terms. But what that writer doesn't need is a new persuasion-in-print education.

Why not? Because with the information in these pages, glued tightly to a professional attitude, that writer can switch gears as easily as trading in one automobile for another.

This book has twenty-four chapters, a conclusion, and two appendices. If you're seriously involved in catalog copywriting, here's a suggestion: for the next month read a chapter a day, twice. For the extra days, reread the chapters you think affect you the most.

Will you write better copy? I *think* so. But even if you don't, I can guarantee you a few laughs as you see what some of the others—even the giants—are doing wrong!

Herschell Gordon Lewis
Fort Lauderdale, Florida

Acknowledgments

Inveterate collectors of books about catalog copywriting will recognize some of this text as the natural descendant of a previous book, *How to Write Powerful Catalog Copy*.

Much of the content of that book, and this one, stems from my copy columns in the distinguished publication *Catalog Age*. Laura Beaudry, Editorial Director, and Sherry Chiger, Managing Editor, have made it possible for me to pretest concepts against a tough and demanding readership. What a marvelous catalytic action the magazine provides: speculation either dissolves or turns into fact!

I'm deeply indebted to Danielle Egan-Miller, the astute and perceptive senior editor at NTC/Contemporary Books, for recognizing two evolutionary procedures: (1) The catalog recipient of the twenty-first century is more sophisticated, impatient, and selective than his or her counterpart of the 1990s. (2) The Internet has added a competitive subdivision to the creative mix.

Heidi Bresnahan, my project editor, and Deborah Roberts, my copyeditor, actually made sense out of the manuscript . . . how, I'll never know.

Some of the wonderful folks with whom I've worked on catalog copy have added immeasurably not only to my knowledge of the craft but to my ongoing struggle (one every copywriter faces) to stay abreast of worthy trends and stay away from unworthy trends. I'm especially grateful to Tom Cross, the genial genius who guides the marketing destiny of Office Depot; Christina Brodie, his brilliant right arm; and Paul Gaffney, who formerly supervised the Office Depot catalog; and Greg Sweeney, who currently does; to Shari Altman of Sara Lee Direct, who can spot a trite idea at one hundred paces; to Lucinda Heekin, who heads the delightful catalog, *The Last Best Place*, for guiding copy into the best place; and to Denise Bovo of Barnes & Noble, maestra of the art of combining high literacy with irresistible rhetoric.

It will be no surprise to those who know how I live and work to know who has been my right arm in the preparation of this manuscript: my wife and business partner, Margo, who not only compiled most of the exhibits but whose knowledge of catalog salesmanship far surpasses mine (and that of anyone else I know). Her mark is on every line of every page, and her unerring eye is responsible for many of the principles codified here.

Thank you all. And especially you.

CATALOG
COPY
That *SIZZLES*

1

What Kind of Copy? We Have Lots of Choices.

Change Our Image? To What?

"Let's change the image of our catalog."

In a meeting . . . over lunch . . . at a board of directors session . . . by edict or memo . . . this declaration generates the reaction "To what?"

The other guy's catalog is always greener. You've been writing straightforward product descriptions. One competitor has been writing chest-thumping copy. Another has been writing "Down Home" copy. Each envies what the others are doing. The versatile writer has to be ready to switch gears.

The Fourteen Kinds of Catalog Copy

I suppose if we were to divide and subdivide and pick hairs and nits, we could come up with fifty types of catalog copy. But in broad categories, we can isolate fourteen varieties:

1. Jes' Folks
2. Down Home
3. You-You-You
4. Shout
5. Quietly Upscale Descriptive
6. Image All the Way
7. Touchstone
8. Narrative
9. Minimalist
10. All the Facts
11. Informational/Educational
12. Snob Appeal
13. I Am the Greatest
14. Plain Vanilla

We might recognize subcategories such as "Good Guy," "Golly, Gee Whiz!" "More Than You Want to Know," and "Internet Bulk," but I figure we have to end the list somewhere.

(Note: samples of each category accompany each description. For this chapter only, figure numbers correspond to category numbers. For example, Figure 1.9 is an example of number 9, "Minimalist.")

1. JES' FOLKS

"Jes' Folks" copy is easy to read. Most copy blocks are first person—"I" or "we." You'll seldom see an uncontracted expression where a contraction is possible, so it's always "I'm," not "I am"; "We're," not "We are"; "didn't," not "did not."

(In my opinion, this approach makes sense for thirteen of the fourteen categories, with the exception being some versions of number 12, "Snob Appeal.")

"Jes' Folks" is the first cousin of the second category, "Down Home," but the difference is clear to both writer and reader.

A "Jes' Folks" description might begin this way:

I went all the way down to Matamoros to sample this Tex-Mex salsa, and danged if it isn't hotter than an El Paso afternoon. We don't call it "Hell-Fire Sauce" for nothin', and if it don't give your taste buds a pretty strong bite, you got us beat before we start.

Some "Jes' Folks" writers would use "ain't" instead of "isn't"—a dangerous game. Maintaining a P.O.C.B. (plain ol' country boy) pace is tough enough without entrapping yourself in jargon.

The benefit of "Jes' Folks" copy: it's highly readable and entertaining.

The drawback of "Jes' Folks" copy: after a couple of pages it gets cloying and too cute to generate solid buyer response. The reader remains reader, not buyer.

2. Down Home

"Down Home" borrows the personalized "I" approach from "Jes' Folks," but it limits itself to conviviality, never lapsing into hay-chawin' folksiness.

The writer tries to draw the reader into a "you and I are a family" attitude—not possible with "Jes' Folks" copy except on the very lowest economic levels (with the very lowest buying power).

The "Down Home" writer would attack the salsa copy block this way:

My aunt Maria vacationed in Mexico and was so excited she phoned me. "I've found the hottest 'Tex-Mex' salsa I've ever tasted," she said. "It's wonderful. I bought a case, and I think you ought to have it in the catalog." Aunt Maria isn't often wrong, so we made an exclusive arrangement with the small Mexican company that makes "Hell-Fire Sauce." If you're brave . . . or if you love *real* Mexican sauce . . . you have to get some.

"Down Home" can include straight talk without seeming preachy. But when the copy lapses into "You'd better . . ." or "You really should . . ." it can alienate readers—without their quite knowing why they're alienated.

The benefit of "Down Home" copy: readers feel the copy is aimed at them, which means benefit *has* to be present.

The drawback of "Down Home" copy: after a few pages, it seems forced. How many relatives, how many trips, how many problems-to-be-solved does this cataloger have, anyway? The writer can be trapped in the device.

3. You-You-You

Advertising writing classes in schools of journalism teach a safe dogma: you the writer can't go wrong by emphasizing *you* the reader.

In catalogs, this sometimes works and sometimes doesn't, because a catalog, even in a Web incarnation, parallels a solo mailing in only one respect: it's part of the direct-marketing family. *You*, revisited hundreds of times in a thirty-two-page or sixty-four-page catalog, becomes wearisome and repetitive.

The "You-You-You" writer would describe the salsa this way:

You think you've tasted hot-pepper salsa? Oh, no, you haven't. That is, you haven't tasted the *real* salsa until you've dipped a spoon into our "Hell-Fire" Sauce and sprinkled a little on your salad. Your tongue will tell you: you never knew a hot sauce could be this good.

In that single paragraph we have the word *you* nine times. Reader involving? You bet. Too heavy a pace for a whole catalog? You bet. And in those two sentences we have the core of benefit and drawback.

The benefit of "You-You-You" copy: readers *can't* feel left out. Copy is aimed like a blunderbuss straight at them.

The drawback of "You-You-You" copy: reader interest buckles under the fatigue caused by artificially heavy involvement.

4. Shout

"Shout" is the easiest of all copy to write. In a great many instances it's the strongest-pulling copy because the shout usually centers around one image: "Bargain!"

A key rule, the Yell-Out-Bargain Rule:

> ✏ When you're shouting "Bargain!" play up price. The very act of shouting implies a price lower than competitors charge, even when it may not be true.

Lots of exclamation points, please! Who ever heard of a quiet shout? But except for the schlockiest copy, don't use more than one exclamation point after any one exclamation.

The writer charged with the responsibility of writing "Shout" copy for the salsa would grind out something like this:

A Hell-Fire Deal on Hell-Fire Salsa!
14-Oz. Bottle $2.49!

- Enjoy the hottest of the hot!
- Make a real Tex-Mex dinner—for pennies!
- Concentrated—a little goes a long way!
- Never before at this low, low price!

You can see the emphasis: it isn't on product; it's on bargain. (Don't mistake me. "Shout" copy can't abandon its responsibility for telling the reader exactly what's for sale. What changes is emphasis, not the informational core.)

The benefit of "Shout" copy: it's an irresistible attention-getter.

The drawback of "Shout" copy: anyone who shouts continuously begins to generate a negative reaction, based on the conclusion that the shouting is a technique unrelated to whether the product justifies shouting or not.

5. Quietly Upscale Descriptive

"Quietly Upscale Descriptive" copy was more popular during the 1980s than it is now, probably because the "yuppies," its principal and most logical targets, are past their status-seeking phase. Many "Generation-X" catalog shoppers, especially online buyers, regard recognizable upscale copy as suspect.

Still, clever catalogers looking for a marketing niche can settle into this posture with some confidence because often the target who responds to "Quietly Upscale Descriptive" won't buy from any other source.

"Quietly Upscale Descriptive" copy usually has a long headline, so the salsa copy might look like this:

For your next party, this unusually hot sauce with the unusually hot name can be the evening's hottest topic of conversation.

"Hell-Fire" isn't for everybody. In fact, we don't recommend its daily use because it makes every other sauce seem so tame. . . .

The writer has to keep the leash on "Quietly Upscale Descriptive" at just the right amount of tension. That's why this approach requires the professional laying on of hands.

The benefit of "Quietly Upscale Descriptive" copy: copy technique itself suggests the advantage of buying and owning what's being described and can sell when yells and screams can't.

The drawback of "Quietly Upscale Descriptive" copy: in an era of price-emphasized online catalogs, the approach is subcompetitive for a large cadre of prospective customers.

6. IMAGE ALL THE WAY

"Image All the Way" differs from "Quietly Upscale Descriptive" in its less-subtle approach to exclusivity. Like its first cousin, "Touchstone" copy, "Image All the Way" depends on a tie to a known and accepted comparative base.

"Image All the Way" copy for the salsa might read this way:

If J. P. Morgan and John D. Rockefeller came to your home, they'd know whether to stay for the authentic Mexican dinner you've prepared. "Hell-Fire" on the table means genuine Tex-Mex on the palate.

"Image All the Way" usually has longer sentences than other types of catalog copy. It doesn't use bullets because excitement and image aren't in the same corner.

The benefit of "Image All the Way" copy: the approach adds cachet to items that either are difficult to describe or don't exemplify a recognizable difference or improvement.

The drawback of "Image All the Way" copy: exposition, necessarily lengthier than typical catalog copy, can lose the reader before making its point.

7. TOUCHSTONE

"Touchstone" copy ties whatever we're selling to a known base. "Touchstone" theory is logical: the reader accepts the touchstone . . . and automatically accepts whatever is tied to the touchstone.

"Touchstone" salsa copy might read like this:

If you had been in the Alamo, you'd have had the opportunity to sample real Tex-Mex food. You weren't there, but the secret of good, hot Tex-Mex salsa is back . . . with Hell-Fire.

The benefit of "Touchstone" copy: it's adaptable. You can intermix "Touchstone" copy with any other type and not destroy the coherent tone of the catalog.

The drawback of "Touchstone" copy: it isn't easy to write and it isn't always pertinent.

8. NARRATIVE

"Narrative" copy tells a story. Depending on the narrator's storytelling expertise the reader is intrigued or turned off. So an effective "Narrative" catalog copywriter has to be a good yarn-spinner. Ability to add a little malarkey to the mixture doesn't hurt, but inserting fiction doesn't work in today's "the reader knows more than we do" marketplace.

"Narrative" copy for the salsa would read something like this:

In 1912 the Mexican bandit and folk hero Pancho Villa escaped to the United States. After his triumphant return in 1913 he formed the famous *División del Norte*. One of the prizes he brought across the border was a recipe for a salsa unlike any tasted before: "Hell-Fire." When Villa became governor of the state of Chihuahua, he served this unique hot sauce to special guests at his dinner table. Now you can serve it to your special guests.

Writing *workmanlike* "Narrative" isn't as exacting a task as writing "Touchstone"; a competent writer with a competent set of reference books or notes from the company's buyer can do a competent job. But writing a catalog filled with engaging narratives requires more showmanship than most journeyman writers can bring to the arena.

The benefit of "Narrative" copy: it holds the reader and generates a buying impulse without pitching.

The drawback of "Narrative" copy: unless relevance of the episode is obvious to the reader, it can seem forced and even stupid.

9. Minimalist

"Minimalist" is the standard for many digest-size catalogs that have eight or ten items on a page. Description is bare-bones.

"Minimalist" copy for the salsa:

Famous "Hell-Fire" Salsa—the very hottest. 14-oz. bottle, $2.49

Photographs accompanying "Minimalist" copy, like the words themselves, have to be no-nonsense.

The benefit of "Minimalist" copy: it's fast and easy to write.

The drawback of "Minimalist" copy: romance has to give way to raw fact.

10. All the Facts

"All the Facts" copy regurgitates any and every scrap of information about the product. The two assumptions: (1) The more the reader knows, the more likely the reader is to buy. (2) The more you tell, the more the reader believes you.

These assumptions become truer in business-to-business catalogs than in consumer catalogs because the business buyer may have to justify the purchase to someone else—and we don't know who that someone else might be or what minor fact might trigger approval.

In defense of "All the Facts" copy in consumer catalogs: some of our customers are catalog "readers" who respond to heavy copy. An example of "All the Facts" copy about salsa:

"Hell-Fire" Salsa—Bottled in limited quantities in Matamoros, this authentic Tex-Mex salsa combines red peppers, jalapeños, green chili peppers, peeled and chopped beefsteak tomatoes, scallions, and a touch of cilantro. Our peppers are transplanted from their original site in French Guiana to a private orchard outside Matamoros, where parallel climate ripens them to produce the hot capsicum extract. Our master chef Pablo grinds the peppers to a fine powder, soaks them in brine to "loosen" the flavor, then marries them to the tomatoes in our special sharp vinegar. . . .

Obviously "All the Facts" demands space. If we were actually selling a $2.49 salsa, it's unlikely a lengthy description would justify a heavy dedication of space.

The benefit of "All the Facts" copy: the copywriter can unlimber heavy artillery, assuming the reader's hot button is in there somewhere.

The drawback of "All the Facts" copy: it eats up a lot of space that might have been used to showcase additional products.

11. INFORMATIONAL/EDUCATIONAL

"Informational/Educational" copy is a specialty. To maintain its integrity, this type of copy dares not lapse into hard sell. The writer has to pick and choose logical subject matter. Probably salsa couldn't qualify for this treatment, but if it did the copy might read:

Cilantro is the fresh leaf of the coriander plant. This delicate fragrant-pungent leaf is one of the oldest spices known to man. When the Romans used finely chopped cilantro to season their bread, the spice already had been known for thousands of years. Each 14-oz. bottle of Hell-Fire Salsa includes both cilantro and. . . .

You can see the value of "Informational/Educational" copy for computer software, garden supplies, electronics, and chemicals. Properly written, this approach will attract readers who don't respond to exhortation—but it can repel readers who do.

The benefit of "Informational/Educational" copy: it appears to be non-selling, while emphasizing comparative advantages.

The drawback of "Informational/Educational" copy: even the slightest lapse into pedantry or preachiness can be a turnoff.

12. SNOB APPEAL

"Snob Appeal" is making a comeback. From about 1975 to the mid-1990s, only a few catalogs dared risk the accusation of outright snobbery. But now, as *need for approval* rejoins the other four great motivators (fear, exclusivity, guilt, and greed), snobbery is in.

The problem with "Snob Appeal" isn't writing the copy itself—although I certainly wouldn't turn loose a beginner on this copy. Rather, it's the need for an exquisite matchup of copy, layout, and illustration. If any of the three falter, the effect is one of stupidity rather than status.

"Snob Appeal" copy for the salsa might be:

Only 1,200 bottles . . . ever, this entire year. Our exclusive "Hell-Fire" salsa is made from such rare herbs, under such rigidly controlled conditions, that only 1,200 bottles will be available this year. We must limit any purchase to two bottles (subject to availability, of course). Each numbered bottle carries the Seal of Elegance. Handsomely gift boxed for your favorite gourmet who cannot obtain this elsewhere. Fourteen ounces, twenty-nine dollars.

Much "Snob Appeal" copy spells out the price. That's why, to the would-be snob, "twenty-nine dollars" has greater verisimilitude than the more pedestrian $28.95. You say the price should be just $2.49? Forget it.

The benefit of "Snob Appeal" copy: professionally executed, it becomes a positioning statement that justifies price, delay, or even substitution.

The drawback of "Snob Appeal" copy: it has to be used in small doses or it becomes apparent as an artifice.

13. I Am the Greatest

A supercilious approach will attract some of the status-seeking buyers who want reassurance.

Unlike "Snob Appeal," "I Am the Greatest" makes a flat statement of superiority. The believing reader buys; the nonbeliever doesn't buy. Gradually the catalog builds a house list of customers for whom the flat statement of superiority becomes a reason to buy. (Once disillusioned, the customer is gone forever.)

"I Am the Greatest" copy for the salsa:

THE BEST SALSA. In comparison tests, our Kitchen Board rated this salsa superior in consistency, palatability, and flavoring. Unlike other sauces tested, Hell-Fire contains genuine tomatoes and fresh spices, producing a greater degree of effectiveness when applied to both tortillas and salads. $2.49, unconditionally guaranteed.

The hedging in "I Am the Greatest" copy turns me off because of the inevitable weaseling—"superior" to what? "Unlike other sauces *tested*"? Which sauces, better than Hell-Fire, didn't you include in your tests?

Still, no one can argue with the ability of "I Am the Greatest" to sell merchandise. Even recognizing the weasel, I've bought from such catalogs.

The benefit of "I Am the Greatest" copy: statements are absolute, so the point can't be missed.

The drawback of "I Am the Greatest" copy: as is true of all editorials, it can raise the hackles of a reader who doesn't respond to a prefabricated opinion posted atop a catalog description.

14. PLAIN VANILLA

An experienced copywriter with lexical imagination is overtrained for "Plain Vanilla" copy.

Actually, "Plain Vanilla"—copy unadorned with hyperbole or puffery—is a pleasant relief after wading through the thick, adjective-rich rhetoric we see in so much contemporary catalog copy. "Plain Vanilla" copy for the salsa rids itself of all but distilled essence:

"Hell-Fire" Hot Salsa—14-oz. bottle. Ingredients: red peppers, jalapeños, green chili peppers, beefsteak tomatoes, scallions, cilantro. $2.49.

If yours is a catalog of exotica—and "Hell-Fire Salsa" would qualify—"Plain Vanilla" copy is too bland to do a competitive selling job. "Plain Vanilla" is the floor under all catalog copy; its primary value is in multi-product catalogs of household staples.

We don't see much "Plain Vanilla" copy anymore. The closest in everyday use is what we might call "Vanilla Ripple"—a touch of sell mixed into the plain description, with an occasional exclamation point added as a rhetorical moisturizer to prevent dryness.

The benefit of "Plain Vanilla" copy: it doesn't glorify one item at the expense of others and is complete when facts are presented, which means the writer doesn't need Meistersinger credentials.

The drawback of "Plain Vanilla" copy: against professional salesmanship, it gets second prize.

Making the Choice

Can you combine copy types within the same catalog?

My answer is an unequivocal *yes*. But consider this suggestion: to intermix a copy approach that differs from the rest of the catalog, set up a section—four or eight pages. It's like a special boutique (or even bargain basement) within a department store. Border the pages differently. Tell the reader this is a special section; don't cause confusion by forcing the reader to wonder whether the printer has bound some wrong pages into the good old catalog.

If your sales have reached a plateau . . . if your universe seems to be shrinking . . . if you have to pass up items because they don't match your "image" . . . then consider a section of "different" copy. You just might attract a whole new cadre of buyers.

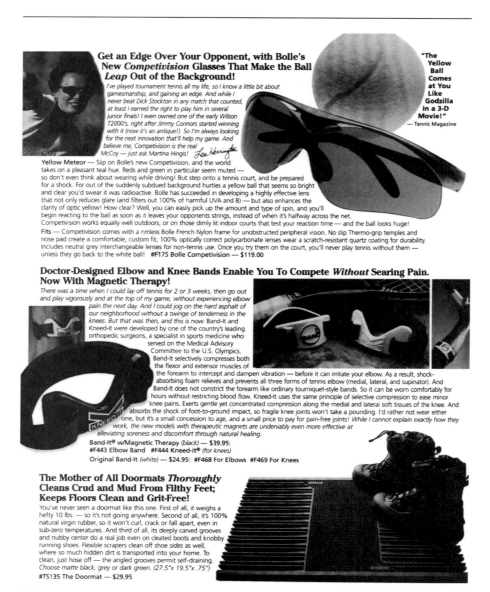

Get an Edge Over Your Opponent, with Bolle's New *Competivision* Glasses That Make the Ball *Leap* Out of the Background!

I've played tournament tennis all my life, so I know a little bit about gamesmanship, and gaining an edge. And while I never beat Dick Stockton in any match that counted, at least I earned the right to play him in several junior finals! I even owned one of the early Wilson T2000's, right after Jimmy Connors started winning with it (now it's an antique!). So I'm always looking for the next innovation that'll help my game. And believe me, Competivision is the real McCoy — just ask Martina Hingis!   *Lee Herrington*

"The Yellow Ball Comes at You Like Godzilla in a 3-D Movie!"
— Tennis Magazine

Yellow Meteor — Slip on Bolle's new Competivision, and the world takes on a pleasant teal hue. Reds and green in particular seem muted — so don't even think about wearing while driving! But step onto a tennis court, and be prepared for a shock. For out of the suddenly subdued background hurtles a yellow ball that seems so bright and clear you'd swear it was radioactive. Bolle has succeeded in developing a highly effective lens that not only reduces glare (and filters out 100% of harmful UVA and B) — but also enhances the clarity of optic yellow! How clear? Well, you can easily pick up the amount and type of spin, and you'll begin reacting to the ball as soon as it leaves your opponents strings, instead of when it's halfway across the net. Competivision works equally well outdoors, or on those dimly lit indoor courts that test your reaction time — and the ball looks huge!

Fits — Competivision comes with a rimless Bolle French Nylon frame for unobstructed peripheral vision. No slip Thermo-grip temples and nose pad create a comfortable, custom fit; 100% optically correct polycarbonate lenses wear a scratch-resistant quartz coating for durability. Includes neutral grey interchangeable lenses for non-tennis use. Once you try them on the court, you'll never play tennis without them — unless they go back to the white ball!   **#F175 Bolle Competivision** — $119.00

Doctor-Designed Elbow and Knee Bands Enable You To Compete *Without* Searing Pain. Now With Magnetic Therapy!

There was a time when I could lay off tennis for 2 or 3 weeks, then go out and play vigorously and at the top of my game, without experiencing elbow pain the next day. And I could jog on the hard asphalt of our neighborhood without a twinge of tenderness in the knees. But that was then, and this is now. Band-It and Kneed-It were developed by one of the country's leading orthopedic surgeons, a specialist in sports medicine who served on the Medical Advisory Committee to the U.S. Olympics. Band-It selectively compresses both the flexor and extensor muscles of the forearm to intercept and dampen vibration — before it can irritate your elbow. As a result, shock-absorbing foam relieves and prevents all three forms of tennis elbow (medial, lateral, and supinator). And Band-It does not constrict the forearm like ordinary tourniquet-style bands. So it can be worn comfortably for hours without restricting blood flow. Kneed-It uses the same principle of selective compression to ease minor knee pains. Exerts gentle yet concentrated compression along the medial and lateral soft tissues of the knee. And absorbs the shock of foot-to-ground impact, so fragile knee joints won't take a pounding. I'd rather not wear either one, but it's a small concession to age, and a small price to pay for pain-free joints! *While I cannot explain exactly how they work, the new models with therapeutic magnets are undeniably even more effective at alleviating soreness and discomfort through natural healing.*

Band-It® w/Magnetic Therapy *(black)* — $39.95:
#F443 Elbow Band   #F444 Kneed-it® *(for knees)*
Original Band-It *(white)* — $24.95: **#F468 For Elbows #F469 For Knees**

The Mother of All Doormats *Thoroughly* Cleans Crud and Mud From Filthy Feet; Keeps Floors Clean and Grit-Free!

You've never seen a doormat like this one. First of all, it weighs a hefty 10 lbs. — so it's not going anywhere. Second of all, it's 100% natural virgin rubber, so it won't curl, crack or fall apart, even in sub-zero temperatures. And third of all, its deeply carved grooves and nubby center do a real job even on cleated boots and knobby running shoes. Flexible scrapers clean off shoe *sides* as well, where so much hidden dirt is transported into your home. To clean, just hose off — the angled grooves permit self-draining. *Choose matte black, grey or dark green. (27.5"x 19.5"x .75")*
#TS135 The Doormat — $29.95

Fig. 1.1:   On this page of a well-known and well-written catalog are three examples of "Jes' Folks" copy. The ability to involve the reader with the writer *as an individual* isn't as common a talent as some who falter with this method believe. Nor is "Jes' Folks" limited to down-on-the-farm rhetoric, which may not sell as powerfully as this copy does. Note the personal touches in each copy block.

Contractor's Clipboard

Take your office with you—jobsite, truck, restaurant or "on the road."

I learned about this product when my plumber made an emergency call to fix the furnace and whipped out his aluminum clipboard, wrote me an invoice for his enormous hourly rate, doubled it because it was in the evening, and got paid a good day's wages for about twenty minutes work. The Contractor's Clipboard made the billing and collection part of his business professional and efficient. I figured if my plumber could use it, so could I. Now I keep all the daily homebuilder's business inside and use the clipboard as my writing surface. Store notebooks, forms, documents, pens, etc. in the 1 1/2" deep case. The 6" clip holds sheets or pads and it even has an auxiliary clip to keep papers from flapping in the wind. 9" x 14".

#99918 $24.99

Separate
section for
pens and
pencils

NEW

Holds forms up
to 8 1/2" by 12"

Fig. 1.2:   "Down Home" copy is a close relative to "Jes' Folks" copy. The difference here is in the recounting of an episode in which the writer shares an unexpected experience.

Fig. 1.3: Variations of "you" and imperatives implying "you" occur at least nine times in the "Learn to speak a foreign language" heading and text. That certainly qualifies as "You-You-You."

Fig. 1.4: "Shout" copy emphasizes bargain pricing. Neatness can actually damage the effectiveness of "Shout" copy. This computer catalog screams "New!" and price. Reverses and exclamation points are generic to "Shout" copy.

Fig. 1.5: For "Quietly Upscale Descriptive" copy to achieve the proper image, illustration has to match. Outlining the watches and never using boldface body copy keeps the presentation coherent. "Quietly Upscale Descriptive" matches a specific reader demographic. The bargain buyer would be puzzled by "make an impression without saying a word." (Is the lowercase *m* in "make" an overdone pomposity?)

The Tradition of Springerle

The origins of detailed hand-carved springerle plaques (pronounced schprin-girl-eh), are lost in Central European history (the first known printed recipe for the dough was in 1688). The plaques, onto which the anise-flavored dough is pressed, took on the same fine detail as illustrations for books, which were also carved on wood. These scenes were taken from mythology, the Bible, folklore, and ancient ornamental patterns. As the illustrated cookies became more elaborate, they became Christmas gifts to favored guests of nobility. Plaques being produced now are less elaborate with mostly seasonal subject matter. Our source, Caroline Kallas, is a scholar and baker who has produced a series of American-made replicas as well as importing plaques. This contemporary selection of high quality plaques is a find for bakers around the world.

Springerle Holiday Plaques

This selection of charming Swiss-made plaques features figures from popular winter holiday tradition. Their style is true to their Central European tradition. You can display these resin replicas of hand-carved plaques as pieces of art when you're not baking springerle. A recipe comes with each plaque.

Angel, 2½" x 2"	#11131	$24.95
Snowman, 3½" diameter	#11132	34.95
Santa Claus, 5" x 3"	#11134	39.95
Mixed Motifs, 6¼" x 5½"	#11135	79.95
Angel with Lute, 9¾" x 4¾"	#11133	79.95

Fig. 1.6: "Image All the Way" emphasizes history and source at least as much as whatever the catalog is selling. Image eats up space, which explains why some catalogers who might want to use the approach feel the laws of economics make it impossible for them. Note the *assumption* that the reader will appreciate what is being made available here.

⑤ FRANK LLOYD WRIGHT*
GARDEN "SPRITE" SCULPTURE
Inspired by decorative sculptures he saw in
Berlin's outdoor concert gardens, Frank
Lloyd Wright collaborated with sculptor
Alfonso Iannelli to create a series of "Sprites'
for Midway* Gardens (1913–14), an
entertainment complex on Chicago's south
side. The Gardens were demolished in 1929;
this lissome reproduction is a testament to
how glorious they must have been. Handcast
in cement, our regal "Sprite" stands 31" tall
and weighs 35 pounds. On her own, she's
impressive; on her matching 11" pedestal
(also 35 pounds), she's spectacular indoors or
out. *Allow 4–6 weeks for delivery. Sorry, no
Rush delivery, Express delivery, or gift box
available.* ($20 shipping per piece.)
Sprite • 61796...$129.00
Pedestal • 61803...$79.00

Fig. 1.7:   Note the multiplicity of touchstones—Berlin's concert gardens . . . Frank Lloyd Wright . . . Alfonso Iannelli.
Could this cast-cement sculpture command its price without those provenances?

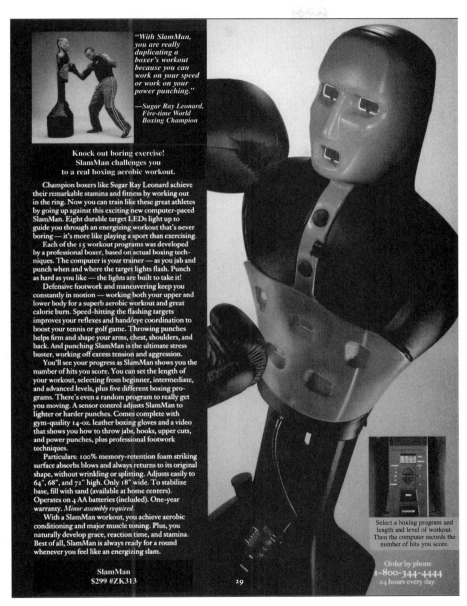

"With SlamMan, you are really duplicating a boxer's workout because you can work on your speed or work on your power punching."

—Sugar Ray Leonard, Five-time World Boxing Champion

Knock out boring exercise!
SlamMan challenges you
to a real boxing aerobic workout.

Champion boxers like Sugar Ray Leonard achieve their remarkable stamina and fitness by working out in the ring. Now you can train like these great athletes by going up against this exciting new computer-paced SlamMan. Eight durable target LEDs light up to guide you through an energizing workout that's never boring — it's more like playing a sport than exercising.

Each of the 15 workout programs was developed by a professional boxer, based on actual boxing techniques. The computer is your trainer — as you jab and punch when and where the target lights flash. Punch as hard as you like — the lights are built to take it!

Defensive footwork and maneuvering keep you constantly in motion — working both your upper and lower body for a superb aerobic workout and great calorie burn. Speed-hitting the flashing targets improves your reflexes and hand/eye coordination to boost your tennis or golf game. Throwing punches helps firm and shape your arms, chest, shoulders, and back. And punching SlamMan is the ultimate stress buster, working off excess tension and aggression.

You'll see your progress as SlamMan shows you the number of hits you score. You can set the length of your workout, selecting from beginner, intermediate, and advanced levels, plus five different boxing programs. There's even a random program to really get you moving. A sensor control adjusts SlamMan to lighter or harder punches. Comes complete with gym-quality 14-oz. leather boxing gloves and a video that shows you how to throw jabs, hooks, upper cuts, and power punches, plus professional footwork techniques.

Particulars: 100% memory-retention foam striking surface absorbs blows and always returns to its original shape, without wrinkling or splitting. Adjusts easily to 64", 68", and 72" high. Only 18" wide. To stabilize base, fill with sand (available at home centers). Operates on 4 AA batteries (included). One-year warranty. *Minor assembly required.*

With a SlamMan workout, you achieve aerobic conditioning and major muscle toning. Plus, you naturally develop grace, reaction time, and stamina. Best of all, SlamMan is always ready for a round whenever you feel like an energizing slam.

SlamMan
$299 #ZK313

Select a boxing program and length and level of workout. Then the computer records the number of hits you score.

Order by phone
1-800-344-4444
24 hours every day.

29

Fig. 1.8:   "Narrative" copy tells a story. This description leads the casual reader into a state of mind in which an original "Who'd be interested in that?" attitude is transformed to an "I'd be interested in that" attitude.

Fig. 1.9a: Copy doesn't get any more "Minimalist" than this: "U119 Backpack, (90) Black $235." Only veteran customers of this catalog will know what the "90" means (it isn't page 90). Copy is totally subordinate to illustration.

What Kind of Copy? We Have Lots of Choices.

21

2A Clear-stemmed goblets with your choice of green or amber bowls. Set includes six of specified color. Imported. 4"Dia. x 7½"T.

2A. Six 7-oz. goblets, 75.00.

Fig. 1.9b: Common to upscale catalogs, bare-bones "Minimalist" copy peels away the frills: "Just the facts, ma'am." This doesn't give the copywriter latitude to omit pertinent selling facts; the technique supposedly forces focus on subject rather than adjectives. In my opinion, "Minimalist" copy is flat and nonmotivating, but some catalogs use it and seem to be thriving.

"Create the fresh fruit and vegetable juices you would find in a commercial Juice Bar in your own home. The delicious, easy way to provide you and your family with great nutrition"

"The Juiceman"

THE COMPACT JUICEMAN JR.® AUTOMATIC JUICE EXTRACTOR

This compact, countertop size Juiceman Jr.® makes delicious pulp-free juice at a very reasonable price. The heavy duty ¼ HP motor is powerful enough to juice most rinds, stems and seeds providing the purest, pulp-free juice possible! Features large feed tube and large pulp receptacle for continuous, non-stop juicing. Includes "Tips on Juicing", an audio cassette and fresh juice recipes and menu planner. Compact 10Wx11Hx7"D. In white.

1221 Juiceman Jr.®, reg. $100.00, special **79.99**

Fig. 1.10:   Can you envision any information about this juicer that isn't included in the description? This example isn't as copy-heavy as many; some catalogs, especially those allotting heavy space allocations, make it possible to combine "All the Facts" with both "Narrative" and "I Am the Greatest."

You made a big investment in your golf clubs. Protect them with the ultimate golf and travel bag.

You could drop 1,000 lbs. on this bag and remove your clubs intact. Yet with all this heavy protection, it only weighs 8 lbs. Golfers say it's the ultimate bag because it offers more security and convenience than either soft- or hard-shell travel cases, yet has all the features of a high-end everyday golf bag. Its hard-shell top cover easily interlocks with the main body of the bag for transportation, plus it has a changeable combination locking system. To streamline the bag for check-in, you detach the carrying strap and pouch to use as a carry-on duffel bag for equipment and personal belongings. When you're ready to tee off, the protective top stays behind so you can access the bag's graphite-lined, divided club compartments, which are roomy enough for a full set of clubs with head covers. The bag has the look and feel of cotton duck with the superior performance of Cordura® Nylon. It's exceptionally resistant to abrasion, punctures and tears, with a lightweight toughness that prevents rot and mildew. Lifetime guarantee.

260030 *Ultimate Golf and Travel Bag* **$229** ✈

✈ *Additional charge for air delivery.*

Fig. 1.11:　When a catalog introduces an item whose use and benefit may not be (a) immediately accepted as useful or necessary, or (b) known to the reader, copy has to educate as well as sell. "Informational/Educational" copy is the right way to present a $229 golf bag.

High Ridge Lodge Jacket

Question: if you saw a beautiful, sultry girl draped in an Adirondack chair reading *Godel, Escher, Bach*, would you be more taken with her appearance or her substance?

Our Lodge Jacket creates a similar quandary. While it's sure to get more than its share of gawks and double-takes, it receives even higher marks when judged against the more substantive criterion of function. First, there are the two big patch pockets. Aside from handling keys, airline tickets, and phone numbers like cargo pockets the world over, these have hidden pockets inside, with zippers for receipts, credit cards, and *special* phone numbers. Of course, there's a chest pocket for a gentleman's handkerchief and, inside, a billfold pocket. Next, there's the collar. If the temperature drops, just take the throat latch from its berth inside the jacket and fasten the neck closed. In addition to keeping you warm it gives you the opportunity to show off the soft, rich leather undercollar. The same leather is used to trim the cuffs, so you can bang around in this jacket for years and never have to suffer a frayed or tattered appearance.

There are other specifics – a cotton mesh half-lining, matching elbow patches, side vents, brass ventilation grommets, horn buttons – that make our Lodge Jacket a useful piece of equipment you'll have for years. But, like the jacket in its entirety, they can't help but to look good while being so functional. Imported. Dry clean.

Regular #4795-98G S, M, L, XL ~~$138~~ NOW $99   Tall #4239-28G M, L, XL, XXL ~~$168~~ NOW $99   Military Khaki

Fig. 1.12a: The first few words of this entry are a pure appeal to snobbery. Note how the text stays in character, combining words such as *quandary* with verbalisms such as *gawk*. Successful "Snob Appeal" copy doesn't repel a reader by saying in totality, "If you don't understand this, you're stupid."

What Kind of Copy? We Have Lots of Choices.

25

PASHMINA EMPEROR'S SHAWL

Extremely rare and prized for its extraordinary softness, this natural yarn is reputed to be the most luxurious type of cashmere in the world. Hand-woven in the Himalayas, Pashmina has been a status symbol in the East for centuries (in Nepal, a Pashmina shawl is an essential part of a wealthy woman's dowry). Still made in the same way it was hundreds of years ago, Pashmina is woven from only the soft, fine wool, culled from the neck and belly of the Himalayan Mountain Goat that is hand-gathered and combed by nomadic herders. Each shawl is hand-woven over a silk warp to strengthen the fabric, then individually dyed in an open vat. Women traditionally roll and knot the yarn ends of the shawl. The one-ply, twisted-fringe shawls are 70% cashmere, 30% silk. Hand wash in cold water or dry clean. Please specify mocha or scarlet. 81" L x 36" W. (1 lb.)
67736J.......$384.95

Fig. 1.12b: Had you ever heard that Pashmina has been a status symbol in the East for centuries? This description combines "Snob Appeal" with minor deception because deep in the description the copy reveals that this shawl isn't pure cashmere; it's 30 percent silk. A less brash description would have glorified the marriage of cashmere and silk.

Deer Valley - The Warmest Woman's Glove

When second best just won't do, this is the glove for you. The shell is made of soft supple Adirondack deerskin leather that has been Scotchgard™ treated and the lining is a cashmere polypropylene blend. The feel is shear elegance and total comfort. Made by Grandoe with over 100 years of experience. Women's Sizes S, M, L See sizing chart on order form.

SL2391 $94.95

Fig. 1.13a: A description calling itself any variation of "The Best . . . "—in this case, "The Warmest . . . "—launches itself into an "I Am the Greatest" competition. Note the first line of reinforcing body copy: "When second best just won't do."

Fig. 1.13b: A catalog's cover is a logical place to make an "I Am the Greatest" claim. This one is lighthearted enough to avoid any accusation of pomposity.

Pea coat Italian wool melton with nylon. Interior pocket. Hits below hip. Import. Dry clean. Navy, charcoal heather, black. XS, S, M, L, XL.   97013A $168. ***catalog only*** *XXL: tall L, XL. 14405A $188.*   *Pea coat with Thinsulate* Insulated with 70-gram Thinsulate®.   22749A $188.

Woodsman jacket Weathered, heavy-duty cotton canvas. Insulated with lightweight 40-gram Thinsulate. Acrylic sherpa button-out lining. Zip front, button-over storm flap. Hits below hip. Import. Machine wash. Khaki, olive. XS, S, M, L, XL.   21269A $168. *XXL: tall L, XL.   21270A $188.*

Wool car coat Our classic car coat in Italian wool melton with 20% nylon. Fully lined; insulated with lightweight 70-gram Thinsulate. Interior chest pocket. Hits below hip. Import. Dry clean only. Colors: black, navy. Sizes XS, S, M, L, XL.   21278A $188. *XXL: tall L, XL.   21279A $208.*

Fig. 1.14:   Find the one word of puffery, one enthusiastic adjective, on this page. Did you see it? It's "classic" in the bottom right description. Unquestionably corporate philosophy dictates a decision to use "Plain Vanilla" copy in a consumer catalog. In a business-to-business catalog, "what it is" may suffice as a description; puffery can irritate the prospective buyer, whose product knowledge may exceed the catalog writer's.

2

Who Hired This Guy, Anyway? Why Doesn't He Use the Good Words?

Nondescript Descriptive Words

Every catalog writer has done it—dozens, maybe hundreds of times. We look at our description of something we're selling, and our brains stagger

6. GLASS JEWELRY
Italian Murano glass "lozenges" in striking colors are
strung on metal chains to create stylish accents for
day and evening wear. Designed by Marina and
Susanna Sent. Made in Italy. Gift-boxed.
26597   Multicolor Necklace. 29"l. $85.00
28213   Amber Necklalce. 17"l. $65.00
28210   Amber Bracelet. 8"l. $60.00

Fig. 2.1:   It's "Snob Appeal" copy, of course. By putting the word *lozenges* in quotation marks, the writer achieves both clarification and acceptance.

out of gear. So we give up. We use the word *beautiful* as a descriptive word, which if we were untainted we'd admit it isn't.

Figure 2.1 calls glass jewelry "lozenges." How many catalog copywriters would have come up with that word?

Beautiful and *lovely* and *ultimate* and *wonderful* and *luxurious*, and their ilk are archetypical *non*descriptive descriptive words. You may have had as an exercise in a primitive creative writing class this project: write a letter to a friend and don't use the word *I*. Okay, try writing a women's fashion catalog without using the word *beautiful*. See? You have to labor to leave it out.

Write in color, not black-and-white.

Give the typical jaded catalog writer the job of writing a single descriptive paragraph about sheepskin slippers and you'll get back copy with the archetypical descriptive words *comfortable* and *luxurious*. Sure, these are adequate adjectives, but they're typical of black-and-white descriptions that don't trigger an emotional firing pin.

More to the point professionally, these knee-jerk-response words are reinforcements for the argument mounted by nonwriters that catalog writers are hacks, mindlessly grinding out copy as though it were hamburger.

That's why the catalog writer who wrote this simple, clear, uncomplicated descriptive sentence—in color, not in black-and-white—has my admiration:

Customers have told us that wearing these slippers is like going barefoot on a fur rug.

The simile strikes home. This copy is infinitely superior to "Comfortable, toasty-warm slippers you'll scarcely know you're wearing," acceptable but uninspired copy the typical writer would have ground out.

Take a look at figure 2.2. What a bright heading, lifting what might have been a nondescript description to a salesworthy height.

Okay, let's try another. Let's suppose you're writing the inside-the-cover letter for a thirty-three-year-old, family-operated catalog business. To

**From Italy! These Eggs Got Legs,
Spice Up The Conversation At Every Meal!**
Salt and pepper shakers are hand-painted ceramic eggs
with yellow legs. Bottom stopper for filling. 5¾" high.
590XLR Egg-Shape Salt & Pepper **$19.98**

Fig. 2.2: Many copywriters would have written only the text under the headline. This writer's headline added tons of appeal to what otherwise would be cute salt and pepper shakers . . . but still just salt and pepper shakers.

excite and inspire the reader, would you write your message in these words?

This season we celebrate our 33rd year of bringing you the best for your casual (or elegant) living style. We're a small, caring, family business, with the efficiency that comes from these years of experience.

I hope you *wouldn't* have written this message. Why? Because except for the word *caring*, this could be standard computer-generated copy. The writer can pour this kind of copy out of the word-can without knowing anything about the company. That's the clue to copy that has no effect on the reader's attitude.

I'm looking at the heading over a copy block in a consumer catalog:

Swissmass Is The Ultimate Massager From Sweden

Now, let's not do what we usually do. Let's not slide around that headline, accepting it as unimaginative puffery. Suppose for once we *don't* accept the statement at face value. Suppose we say to the writer, "All right, my friend, you've said this is the *ultimate* massager. Mr. Webster says that means no massager ever will match yours. This is as far as massagers can go."

So what's the first sentence of body copy?

You'll imagine you're being professionally massaged by the skillful touch of a trained masseur.

If that's so, and if that's the comparative benefit of this device, the headline not only misuses the word *ultimate*; it misses the boat by using generalized puffery as the point of emphasis instead of specifying what this is and does. Buried in the copy is the key—the unit has five $1\frac{1}{4}$-inch finger-like nodules that simulate the action of human fingers.

The effectiveness of the copy is blunted by the tired puffery of the headline, which draws no word image to help convince the reader and ignores the unique selling point.

A catalog writer's total description of a necklace made of semiprecious stones:

Blue lapis is enhanced with the finest touches and 14K gold lustre.

What if the person paying this writer said, "Hey, hold it. What does 'enhanced with the finest touches' mean? Rewrite that description to make it descriptive." *Whatever* would have resulted would have been an improvement.

Don't overcomplicate your copy.

Describing an item within a predetermined amount of space is a discipline . . . but not necessarily a talent.

That's why so many writers can write acceptable catalog copy but stumble when they shift to some of the more dynamic forms of force-communication. It also explains why some writers who have powerful creative talent but little professional discipline can't write effective catalog copy.

The Clarity Commandment—Friend or Foe?

Anybody who supervises the creative process for a catalog has faced this dilemma:

It's catalog writer hiring time. The company runs an ad or posts a notice, and candidates troop in to compete for the job. Each has samples, which may or may not be indicative of personal talent.

So we give the candidates a standard writing test. They know, as they sit at a foreign keyboard, how much of their future lies in the hundred or two hundred words they'll write.

What they *don't* know is what we want them to do, unless we give them samples.

Like most who read these words, I've been a lot of different people at the keyboard. I've written catalog copy so deliberately pompous it wears a monocle . . . "Y'all be good naow" P.O.C.B. (Plain Ol' Country Boy) copy worded on a level far less sophisticated than "Jes' Folks" . . . no-nonsense here's-what-it-is-and-you-make-up-your-own-mind copy . . . poetic and rhapsodic copy . . . hi-tech copy . . . artificially bright copy . . . bulked up Internet copy . . . double entendre E-mail copy. In each case my goal was to match copy into a four-piece jigsaw puzzle:

1. buyer demographics
2. our intended position, actual image, and history
3. production limitations
4. corporate or CEO ego

Within all these strictures and limitations, a battle-scarred copy chief still has to warn the beginner: keep your massive vocabulary in check.

Why? Because job applicants usually feel they will lose unless copy shows the potential for spectacle. Out comes copy that violates the Clarity Commandment:

> ✐ In force-communication, clarity is paramount. Don't let any other component of the communication mix interfere with it.

Then whoever administers the writing test draws a conclusion: this person is too vocabulary-conscious to write catalog copy. The conclusion is logical only if proper instructions preceded word regurgitation.

If you can write copy such as in figure 2.3 you've mastered the art of adding color without sacrificing clarity. That's a major indicator not only of professionalism but of superior talent.

Let me make a modest proposal.

If your copy tests have been one-string fiddles, I suggest this modest change:

Ask applicants to write the same copy block at least two ways—"straight" and lyrical. It's been my experience that (1) a copywriter who can write lyrical copy can, with minor deprogramming, write straight copy; (2) the copywriter who can write straight copy but who stumbles when writing on-demand lyrical copy has about a 50 percent chance of ever being able to make the switch if needed; (3) left alone without instructions, copy-

A zillion Christmas memories ago, I remember lying on the floor beside the tree at the Atwaters' house on Court Street. I was nine or ten. The room lights were out and their tree was trimmed with Bubble-Lites. I was enthralled, mesmerized…the tree was magical. Each 7 ft. long, seven-light strand is still made by the same company who first introduced Bubble-Lites in the early '40s. Share the wonder with a new generation or rekindle your own memories. Connects up to 50 lights (seven strands).
Noma Bubble-Lites 3310.0083 $22
Extra Bulbs, set of two. 3310.0084 $6

Fig. 2.3:   Can you think of a more appealing way to sell these Christmas lights?

writers will write (or try to write) lyrical copy because they think it's a better exemplar of their talent.

While I'm ranting about copy tests, three other suggestions:

1. Always prescribe the copy length of the test.
2. Ask the writer to describe two unlike items, to prevent disqualification based on lack of product familiarity.
3. Show an example of the kind of copy you're looking for.

Is it a sad commentary on our profession that the most dependable catalog copywriters are parrots? I don't think so. The copywriter who changes the entire face and image of a catalog isn't a copywriter at all; that person is a copywriter-*plus*. Catalogs such as *Hello Direct*, which in a business-to-business ambience achieve the near-impossible miracle of producing a thoroughly down-to-earth yet entertaining compendium of product descriptions, aren't the result of an individual copywriter saying, "And now for something completely different."

Mud isn't a clarifier.

Here's the opening of a one-paragraph copy block for a mailbox:

It's copper. And it will have your name and a scene of landing ducks embossed on it, both sides. And, fittingly, it's big . . . 21″ long, 12″ high, 8″ wide. What isn't gleaming copper is steel enamelled in earthy green. It will last long and weather beautifully, to a lovely soft patina.

Well, so the writer used "lovely." It's a second-echelon word, after all; it might have been "beautiful." My question is about two other components. First, why "fittingly"? What prior reference makes this "fitting"?

Second, "What isn't gleaming copper" is a negative way of putting a positive thought. In this era of advanced word processing and instant corrections, we no longer can justify writing ourselves into a corner. While we're chewing on that description, "steel enamelled in earthy green" reads wrong. We read "steel enamelled" as a unit, which we couldn't do if the writer threw in a comma after "steel."

Consumer catalogs don't have a lock on muddy writing. In business-to-business catalog writing, "I know something you don't" arrogance and "I'd rather entertain you than sell you something" insecurity eliminate a host of potential buyers who just don't know what the writer means.

An example is this catalog copy for—well, you guess what it's for:

WHEN THINGS GO BUMP IN THE NIGHT, *MIGHTY MO* DOESN'T EVEN HAVE AN A.C. BLINK

You may have milliseconds to waste, but your micro doesn't. *Mighty Mo* keeps micros up to snuff with power on when power's off. Old Jim Watts lent his name to the *Mighty Mo* 400 and the *Mighty Mo* 800, depending on how many goodies you hook into your micro's guts.

Want ultimate protection? Want to sleep, even sitting at the board? *Mighty Mo* just might keep you from becoming "mighty po'"!

The CIA's cryptography department helped decode this message. "Micro" stands for "micro-computer," and "Mighty Mo" is an uninterruptible power supply. Once you know this, figuring out the Jim Watts reference is duck soup. It's James Watt (not Watts, but don't we wish this were the only flaw in the copy?), whose name is immortalized as the measurement of electric power; so Mighty Mo 400 gives us 400 watts of power and Mighty Mo 800 gives us . . . aw, what the heck, who cares?

If you're of a mind to defend this copy, saying, "At least it's different," I point out that painting your face purple and your hair green also are "different," but please don't come to my dinner party.

Compare that with figure 2.4. It also uses episode. Is it *over*written? Some may think so because it takes a while to get to its point. Others will think it's charming.

What's wrong with "An Elegant Gift"?

What's wrong with this, the total description of a designer scarf?

An elegant gift that's certain to be appreciated and used with pride.

Right. It's more of that boilerplate copy some infernal artificial copywriter is excreting. Proof? Try it on just about anything you're describing in your catalog.

This gives us another component for a catalog copywriting test: look for boilerplate copy.

Turning this mild tip inside out, we have, for journeyman (journeyperson?) catalog copywriters, the Boilerplate Avoidance Proposition:

> The possibility of depersonalized, interchangeable, nondescriptive copy decreases in exact ratio to an increase of usable fact presented to the writer.

Beneath the Chandeliers.

She was a little tired of modern life right now, she said.

The beep of the fax, the click of the cell-phone, the incessant flood of information which is not really urgent, in fact, barely of interest, had been getting her down.

My prescription: 48 white roses. Ellington. Perrier-Jouet. The only sound: our bare feet against the marble floor.

Just a suggestion.

Dress for Romance (Nº. AAG8014). Color: Earth Purple. Women's sizes: 4 through 14. Price: $295. Imported. Tea-length, full-bodied velvet trimmed with charmeuse satin. Wide, wide, neckline. Sweetheart style, siren impact. Satin covered buttons. Empire waist (understandably popular for 2,000 years). Posh dinner parties. Winter weddings. Or just little spells of murmuring, nibbling.

Fig. 2.4:   Are you enchanted or annoyed by this description? You're enchanted if you're a fan of this catalog or like leisurely romance. You're annoyed if you're a "Get to the point" person or if you feel the tie between the opening and the garment is tortured. (Annoyances outvoted enchantments; this catalog company went out of business.)

To validate the proposition, try writing two parallel pieces of copy. For the first, you have bare-bones information—colors, sizes, and a product photograph with no cutline. For the second, you have all the information the buyer would give to the department manager of a retail store.

Sure, the second piece of copy is easier to write. But that isn't the way a printed-catalog recipient or online-catalog reader keeps score. The second piece of copy invariably has more meat in it, and that's a powerful way to keep score.

The catalog writer who lazily uses the first available word is just as unprofessional as the cabinetmaker who uses the first available scrap of wood, whether it fits or not.

The catalog writer who egocentrically says, "Let me entertain you," had better tie a string around every finger that might hit the keyboard, as a reminder of the Catalog Copywriter's First Charge:

> ✐ The purpose of catalog copy is to sell the item you're describing. *Every* other facet of creative copywriting is subordinate to this, except maybe the Clarity Commandment, without which copy isn't copy.

We Have Catalog Copywriters . . . and Catalog CopyWRITERS!

Catalog writers instinctively take a competitive, comparative view of the copy in other catalogs. It's almost a Pavlov's Dog reaction.

Maybe that's why we seize upon nondescript and ineffective word-smithery and let good copy slide past us. On an educational level, rewriting a random copy block from a competitor's catalog is an effective exercise. Recognizing, admiring, and emulating a colorful or powerful piece of copy is just as effective an educational procedure—and probably more advanced as well.

Figures 2.5 and 2.6 illustrate contrasting approaches. Figure 2.5 is straightforward but doesn't "romance" the lights; 2.6 makes a claim of exclusivity that states uniqueness from its first three words.

Are they good writers? We may never know.

Only a select few catalog writers achieve celebrity status. This isn't necessarily because they're the only ones who can write stirring prose. No, I don't doubt for a moment that deep in the catacombs of many catalog

D. Mesh Lights—the easy, tangle-free way to add lights to a tree, shrub or fence.
This net of 150 steady-burning, super-bright white lights covers approx. 28 sq. ft.—a 4'x7' area! Includes flasher bulb. If one bulb burns out, the others remain lit. Only two sets of Mesh Lights can be used per outlet or extension cord. 20-gauge wire; UL listed. **#13195 $24.50 per set SAVE! 3 or more sets $22.50 ea.**

Fig. 2.5: All the necessary information is here, but an item with implicit emotional overtones can warrant "holiday" treatment.

© LVC 1998

EXCLUSIVE
You Won't Find This Clock Anywhere Else In The World. It was designed just for us by Parisian artist Regis Dho. Ceramic clock has a charming country design, black metal hands and large, easy-to-read yellow numbers at 12, 3, 6 and 9. Takes 1 "AA" battery (not included). 10½" across. Hang from back hook.
194XLR Apple Clock **$24.98**

Fig. 2.6: Whenever you can claim, "You won't find this anywhere else," you're on your way to attention-getting, winning copy. But catalog copywriting is neither that easy nor that automatic because in a competitive ambience it's rare to be able to make that claim without hedging.

houses are writers who have "the gift" but who are trapped in *format*. When we have six lines of forty characters in which to empty our verbal baskets, how poetic can we be?

So the titans of catalog writing—the Babe Ruths, the Mark McGwires, the Michael Jordans—invariably are those whose good fortune or talent lands them at *The Sharper Image* or *Herrington* or *Field Trips* or *Lillian Vernon*. There they can stretch their creative muscles to match the stretched-out copy blocks that tight little catalogs don't make available.

How many free spirits are trying to pop the cork out of their restrictive six-line–forty-character bottles and show us how much talent they really have? We'll never know.

Here's a different set of yardsticks.

Our counterparts who write solo mailings and space ads might list these as professional requirements:

> salesmanship—30 percent
> vocabulary—20 percent
> grammar—15 percent
> writing discipline—15 percent
> knowledge of relationship to graphics—10 percent
> speed—10 percent

I've omitted product knowledge because this is impossible to measure. As hired Hessians, expected to go forth to successfully attack "somebody," we'd better be able to write effective copy for insurance one day, insecticides the next day, and insulated underwear the next. That's why salesmanship tops the list.

Because we have to kill with one blow, our copy for solo mailings and space ads depends heavily on our ability to match vocabulary with our targets. That's why vocabulary ranks second.

Every word is "page 1" in a solo mailing, so grammar is significant. (Actually, I don't ever see a need to justify decent grammar as a starter requirement for *any* writer.)

Writer discipline isn't a big deal. Yes, we have to get the mailing package out in time. But nobody expects us to hammer away at the keyboard for eight solid hours a day. That, too, is why speed isn't a major consideration. Mailing dates often are flexible.

Usually, an ad or mailing piece has art direction. So the writer has a companion in the hot seat, figuring out the graphics.

Now let's assemble a similar list for catalog writers, *excluding the copy-heavy catalogs*. In my opinion, the ratios would be:

writing discipline—35 percent
speed—25 percent
salesmanship—15 percent
vocabulary—10 percent
grammar—10 percent
knowledge of relationship to graphics—5 percent

If you don't believe this shift, apply for a writing job at the typical catalog house and see how long you last without writing discipline and speed. Ex-catalog writers can increase the departmental output but may stumble over the salesmanship barrier when they're appointed creative directors at mail-order companies: they're more discipline-oriented.

If we move those writers over to copy-heavy catalogs, we see an obvious change:

writing discipline—25 percent
salesmanship—25 percent
speed—20 percent
vocabulary—15 percent
grammar—10 percent
knowledge of relationship to graphics—5 percent

Salesmanship moves up and discipline slacks off because, although they still have catalog deadlines, these writers don't struggle inside the straitjacket of having to grind out an eight-item page. And with one or two items on a page, salesmanship surges forward; without it, the page won't pay for itself.

"A HAND-PUSH lawn mower? You're kidding!"

With those ratios as yardsticks, I'll pay homage to some catalog writing I regard as superior.

I can't comment on speed because I wasn't there with a timer. I'm taking discipline for granted because this *is* catalog copy. But salesmanship—no question about the talent.

Most of us, asked to write catalog copy for a hand-push lawn mower, would snort, "You're kidding! My grandfather had one of those." Not the writer of this gem, who knew the magic equation: successful salesmanship = projection of benefit.

The heading:

The Hand Push Lawn Mower is perfect for small lawns, trimming tight corners, and a little peace and quiet on a Sunday afternoon.

What an elegant headline! It's pure benefit, relating to the reader, not the manufacturer (and that's a welcome relief after some of the chest-thumping braggadocio copy we see).

When you get to chapter 24, remember this example because it's two-thirds of the magical Benefit-Benefit-Benefit Principle described in that chapter.

I have a simple way of judging copy: would I be proud if an outsider asked, "Did you write that?" and I could answer, "Yes."

Is it because the copy attacks a specific prejudice?

I'm looking at another copy block I admire. The heading:

Why You Should Spend $125 for a Golf Bag That Weighs a Mere 2-lbs., 15 oz.!

I don't understand why the writer stuck a hyphen between "2" and "lbs." and not between "15" and "oz."—but, heck, we're being picky; it isn't as though the writer used "it's" for "its." And we only rate grammar at 10 percent anyway, for this kind of writing.

The copy immediately attacks our negative reaction, which is based on human prejudice against something lightweight costing more than similar items weighing considerably more. The very first sentence isn't descriptive; it's the smooth opening of a seller who knows rapport can't be established until implicit prejudice is dissolved:

Based on cost-per-pounds, our Balance Bag™ may be the most expensive golf bag you can buy.

The next word, of course, is *but*.

Can YOU do it?

Can *you* sell a hand-push lawn mower for $86.80? Can *you* sell a lightweight golf bag for $125? Can *you* sell a standard-looking clay pottery figure for $350? And can *you* get this copy out of the printer by deadline date?

Then you're the most desirable of all catalog copywriters, the magical amalgam of salesmanship and discipline.

You're innocent until proved guilty.

Anyone who reads catalog copy with a critical eye will agree: catalog copywriters are guilty of many sins. Sloth, dullness, and an accordionlike imagination that either puffs itself full of air or goes flat are a few.

Consider, though: before you blame the copywriter for all the communication sins, ask around. You have three logical questions:

1. Did the copywriter get as much selling weaponry as the buyer or product manager had at hand?
2. Has corporate policy stifled the copywriter's ability to ask for information that surely exists but wasn't included?
3. Who hired this guy, anyway?

If your copy is strong-selling *and* clever, may the Lord bless and keep you. But if it sacrifices salesmanship for cleverness, may you spend eternity restocking the shelves of catalog houses who knew better and hired writers for whom moving merchandise is a more worthy goal than showing off.

3

It's *Force-*
Communication,
Baby!

First, *You* Try It!

Your assignment . . .

You're selling a "Doubleheader" ballpoint pen that has a hidden built-in seventy-five-second recorder. Write a headline that will stop the reader and generate a buying impulse.

Take thirty seconds. No longer than that.

What was your headline? If it was something such as "While you're writing it down, your pen is recording it"? Professional! If it was "Not only a pen. It's also a recorder," not so professional. Take a look at the description that appeared in a well-written catalog. (Figure 3.1.)

The Power of Verbs

We who write catalog descriptions are perpetually adjectival. We thumb our thesauri, or we click the on-screen "Thesaurus" menu, looking for adjectives—synonyms for *beautiful* and *tasty* and *durable*.

But after we've exhausted *lovely* and *handsome*, *delicious* and *delectable*, *heavy-duty* and *sturdy* . . . we begin to run out of gas.

That's because adjectives, while the obvious and most convenient describers, aren't the most powerful.

Nor are nouns.

Verbs have the power. But it's a two-edged sword because verbs are the toughest to use. *Strut* creates a word image *walk* could never match; *grab* generates a mini-excitement far beyond *take*; still, how often do we get the opportunity to strut or grab in a catalog description?

More often than you might think if you aren't verb-aware.

You can be effective without being tricky.

The Kingdom of Heaven is the ability to summon up verbs that have an imperative overtone, *without becoming strident*. If we start to shout or preach, we move outside the orbit of catalog copy and into the more savage world of direct response. Now, that isn't necessarily bad, but two problems arise: (1) You can't preach throughout a catalog. (2) A description making a heavy demand can cast a pall over other descriptions that don't.

(An exception: a "magalog"—a catalog that looks and reads like a magazine—which by its hybrid nature requires commands.)

Gentle imperatives are an art. This came home to me as I was looking through a catalog of "products for country living." I had to ask myself whether, charged with writing the same description for a "slumber sack," I'd have been able to match this:

Snuggle Into Our Slumber Sack And Say Goodbye To Drafts

Read your favorite book or watch TV in cozy comfort. Step into our Slumber Sack, zip up, and let the soft Polartec® fleece warm your whole body like a blanket, but without gaps that let in the cold. . . .

Count the imperative verbs: *snuggle*, *say*, *read*, *watch*, *step*, *zip*, *let*. Quietly and seamlessly, the writer has injected a command we recognize *not* as a command but as a self-suggestion. (Off the point: the heading would have had greater strength without all the artificial capitalizations.)

Compare the lushness of that description with this one, from a catalog of women's wear:

Not-so-basic Metallic Turtlenecks

Turn a simple jumper or suit into a stunning holiday outfit with the addition of a gold or silver ribbed metallic turtleneck. . . .

What's wrong with that? Oh, nothing much, because calling it "wrong" (an adjective, easily changed to "imperfect") is too harsh. So a mild ques-

That remark was off the record.
And recorded on this pen.
For those who have gift-giving in mind, the Pencorder may just be the talk of the town. This remarkable device has a 75-second recording capacity, so you can record one long memo or multiple shorter ones. The Pencorder allows you to skip forward and backward through your messages or repeat them, and it can even retrieve accidentally erased messages. Inside its elegant protective brass housing with a sleek nickel/palladium finish, there's a miniature recorder/playback microchip, batteries and a ballpoint pen cartridge. Arrives gift-boxed with batteries and a spare ink refill.
230023 Pencorder $79
230024   Ballpoint Ink Refill (5 pack) $4.99

Fig. 3.1: The casual reader may not reflect, "This is superb catalog copywriting." The intensely aware catalog copywriter certainly should reflect, "I wish I'd written that."

tion: if you or I had written the text, we wouldn't have used "Turn," would we? We'd have moved up to a power verb and written "Transform," or if we were very brave and not worried about getting fired, "Revolutionize."

It's your call.

As is true of so many rules of communication, using action verbs isn't universally desirable. For example, a catalog of home furnishings had this as the complete description of a table:

Shaker Country Table

Our Shaker inspired table is made in Maine of solid poplar. Simple assembly required. Cherry stained top with your choice of colors for the base. Colors: Stain (shown), Black, Burgundy, Forest, Unfinished.

Does this description leave you vaguely dissatisfied? Me, too. It isn't because the copy desperately needs a hyphen between "Shaker" and "inspired" and between "Cherry" and "stained." That's another topic. No, I think it's because "Simple assembly required" not only is in the wrong place but is worded wrong. "Simple" and "required" don't match up. You or I would have put that at the end and worded it with a benign imperative— "Assemble it in a few minutes."

But wait: is an imperative in order here, based on what action or reaction we intend? Would "Assembles in a few minutes" propose *less* of a challenge than "Assemble it in a few minutes"? I think so. And we have the exception that verb power itself necessitates, the Imperative Exception Rule:

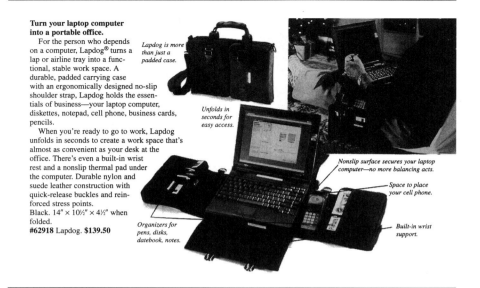

Turn your laptop computer into a portable office.

For the person who depends on a computer, Lapdog® turns a lap or airline tray into a functional, stable work space. A durable, padded carrying case with an ergonomically designed no-slip shoulder strap, Lapdog holds the essentials of business—your laptop computer, diskettes, notepad, cell phone, business cards, pencils.

When you're ready to go to work, Lapdog unfolds to create a work space that's almost as convenient as your desk at the office. There's even a built-in wrist rest and a nonslip thermal pad under the computer. Durable nylon and suede leather construction with quick-release buckles and reinforced stress points. Black. 14″ × 10½″ × 4½″ when folded.

#62918 Lapdog. **$139.50**

Lapdog is more than just a padded case.

Unfolds in seconds for easy access.

Nonslip surface secures your laptop computer—no more balancing acts.

Space to place your cell phone.

Built-in wrist support.

Organizers for pens, disks, datebook, notes.

Fig. 3.2: "Turn your . . ." is always workmanlike, because the concept of upgrade transformation is a universal motivator.

> ✎ When the desired action implies work, or difficulty, or the need for capabilities the reader may not possess, an imperative can cause unease.

With that little rule in mind, evaluate this copy from a discount health-care catalog:

Electric Callus Remover

Keep your feet smooth and sleek with hardly any effort! Simply press the electric callus remover gently against corns or calluses . . . and watch them vanish! . . .

Okay, how would you have opened this description? I'd have tossed out "Keep"—which suggests ongoing work—and written something like this: "Smooth, sleek feet are yours with no effort at all." (I'm trying to stay inside the original concept.)

A Bookseller-by-Post catalog really knows how to use the gentle imperative as the opening gun. Here are just three of the many gems from its pages:

- Wow, get a load of that schnozzola! Bizarre and Beautiful Noses investigates. . . .

- Forget the cherry tree. Where did George Washington learn the patience that. . . .

- If you've thought of France as not particularly user-friendly, you need to read Polly Platt's entertaining little treatise. . . .

The word *can* is an easy compromise.

For generations, product introductions have leaned on "Now you can." The word *can* is a bridge between the imperative and the blandly descriptive. It implies advance, new capability, and ease in a single word.

An "outfitting" catalog uses *can* effectively for many descriptions in which an imperative might seem harsh or grating . . . and a straightforward description would lack personality.

One example:

Soft, comfortable, and heroically wrinkle-resistant, these knits are so adaptable that you can wear them from the airport to the open air market to the opera with just a change of accessories.

This is truly superior copy. Most catalog writers wouldn't have included "with just a change of accessories"—a parenthetical phrase that forces a standard and often disbelieved claim to ring true.

Another "can" description in this catalog raises an interesting question, albeit a somewhat abstruse one: should the word refer to the product or to the reader? The Imperative Exception Rule works here, too (I could have said "can work here, too"). A description of a "Correspondent's Jacket" includes this sentence:

The tightly woven microfiber twill sheds creases and can be worn on overnight flights or crowded trains, and then washed and worn right out of the dryer without ironing.

Here, the writer uses *can* as a product reference. Would the copy be fractionally stronger worded this way?

The tightly woven microfiber twill sheds creases. You can wear it on overnight flights or crowded trains, and then wash it and slip it on again right out of the dryer without ironing.

Stew's Gift Clubs ...when one gift is not enough!!!

**Stew's Gift Clubs
are perfect for:**
- Extra-special Clients
- Family members and friends who live far away
- Kids away at college
- Valued Employees
- Friends who have moved away from Connecticut

Thanks to our high purchasing power, we're able to go direct to the coffee plantations to buy our coffee beans. By going to the source, we are able to see our coffee grown, picked and dried in the sun. We can cut out the "middle-man" expenses, and pass the savings on to you.

Every year, we roast over 200 tons of Arabica coffee beans in our store. Master Roasters supervise the slow baking of green coffee beans, then carefully mix different beans to make our special Stew Leonard's blends.

"Stew's has the largest in-store coffee roasting operation I've ever seen!"
**Sterling Gordon,
Coffee Importer**

*Dear Mr. Leonard,
I love to drive up up to your store from Long Island because you have the best Costa Rican Coffee I can find anywhere!!!*

Thanks to Daniel's superior customer service, I just bought 10 pounds!!!
**Al Henderson
Long Island, NY**

Now you can give a Stew-pendous gift that keeps on giving, long after the Holidays!!! You decide how many months — 3, 5, 8, or a full 12 months of delicious Stew Leonard's gourmet goodness shipped to a very lucky gift recipient. A certificate of the selected Stew's Club will be sent with the first gift — shipped to arrive for the Holidays. We can add custom gift messages, so you can send along wishes for birthdays, anniversaries, and seasonal holidays!! Plan a full year of gift-giving, and let Stew's take care of the details.

3 Month Club / Gift 903 - $59⁹⁵   *8 Month Club / Gift 908 - $159⁹⁵*
5 Month Club / Gift 905 - $99⁹⁵   *12 Month Club / Gift 912 - $229⁹⁵*

DECEMBER — *Bethy's Traditional Style Ruggalach*
JANUARY — *Stew's Choice Coffee with Decorator Tin*
FEBRUARY — *Deluxe Valentine's Tower*
MARCH — *Bethy's Brownie Sampler*
APRIL — *Perfect Fruit Bowl*
MAY — *Bucket O' Candy*
JUNE — *All Butter Popcorn Tin*
JULY — *July 4th Snack Box*
AUGUST — *Bethy's Bakery Chocolate Chip Cookies*
SEPTEMBER — *Sweet Treats Basket*
OCTOBER — *Halloween Popcorn Tin*
NOVEMBER — *Gourmet Mixed Nut Tin*

FRESH Roasted Coffee

You don't have to live in Connecticut just to have a delicious cup of Stew's fresh-roasted coffee each day!! All coffee available in Regular (R) and Decaffeinated Swiss water (D). All coffee is roasted and ground to order, then packed in one pound vacuum-seal bags. *$9⁹⁵*

**Stew's Choice / Gift 972R - 972D
French Roast / Gift 977R - 977D
Hazelnut / Gift 970R - 970D
Colombian Supreme / Gift 974R - 974D
Stew's Coffee with Decorator Tin
Gift 943 - $12⁹⁵**

ADD to any Gift purchase at a Savings of $2.00 lb. off each pound.

Fig. 3.3: The first line of body copy begins "Now you can." In this instance, the device seems to be an artifice because nothing in the text suggests "Now you can" as a new or breakthrough development. Might starting with "Give" be stronger? What's your opinion?

Aside from avoiding repetition of the word *worn* or *wear*, the second version with its "You can" thrust is more salesworthy than the original, both because "can" refers to the reader and because our version eliminates passive voice. Actually, moving up to a full imperative makes it even more convincing:

The tightly woven microfiber twill sheds creases. Go ahead and wear it on overnight flights or crowded trains. Then if you like, wash it and wear it again, right out of the dryer without ironing.

Creating the Instant Impulse

If you had your druthers, would you rather sell or describe?

Careful, now. Before any "Of course" knee-jerk response, consider: we're in the catalog business. The same professional copywriters who pile every selling adjective they can muster into a solo mailing will ease up and put a silk glove on copy for a catalog. The two selling media aren't parallel.

But what *is* parallel is the adjective before "media"—*selling*. A catalog doesn't succeed by winning a bunch of awards for artistry; it succeeds if somebody reading it sends in an order. (Witness the ever-professional *Camp-Mor*, which seems refreshing not only because of its no-B.S. copy but also because it's printed in monochrome on newsprint.)

You don't need high pressure to sell.

Every now and then I come across a catalog whose copy approaches the poetic, bright and shining and thoughtful and graceful. Ever have the good fortune to look through *A Common Reader*, a digest-size catalog—and yes, except for the cover it's black-and-white on newsprint—issued by James Mustich Jr.?

I don't know Mr. Mustich, but I suspect he's a gentle soul who loves books. That's what his catalog sells—books. Copy doesn't pitch. It's quiet, never shrill.

Each book is awarded one long paragraph of text—I'd guess one hundred to one hundred fifty words, in eight-point type. You can see how many of our standard rules *A Common Reader* violates: single, unbroken paragraphs, plus type far smaller than we'd ever allocate to a catalog catering to "mature" targets. So what? The miracle of this copy is that as we share his enjoyment of a book, the buying impulse rises up in us. Now, *that's* professional catalog copywriting.

So yes, it's possible for catalog copy to create the instant impulse to buy; I don't know why more catalogs don't lean in that direction.

Instead of labeling, why not suggest use?

I'm looking at similar items in two catalogs—home intercom systems. The headline on one:

Wireless Home Intercom System

The headline on the other:

No more yelling! Simply plug in these Wireless Intercoms and *talk*.

Oh, sure, the second one has more words. But I'd give up a line or two of body text in favor of a headline that generates the buying impulse. (In answer to your obvious question, I, too, would replace "Simply" with "Just.")

Here's another headline that replaces bland description with a buying-impulse breeder:

Chair protector takes the stress out of mealtimes with kids.

Can't you see a typical wage-slave copywriter missing an opportunity by grinding out "Protect your chair cushion with this heavy-duty vinyl cover"? Can't you see a jaded cataloger putting an okay on such a heading because the creative atmosphere is one of clerkdom, not salesdom?

Tell 'em what to do.

One of the great laws of force-communication is "Tell the reader/ viewer/listener what to do." And it's the easiest of all the great laws to implement because we couldn't have reached adulthood if we didn't have a ton of experience both in telling people what to do and in being told what to do. We know what the signals are.

Combine that great law with benefit and you have an automatic impulse-generator. Guaranteed. Can't miss.

Here's an inflatable neck pillow. We've seen it for years, usually described as "Inflatable Neck Pillow." Now comes a newcomer to the arena, with this headline:

Say "bon voyage" to cricks and stiff necks when you travel!

Here's a long-handled bulb changer. One catalog shows it in use, with this headline:

Change ceiling bulbs without a ladder.

No, it isn't terrible, and it's light-years better than "Long-handled bulb changer," but it isn't even close to being in the same league with this one:

Change overhead bulbs and floods with both feet safely on the floor.

So how would YOU have written it?

Here's an office chair. The heading:

After Many Years, Still a Popular Seating Choice

Okay, what would you have done with that? I'll bet three bucks if somebody handed the copy to you and asked you to give it some octane, at the very least you'd have added a couple of words, if only "The reason why" in front of a flavorless headline that can repel as many as it attracts.

Avoid putting your worst foot forward.

A catalog I usually admire has this heading for that facial toning gadget we've seen advertised everywhere:

Uncontrolled clinical tests show Facial Flex® can tone and firm your face in just 8 weeks, with no drugs, no surgery

---

"*Un*controlled"? All right, let's assume they can't claim a controlled test because . . . well, because it's their own self-serving test. Do they have to emphasize the wildness of the claim? How would *you* have handled the statement?

First of all, I'd have put a period at the end because it's a complete sentence. Next, I'd have used "Our tests"; or, if the legal department raised its hackles, "If Facial Flex® doesn't tone and firm your face in just 8 weeks, we'll refund every cent you paid for it"; or, for an easy solution, a transformation into a question such as "Will Facial Flex® tone and firm your face in just 8 weeks? We have lots of evidence that says it will." Brilliant copy? You know better than that. But it's infinitely superior to hoping the reader won't read "Uncontrolled" the way we just have.

You can generate a buying impulse from Ground Zero.

One of the jewels of our business is a catalog called *Art & Artifact*. One reason I like this catalog is its ability to treat highbrow items with grace and clarity. Most of their headlines are at variance with all we've just been reading about, but to object to an understated position of culture would be objecting to elegance itself.

At what point does an understated position of culture, indicative of supreme elegance, lift itself outside the buying realm? It's a genuine problem for catalogs whose list selection has to be an exquisite match.

Let's suppose—and it's a totally valid supposition—you have no preconceived desire to buy a tapestry. You chance upon this description (I'm quoting only the opening):

WATER LILLIES [sic] TAPESTRY

First your eyes, then your soul will be irretrievably drawn into our stunning tapestry replicating a Monet canvas of water lilies with a Japanese footbridge. . . .

Would this spur you to lift the phone? Probably not. But it might well spur you to take a closer look at the illustration. (Misspelling of the word *lilies* is the catalog's.)

In the same catalog is a different, more pedestrian call to action:

PORTOFINO TAPESTRY

Give your room a view with our captivating tapestry portraying the sunwashed village of Portofino. . . .

In this instance, the suggestion of a tapestry as substitute for a window might well be a buying spur.

Suggestion of use is even more significant for B to B.

Suggestion of use becomes a profound selling instrument in a business-to-business ambience.

Here, on the same page of *Hello Direct* (always a bellwether of superior copy), are two telephone headsets. Each headline solves a specific problem. Headline A:

———————————

So much noise you can't hear your caller? This headset covers both ears.

———————————

Headline B:

———————————

Don't want anything on top of your head? Try this on-the-ear headset.

———————————

The technique is impeccable: each headline suggests both problem and solution.

And that's a huge key to creating the instant buying impulse. Let the academic researchers state a problem without offering a solution. Stating a problem and then offering a solution *without giving the reader time to look elsewhere?* That's high professionalism in catalog copy.

And that's what our mission is, right?

Confusion? In Catalogs? Not Possible. Oh, Yeah?

We have a far more disciplined playing field than the marketers who deal in direct mail. So we'd never louse up pricing nor pagination nor, for Pete's sake, a description. Would we?

Sigh.

Yes, we would, and yes, we do. How and why this happens is beyond the realm of logic.

I'll tell you what else is beyond the realm of logic: when we ask some of the catalogers whose logic we question what was in their minds, most of the time the answer is, "Oh, sure. We meant to do it that way." Is a puzzlement.

What about obfuscation fascinates some catalogers? Here's a catalog whose cover says it's "Vol. 5, No. 3." Okay, fellow puzzle fans: what period of time in what year is it supposed to represent? Any reason why whoever excreted this concept couldn't have put a date instead of arcane numbers on the cover? I know . . . we've always done it that way.

How can it be that in the date-conscious twenty-first century we still see printed computer-equipment catalogs that not only don't have an index; they don't have page numbers? The only answer is that a misguided sense of artistry ranks above clarity and reader comfort.

How can it be that we have online catalogs that require three to five clicks to get you to a place where you can specify what you want to see? The only answer is that to these people technique ranks above clarity and Web visitor comfort.

How does it run? And how much is it?

Here's a travel clock. I'm advised to "Take it anywhere in the world." Okay, I'll do that. Do I need a plug for it? You don't tell me if it's AC or runs on batteries. And if it runs on batteries, what kind and how many? Instead of "Batteries not included" your copy really says, "Information not included."

Here's a handsome catalog of electronic stuff—digital cameras and scanners and CD-ROM players and monitors and printers. Nice color, fine paper. Thanks for sending me three of them.

With three copies, I'd better take a look. Yeah! Here's a Toshiba digital camera. And on the facing page, here's an Olympus. Oh, and you also show Minolta and Nikon. Which one to buy?

Who the hell can tell? There isn't a price in the entire catalog.

Whoa, don't tell me the catalog has a separate price list. I've written such catalogs. Sometimes a separate price list is necessary. But this one has *no* price list. None. I've verified that three times because they sent me three catalogs. Nor is there any reference to where a price may be.

At the bottom of each page is the suggestion: "For more information visit our Web site." Masochist that I am, like an idiot I did that. Here, word for word, is the entire site (I've changed the company name and numbers to protect the guilty):

———————

Winners inc.

Welcome to Winners online. Winners is a national distributor of computer peripherals from manufacturers such as Canon, Epson, Kodak, Toshiba, and Hitachi to name a few.

Until our Web Site is complete you may call us at 1-800-555-9648, or by fax at 555-437-0432 or email us at *info@winners.com.*

———————

It's actually funny, because this message ends:

———————

© Winners Inc. All rights reserved.

Site design by *Independent Digital Communications*

———————

What in heaven's name are you claiming a copyright for? And why would anyone want credit for designing a non-site?

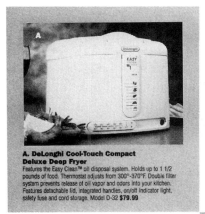

A. DeLonghi Cool-Touch Compact Deluxe Deep Fryer
Features the Easy Clean™ oil disposal system. Holds up to 1 1/2 pounds of food. Thermostat adjusts from 300°-370°F. Double filter system prevents release of oil vapor and odors into your kitchen. Features detachable lid, integrated handles, on/off indicator light, safety fuse and cord storage. Model D-32 **$79.99**

B. DeLonghi Classica Chrome Two-Slice Toaster
Classic styling and unique design. "Cool-touch" metal surface. Extra-lift mechanism raises small items higher for easy removal. Self-adjusting grips automatically center bread in slot. Slide cut crumb tray, defrost feature.Model CT-12 **$49.98**

A full line of DeLonghi's Toaster Oven Broilers is available.

C. DeLonghi Air Stream Convection Chrome Toaster Oven
Large .5cu ft capacity oven accommodates virtually all your family's cooking needs: baking, roasting, broiling, top browning, defrosting and dehydrating. Two tier cooking. Fully adjustable thermostat from 200°F to 450°F. Thermostat indicator light. Interior light to monitor cooking performance. Durastone enameled porcelain interior and convection fan distributes heat evenly for consistent cooking results. Includes durastone bake pan, broil rack, two oven racks, two cookie sheets, hand grip and instruction booklet.
Chrome Model AS-690 **$179.99**
Also Available:
White Model AS-670 **$159.99**

S *Crossed out prices are list prices.*
Call for Zabar's low, low prices!

D. DeLonghi Griglia Tutto Contact Grill
Quickly sears the food outside, sealing natural juices and flavors in. 3 variable cooking positions: closed for contact grilling, semi-closed for broiling plus top-browning, fully open for "barbecue" grilling. 2 interchangeable non-stick surfaces, cool touch handles, 3 power levels, thermal safety cut-off, on/off switch with indicator light. Model CG-18 **$99.99**

E. DeLonghi Alfredo Convection oven
With broil function. This large .99 cu ft capacity convection oven features porcelainized interior walls, internal light, double walls for heat retention, and controls for baking, broiling, top browning, defrosting and warming. Model E0284 **$299.99**

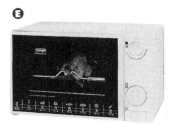

Fig. 3.4:   We can understand and empathize with two circumstances in which a catalog says, "Call for prices": (1) an annual catalog showing a commodity such as bulk paper, whose prices may go up or down dramatically over the year; (2) a pre-introduction description in which the retail price hasn't yet been set. Can a cataloger justify showing list prices and not actual prices with a half-hidden "Call for our low, low prices!" Nah. (If these are items for which the manufacturer forbids quoting a lowered price, say so, *emphatically*.)

Fellows, a mild suggestion: get your promotions in sync with one another. The cross-reference was yours, not your prospects', and not being ready to handle Web inquiries is even less justifiable than running an inquiry ad and not having catalogs to send.

The cataloger and the copywriter can eliminate all these problems easily by recognizing and implementing the Rule of Spartan Avoidance:

> ✏ When illustrations don't clarify the difference between similar items, copy must clarify the difference between similar items.

Here are a few more bits and pieces of confusion.

Then there's the catalog with my very favorite description in the entire world, for a Schwinn bicycle:

———————

Ships pre-assembled—about 15 minutes assembly required.

———————

And then there's the one with a "Nature Colored Knit Polo," in color, full bleed. Uh-oh, what's this line at the bottom of the description, after the all-too-telling line "And you'd be hard pressed to find construction like that on a shirt costing three digits"?

———————

Sorry, not available.

———————

Oh. I guess I'd be hard-pressed to find construction like that on a shirt costing any digits. How statesmanlike of you to describe it anyway.

Is it much ado about nothing?

We're wordsmiths. Words are our weapons. A difference of a fraction of 1 percent in our ability to generate or intensify reader involvement is worthwhile. Knowing how and when to plumb for power verbs and imperatives is just one more indication of our professionalism. Enough said.

Baroque Brass Candleholders Are Weighted Not To Tip. Inspired by a Dutch antique, they brighten decor even when candles aren't lit. Lacquer-protected against tarnish. Set of 3 to group or spread around: 4½", 7½" and 11¼" high. ¾" spike secures candles to 3" wide.
646YLR 3 All-brass Candleholders **$39.98**
115ZLR 3 Ivory Pillar Candles are the safe and elegant way to create a beautiful glow. Each is 3x3" tall, burns about 25 hours, shrink-wrapped. **$12.98**
Save $6.00! 2 Sets (6 Pillar Candles) **$19.98**

Fig. 3.5:   Mild confusion here. What might you have written to make "Weighted Not To Tip" clearer?

★ The secret the leading auction houses don't want you to know.

The ancient art of iconography.
For centuries, hand-painted icons occupied an honored place in Russian Orthodox churches and homes. Serving as a shrine and a source of inspiration, they became cherished family heirlooms. To destroy any threat to their power, Lenin and Stalin demolished hundreds of churches and with them, thousands of antique icons. As icons became scarce, values skyrocketed (especially abroad).

To capitalize on this, KGB agents launched a top-secret operation during the '60s whereby antique icons were recovered and retouched (often duplicating styles and signatures of famous masters). They were then passed off as 17th century originals. Antiquities experts tell us it is virtually impossible to distinguish the clever KGB forgeries from the 300-year-old, unadulterated masterpieces.

The icons we have may be authentic or they may just be top-notch forgeries. We don't know. We do know that the wooden panels they're painted on are 300 years old (we paid 100% duties to the Russian Ministry of Culture after they carbon-dated them and categorized them as 17th century vintage).

Exquisite art objects, each features the Madonna with Child with gold leaf border. Approximately 9"x12". *No two exactly the same.* A rare and wonderful collectible, at a fraction of the thousands you'd pay at auction or in an antique shop for a so-called "original." Your money back if not completely satisfied. #150231 **$650**

Attention Collectors! Also available, a few icons depicting St. George Slaying the Dragon (a classic Russian symbol and the emblem on Moscow's crest) and St. Mikhail. St. George is on horseback with his spear held high. The dragon, beneath the horse's forelegs knows the end is near; angels watch from above. Good overcomes Evil as a winged St. Mikhail, holding the orb and sceptre, sits atop a winged Pegasus. Both icons are accented with gold. We have just a few of each style, so please call before ordering. #150239 **$650**

Fig. 3.6:   Utter honesty works when it's tied to salesmanship. To say, "The icons we have may be authentic or they may just be top-notch forgeries" indicates a less-than-professional look into provenance. (The Lewis household has an icon whose validity was verified by an expert, using what he described as "standard techniques to winnow out forgeries." For icons selling at $650 this catalog should have done the same.) For a more salesworthy way to sell a replica, see figure 3.7.

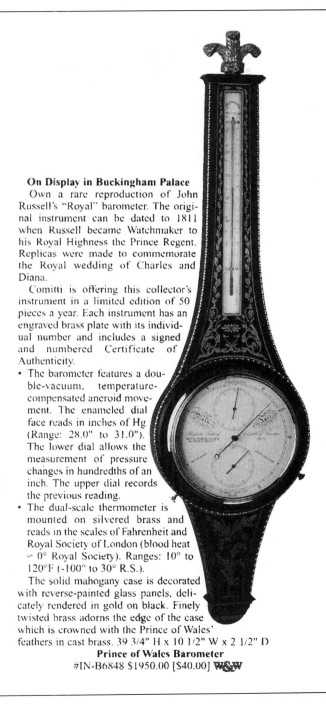

On Display in Buckingham Palace

Own a rare reproduction of John Russell's "Royal" barometer. The original instrument can be dated to 1811 when Russell became Watchmaker to his Royal Highness the Prince Regent. Replicas were made to commemorate the Royal wedding of Charles and Diana.

Comitti is offering this collector's instrument in a limited edition of 50 pieces a year. Each instrument has an engraved brass plate with its individual number and includes a signed and numbered Certificate of Authenticity.

- The barometer features a double-vacuum, temperature-compensated aneroid movement. The enameled dial face reads in inches of Hg (Range: 28.0" to 31.0"). The lower dial allows the measurement of pressure changes in hundredths of an inch. The upper dial records the previous reading.
- The dual-scale thermometer is mounted on silvered brass and reads in the scales of Fahrenheit and Royal Society of London (blood heat = 0° Royal Society). Ranges: 10° to 120°F (-100° to 30° R.S.).

The solid mahogany case is decorated with reverse-painted glass panels, delicately rendered in gold on black. Finely twisted brass adorns the edge of the case which is crowned with the Prince of Wales' feathers in cast brass. 39 3/4" H x 10 1/2" W x 2 1/2" D

Prince of Wales Barometer

#IN-B6848 $1950.00 [$40.00] W&W

Fig. 3.7: This is the proper way to relate a replication to the original. After describing the original instrument, the copywriter then establishes a *separate* logical value to the limited-edition reproduction.

Leatherface™

One tough mother scratcher of a knee pad.

The dinosaur of knee pads finally met its maker. Those old-fashioned, felt-lined, rub-the-backs-of-your-knees-raw pads have finally been updated. Great design means extreme comfort. Flexible heavy leather exterior now comes with high density padding against the knees. An inner plastic shield eliminates spot pressure points. Quick-release fastening system replace those gnarly leather straps.

#55006 $39.99

Fig. 3.8:   What professional copywriting! Here is as mundane a product as anyone could be asked to describe. As the reader smiles, he or she also recognizes the enhancement over "the dinosaur of knee pads."

Fig. 3.9: Whom to blame? The headline says, in almost unreadable type, "All Eureka Lightweights On Sale!" Is the "Powerline Superbroom" a lightweight? What reason might anyone have to buy any of these? Even one descriptive line would help. Probably the copywriter *wasn't* to blame because the command was to have simple listings.

4

I'm Awfully Tired Today, So Please Don't Challenge Me.

First, *You* Try It!

Your assignment . . .

Rewrite this headline for communication—connecting with your readers—assuming your targets are upscale consumers who don't have a lot of technical background.

Acoustic Masses Parallel Room-Dominating Speakers

In place of massive vibrating woofers you'll find inexpensive production-line speakers, the Olaf Acoustrong OA-67X Speakers use two acoustic air masses to reinforce the base while reducing harmonic distortion. Omnidirectional $2\frac{1}{2}''$ wide range speakers work anywhere in the room.

Okay, what's your first decision?

Right! You're going to tell the reader what you're talking about . . . which is . . . what?

Speakers? If that's your decision, you're selling metal, not romance. The alert copywriter asks himself what interests the *reader*?

Okay. You're selling these speakers. Suggest a more salesworthy headline.

Take thirty seconds. No longer than that.

What's your headline? If it's something like "Big Speaker Sound" or "Technological Break-through," you're safe. But you aren't on the main line because you're just repeating a tired cliché. Here's a different tune, a dialogue:

- "Close your eyes and listen."

- "Hmmm. I'd guess it's a 15-inch woofer."

- "Nope. The whole speaker is $2\frac{1}{2}$ inches."

- "You've gotta be kidding!"

You can't even consider a heading such as this unless you have LOTS of space. In small space, how about:

In 2010 Your Neighbors Will Have These Speakers, Too.

Whatever you wrote, I hope you sold *benefit*, not metal.

Lip Service Doesn't Serve Clarity

Do you, struggling through the day's catch of catalogs, sometimes feel as I do . . . the writer is daring you to clarify the muddy message?

A single constant theme, running throughout this book, is my slavish worship of the Clarity Commandment:

> ✐ In force-communication, clarity is paramount. Don't let any other component of the communication mix interfere with it.

Catalog copy is as grass-roots force-communication as any copywriting could ever be. Catalog copywriters, who have smaller space and fewer words than advertising, direct-mail, or editorial writers, have to brand the commandment on their foreheads.

I really hope this isn't like a seat-belt law, which gets lip service from drivers who then ignore it.

Add to the Clarity Commandment another venerable maxim, the Whose Message Is It Anyway? Rule:

> ✐ Your message should operate within the experiential background of the message recipient, not within your own experiential background.

Together, these stainless, rustproofing principles will lead a catalog writer through the muddy rhetorical waters of overwritten, overcolorful, and self-contradictory copy.

Overwriting, overcolorful word use, and copy engendering an "Is it A or is it B?" reaction didn't exist when Sears', Ward's, and Alden's were the only catalogs most of us saw. Those were companies that took the long view. Their product lines, though extensive, were slow to change; description was paramount and benefit was left to the buyer's imagination (which in those bygone times was far more self-corruptible than the writer's).

So a description such as figure 4.1, in those catalogs, wouldn't have left the reader wondering what the relative percentages of silk and wool were in that jacket.

Internet copywriters who migrate to printed catalogs can bring some nasty habits with them. They see nothing wrong with taking forever to get to a point, or making a reference that requires three or four clicks to clarify. Don't emulate those semi-writers who regard the medium as paramount over the message.

Sophistication grows . . . clarity goes.

What could be clearer than the classic Sears "Good, Better, Best" labeling? When catalog merchandise is competitive only with itself, clarity is recognized as the asset it is.

A. Silk/Wool Herringbone Blazer *An Orvis Exclusive.* From workdays to weekends, across seasons and time zones, our adaptable jacket pairs as perfectly with denim pants as it does with a tailored skirt. The spring-weight blend of silk and wool is a subtle herringbone weave of soft blues, styled with two buttons, set-in flap pockets. Fully lined. Sizes 6-20; about 28" long. Dry clean. USA.   LA147X **$159**

Fig. 4.1:   It's a "silk/wool" blazer. Copy sells correctly if the percentage of silk is negligible. If the percentage of silk is substantial, the writer should give us the ratios. Buyers want that information.

In these darker days, with our tables and desks covered inches deep with catalogs, competition is external, not internal. Each catalog fights for its life in one of the most brutally competitive marketplaces the wily brain of humankind could invent. An endless fight makes clarity a victim, like a pedestrian crossing an expressway that has no stoplights, no speed limit, no lane markers, no direction signs.

Our job: preserve the victim.

This is why clarity suffers.

Clarity suffers because of . . .

1. the fight for attention
2. the fight for item-by-item desirability
3. the fight for reader involvement
4. the fight for colorful word use
5. the assumption that *where* it is (in a particular catalog or on a website) equals *what* it is

How far we've come down the muddy road! The struggle to create clarity in the midst of the raging maelstrom of rhetorical tricks isn't at all parallel to sweetly innocent product descriptions. Nor should it be. We couldn't be content with 1950-ish catalog writing, anymore than we'd be content with 1950-ish novels or movies or luxury cars. They're charming curios, not dynamic competitors.

So clarity becomes a petunia in an onion patch. It's out of place when the writer, after the fact, tries to go back into copy blocks created for a different purpose—flair, corporate image, ultra-high fashion—to bring clarity bubbling to the surface. Copy is skewed because clarity wasn't a primary intention of the original message mix.

Proofreader, Where Are You?

Fashion catalogs are especially prone to sacrificing their descriptions on the "We're Different" altar. Probably this is because this is the toughest field in which to stand apart, not only from competitors but from internal competition within the catalog's own pages.

That's where proofreading should become a factor.

A copywriter falls in love with a phrase and unconsciously overuses it. Days or even weeks may elapse between product descriptions, but the reader sees them in one piece.

So we have, on page 10 of a fashion catalog:

Fresh pastels weave their fashion magic in this versatile braided cotton belt. . . .

---

and on page 12, same catalog:

Fiesta-bright colors weave their fashion magic in this cotton braided belt. . . .

Okay, it's possible that fresh pastels and fiesta-bright colors both weave fashion magic. But don't the two descriptions *detract* from each other's impact? (I didn't scan the catalog for other fashion-magic weavers, but they may have been there because obviously nobody said, "Hey, we've used that phrase before. Make up another description.")

"Who cares if you know the words? I'm the writer and I know them."

The Whose Message Is It Anyway? Rule popped into place when I heard one woman I regard as knowledgeable in fashion ask another, "What's a dobby pattern?" Neither knew. They guessed "nobby" or "nubby" pattern, but the product photograph didn't bear them out.

I thought—if it shows horses, maybe it's a *dobbin* pattern. It didn't show horses. The copy read, "Our pleat-front cotton blouse has a dobby pattern, Peter Pan collar and concealed button front." No clues there.

That's one of the no-clarity keys: hit-and-run description, using a word and telling the reader, "If you're not fashionwise, you don't deserve to understand my copy." Uh-uh. Copy should say, "Dear, Sweet Reader, This is for you, and because you feel comfortable and secure with my description you'll buy." (More on hit-and-run in chapter 23.)

The dictionary gave us the definition of dobby: "A spirit like a brownie, but often malicious." I don't want that pattern in my house.

Okay, I'm being wry. But how difficult would it have been for the writer of this medium-price fashion catalog to say, "*I* know what dobby means, but maybe some of my readers don't. So I'll inject a four- or five-word description: 'Our pleat-front cotton blouse has a dobby pattern (SHORT EXPLANATION) . . . '"?

In Search of an Ombudsman

I long have preached the doctrine of having an outsider—someone not involved in product acquisition or description—check catalog copy for logic.

No, I'm not referring to a proofreader. I'm suggesting a designated ombudsman.

I'd compare this with the role of independent counsel, although not in as dogged nor agenda-laden a mode as one hired by the government. The ombudsman is responsible to only the highest authority, the CEO. The creative director, the art director, the head of merchandising—none of these should have any influence or control.

Why shouldn't they have any control? Because if they did, the job would be for window dressing only, not for serious reinterpretation of how what appears in print, or on the Web, represents the company. And how about clarity?

Yes, how about clarity?

Here's catalog copy with a heading "The skinny on bed and bath."

They need an ombudsman.

I'm aware of current slang. I'm also aware that by the time it filters down to the bedrock over-thirty-fives, it's already worn out among its originators. To many—or maybe even to most—who see a photo of a king-size bed next to a headline starting with "The skinny . . ." the reaction has to be, "Huh?"

I'll bet four dollars whoever wrote that is under thirty. So the writer generated copy not for the catalog's readers but for the catalog's creative department. And somebody approved it. That's why the ombudsman shouldn't have to answer to a creative director or an art director, who may share an oblique attitude.

Which Scottish soap do you want?

Here's a catalog that, on page 2, has "Pure & Simple Tropical Sampler." It's twelve seven-oz. bars of soap, made in Scotland. Regular price is $36, sale price $29.99.

Okay, that's page 2. Now, here's page 24, with a heading, "Pure & Simple Floral Sampler." Yep, it's twelve seven-oz. bars of soap, made in Scotland. Price is $38.

To which the typical soaper puzzles, "Huh?"

They need an ombudsman.

And what might that ombudsman have suggested, in this instance? If these two soaps differ—and from the photographs they don't seem to—he or she would have insisted they be given adjacent positions, with the differences explained. If they don't differ, the ombudsman would have earned his or her salary for the month then and there.

Are there a few subtleties a proofreader might miss?

Not every call on an ombudsman's talent is obvious. But certainly, anyone qualified to be a catalog ombudsman recognizes the necessity of a quick link from headline to body copy.

So a proofreader certainly would catch the ghastly grammatical error but might find nothing wrong with the logical error in this next one; in fact, *wrong* is too harsh a word. Rather, the proofreader might miss or discount the lack of linkage. The ombudsman wouldn't. The heading:

Get a light or vigorous workout with our electronic monitored Mini Stepper.

And the body copy:

Step up to better health in the convenience of your home as you tone waist, calves, hips, and thighs with this Mini Stepper. It's extremely smooth pulley system uses resistance from hydraulic cylinders to improve your endurance and cardiovascular performance as well as muscle tone. A built-in computer records elapsed time and counts number of steps taken. Made of durable steel . . . [rest of copy is mechanical].

I certainly hope you aren't wondering what the grammatical error is. Somebody who doesn't know the difference between *its* and *it's* is grammatically challenged beyond any help we might offer. The mini-problem an ombudsman would catch and rectify is the "light or vigorous" reference, never covered in the text although ample opportunity abounds. The elapsed-time computer provides a perfect *refer*-back opportunity, such as: "Whether for a couple of minutes between conferences or for your daily tone up. . . ." And this should be first in line since it's the headline reference.

Figure this one out!

Titanic mania may not end until they raise the thing from the ocean floor. Here's a ship model, and it isn't cheap. The heading:

Limited Edition *TITANIC!* $699.00 Length overall 24.5″

The picture is a ship model that doesn't quite look like the *Titanic* but has four stacks and the name *Titanic* on it. Any question about what this is? Keep reading. Here's every word of one of the strangest ombudsman-ready copy blocks you'll see today:

TITANIC! 15 April 1912! The ship that wouldn't sink . . . Amazing, the movie cost more than White Star Lines paid Harland & Wolff, Belfast to build the original. 46,439 tons, 882.5′ LOA, 92′ beam, triple screw, combination triple expansion engines and turbine, 23 knots. Her sister, *Olympic*, was also bad luck! Collided with HMS *Hawke*, 1911; rammed by German U-103, 1918; rammed and sank the *Nantucket Lightship*, 1934; demolished 1937. Tucher & Walther couldn't resist. Four funnels, but only twin screws, with big wind-up motor. Limited edition of 750, with Certificate and box. Hopefully proving that a pool is somewhat safer than the North Atlantic! Mea culpa! "Oops . . ., I goofed when I wrote the original copy. *Titanic* fans, please accept my sincerest apologies."—Slim

---

Okay, we'll accept your sincerest apologies if you'll accept the sincerest advice that you need an ombudsman.

Look for a mis-mix *and* mis-match.

Should we be upset by these two references from the inside-the-cover letter in a recent fashion catalog?

Turn to page 5 for the New Romantic look, in our red calico suit . . .

Remember, you can find your size—whether it's Misses, Petites (5'4" and under), Women's or Half Sizes. Our new emblem makes shopping for your size range even easier.

Page 5 had a red suit, which *probably* was calico. But nowhere in the description did the word *calico* appear, making letter and description a mismatch for those who may not have a one-on-one knowledge of calico other than the childhood poem about the calico cat.

And how does the emblem make shopping for a size range easier? Scouring the catalog, we do see an occasional wedge, usually facing the other direction, with phrases such as "Also petite" and "Also women" set inside. Wouldn't it have been gracious of the copywriter to tell us *how* the emblem (that word also bothers me: it isn't an emblem) works, explaining that it appears when the range of sizes is expanded? "Makes shopping easier" is the muzzy phrase that throws us.

Your turn. You be ombudsman for any catalog on your table. If you're especially stouthearted, make it your own.

The Adjectival Morass

As usual, it's the adjectives and adverbs, not the nouns and verbs, that cause copy to grunt and heave instead of flowing smoothly. Read this product description:

F. Shrimp basket. Georgia artist Kate Lloyd has created yet another virtually irresistible basket of natural reed and papier-mâché. The pale peach basket is freshly decorated with coral-colored shrimp and highlighted in blue and green. Hand painted and signed by the artist, our shrimp basket is just as comfortable in traditional settings as it is at the beach. . . .

Colorful writing causes kinks here. Our "How's that again?" reaction isn't generated by "coral-colored shrimp"; we know perfectly well, and the photograph verifies, that they're painted on, not real. What raises the first question in comprehension is "freshly." How does that word fit? How does it enhance the description? We'd understand "decorated with fresh, coral-colored shrimp," but "freshly decorated with coral-colored shrimp," suggesting wet paint or fresh shrimp, is hard to compute.

Then we hit "just as comfortable in traditional settings as it is at the beach." Does that mean we've been wrong? It's a *real* shrimp basket? No, it can't be, because it's papier-mâché, and that means fragility.

Conclusion: it's a case of overwriting, stemming from emphasis on colorful rhetoric rather than the Clarity Commandment and the Whose Message Is It Anyway? Rule.

How sweet it is!

The writer who says, "Here's mud in your eye," and the writer who struggles like Hercules in the Augean Stables (see the next paragraph) for word color can damage the catalog reader's desire to buy. What a paradox! It's exactly the reverse of what the writer is paid to do.

(If you don't know the story of Hercules and the Augean Stables, consider: if I'd used the reference in catalog copy, I'd have killed you off. Even in a trade book, showing off for no purpose makes the reader uncomfortable, doesn't it?)

Like a virtuoso violinist who makes impossible fingering seem easy, a good catalog writer creates descriptions so clear and appealing the casual reader doesn't recognize the talent behind it. The writer has done what he or she is paid to do—call attention to what's being sold, not *how* it's being sold.

This near-perfect piece of copy, in lesser hands, might have repelled the reader instead of attracting her:

STRIPED TUNIC

In India, where temperatures often reach scorching, unbearable heights those in the know on how to keep cool wear the traditional tunic called a "kurta." We've designed ours in 100-gram *Bengal Silk*, to keep you cool in the sizzling days of summer, and glide just as easily into autumn's chillier clime. With deep, gusseted armholes, pullover placket front, and. . . .

Yes, I know a comma is missing and I know the phrase "those in the know on how to keep cool" is a shade tortured. What I admire is the writer's restraint in not hitting us in the eye with the word *kurta*, bragging at once, "I know something you don't, dummy."

Effective force-communication often demands vocabulary *suppression*. If this bothers you, write textbooks.

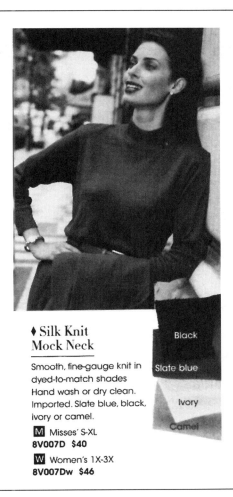

♦ Silk Knit
Mock Neck

Smooth, fine-gauge knit in
dyed-to-match shades
Hand wash or dry clean.
Imported. Slate blue, black,
ivory or camel.

M Misses' S-XL
8V007D $40

W Women's 1X-3X
8V007Dw $46

Black

Slate blue

Ivory

Camel

Fig. 4.2:   Here's another silk garment. The fashion-conscious young woman who showed it to me said she *couldn't* order based on this description because it doesn't state the gauge, thickness, weight, and whether it's to be worn as a T-shirt or as a light sweater.

Clinically proven

New! Keep most foods in your refrigerator fresher and tastier from 10-100% longer

Unlike baking soda, which can only control food odors, clinical tests prove that our 100% natural, non-toxic FoodSaver extends the life of most foods; fruits and vegetables stay crispier longer, baked goods stay fresher longer, leftovers and meats taste better and last longer. Simply place a box of FoodSaver in your refrigerator. The proprietary blend of minerals helps regulate humidity in your refrigerator as air circulates through small holes in the box. Once humidity levels are regulated, lower temperatures are maintained, bacterial and mold growth is slowed by up to 60% and odors are eliminated. FoodSaver even helps your refrigerator run up to 15% more efficiently! 3-pack lasts an entire year.

FoodSaver 3-Pack   LP0100 $19.95

Fig. 4.3:   In a direct-mail presentation, "Clinically proven" has to be justified. In a catalog, a question about the validity of the claim is seldom raised. Note how copy dismisses the principal competitor, baking soda.

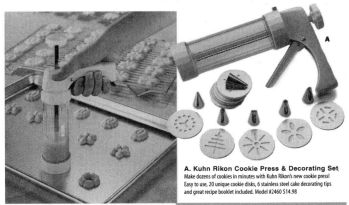

A. Kuhn Rikon Cookie Press & Decorating Set
Make dozens of cookies in minutes with Kuhn Rikon's new cookie press!
Easy to use, 20 unique cookie disks, 6 stainless steel cake decorating tips
and great recipe booklet included. Model #2460 $14.98

B. Kuhn Rikon Duromatic Pressure Cookers
Kuhn Rikon brings pressure cooking back to your kitchen. Your grand-
mother knew the fastest, easiest and most delicious way to cook was in a
pressure cooker. We bring you that method back with 20th century technology, innovation and European design. Free cookbook $14 value!
5 Ltr. Model #3342 $164.00
7 Ltr. Model #3344 $172.00

C. Kuhn Rikon Duromatic Duo Set
Fast, for busy people who love great food this set offers you all the cookware for a
great meal. These new generation cookers come with six built in safety features for
complete peace of mind.
Set includes: 5 Lit Body, 2 Lit Frypan Body, Pressure lid, Glass lid.
Free cookbook $14 value plus Fresh Food Menu Planner/Recipe booklet.
Model #1588 $299.00

**Kuhn Rikon
Duromatic
Pressure Cookers**

Safe
The integrated lid-locking system
and no fewer than 5 safety steam-
release systems make the UL
approved Duromatic the standard of
safety worldwide.

Fast
Compare cooking times! Cooking
with Duromatic takes an average
of 1/3 the cooking time of conventional cooking methods.

*Crossed out prices
are list prices.*

*Call for Zabar's low,
low prices!*

**D. Duromatic
Pressure Frypans**

It's a pressure cooker . . . it's a
frypan . . . it's a braiser! Our unique
honeycomb waffle bottom lets you
brown meat without the use of oils
or fats. These shallow, wide cookers
are ideal for braising and sautéing
before pressure cooking. The right
size for a 1–2 person household. All
Kuhn Rikon Pressure Cookers come
with a 10-year warranty and a free
cookbook.

Pressure Frypan
2.5 Ltr. (long handle)
Model #3346 $160.00

Braiser
2.5 Ltr. Model #3347
$160.00

Fig. 4.4: Crossed-out prices suggest a lower actual price. What is it? Not particularly prominent is the suggestion to call for the company's "low, low prices." Call what number? It isn't on this page. Curiously, on a page that does list a phone number the company also lists a fax number—not a toll-free one—"To order now." How can anyone fax an order, not knowing what the price is? Suggestion: don't play a guessing game with your customers, and if you want calls and faxes, put that number directly adjacent to copy asking for the call or fax.

5

The Clarity Commandment Revisited

First, *You* Try It!

Your assignment . . .

Replace this headline, which actually ran, page after page, on an upscale catalog:

The Season of Quintessence

Before replacing these four words with one to ten *clearer* words, ask yourself: what was this writer trying to transmit?

Yes, the impression is one of a beginner who learns a new word and has to launch it at every possible target.

If we look up *quintessence* in *Merriam Webster's*, we get little help:

1. The fifth or last and highest element in ancient medieval philosophy. The ancient Greeks recognized four elements, fire, air, water, and earth. The Pythagoreans and Aristotle added a fifth, ether. Heavenly bodies were said to be composed of this additional element. *2.* The essence of a thing in its most concentrated form. *3.* The most typical example.

How do we tie any of this to *season*? We don't . . . and not just because it's a wild stretch. No, we don't tie it to *season* because we, as clarity-seeking copywriters, wouldn't use *quintessence*. What percentage of our readers know the word at all? What percentage won't buy from us because we've made them feel uncomfortable?

So let's have your replacement.

Take thirty seconds. No longer than that.

Okay, what do you have? "The Heavenly Season"? Great. "Procession of the Ultimates"? Much as the word *ultimate* is overused, it's an improvement. In fact, I'll bet *anything* you created is an improvement.

Form Over Substance: A Dangerous Direction

Depending on whose catalog you're writing, you have lists of rules, constraints, and no-nos at your elbow.

"You can't say this." "You have to put it this way." "You can have only twelve words of two syllables or more in a copy block." "The first word has to be a verb."

What's wrong with every one of these rules?

Right! They emphasize form, not substance.

But *we* know better. We have the Clarity Commandment. It's at our elbow, pasted onto our keyboard, scrolled on the doorposts of our house, and etched onto our foreheads.

With the Clarity Commandment in place, emphasis shifts to where it should be: communicating on the reader's level.

What are the benefits of clarity?

Clarity adds a key ingredient to the catalog copy mix: the reader knows what you mean.

Ever travel to Europe without your voltage adapter and unwittingly try to plug your electric appliance into a wall outlet? It didn't fit.

The same problem confronts catalog writers who try to plug their rhetoric into the reader's consciousness. Unless writers are equipped with rhetorical adapters, their rhetoric won't fit. No current flows through the line because the rhetoric isn't plugged in.

Okay, enough metaphor. The adapter is the Clarity Commandment, and if you keep it at the ready and plug it in to clarify a violation, copy can only be improved.

Another benefit: you'll cut down returns and "white mail" (complaints, curses, and occasional threats, usually sent in your postage-paid envelopes) because what you ship will be what you've described.

Figure 5.1 won't win any awards for brilliant copywriting. But it's clearer and less likely to generate returned merchandise than many "brilliantly written" pieces of copy. As you read it, you'll see that it tells you exactly how this clock radio differs from ordinary clock radios. Every

Very smart clock radio always knows what time it is and never needs setting!
You need it to know the precise time when you wake up in the morning, but this amazing clock radio sure doesn't need you! Plug it in and it automatically sets the time, month, date, and day of the week. During a power failure it keeps track of the passage of time, and even readjusts itself to daylight savings and leap years. How does the Emerson Research "SmartSet" do it? It comes with a factory-programmed micro chip that's automatically activated by a lithium button-type battery (included). Dual alarms can be programmed separately for weekdays, weekends or everyday operation. With bold green LED display lights. Lull yourself to sleep and wake with music or alarm. Perfect for your night table: measures 8½" x 4" x 3¼" deep.
Emerson Research SmartSet™ Clock Radio
#ASS340 $39.95

Fig. 5.1: With just enough sell to be convincing (words such as *amazing* and *perfect*), this description is factual and clear. The exposition cleverly leaves it to the reader to self-convince that this clock radio is next-generation, a logical replacement for the old one now on the nightstand.

necessary bit of information is included, with an economy of words and a minimum of puffery.

What *is* it?

I'm looking at a catalog page describing scrimshaw pocket knives, money clips, belt buckles, and other novelties.

You and I know: we can find two types of scrimshaw. The first, the expensive type, is hand-carved ivory. The second, the inexpensive type, is molded plastic. Which are these?

This writer ignored the Clarity Commandment. Copy says, rather cleverly, "original scrimshaw designs" and "carefully etched and hand-finished." The word *ivory* appears, but its use could be interpreted as a color, not a medium—which may be a sly attempt to *avoid* clarity.

Might this be a trade-off? We'll attract some buyers who don't know the difference . . . and handle forthrightly any complaints from buyers who think they're getting real ivory.

Had the Clarity Commandment been in effect, the writer could have served both God and Mammon by using phrases such as "in the tradition of" and "the look and feel of." I recommend this only because, having read the copy three times, I'm still only 99 percent sure it *isn't* real ivory, and without the key we won't open as many doors.

Can you say *vol-au-vent?*

Quick! What does *vol-au-vent* mean?

If you answered, "It's pronounced 'vol-oh-vahn' and it's pastry filled with meat or vegetables," skip this section.

If you answered, "Huh?" you parallel every person I asked, except one, whose guess was oblique to the target but close enough to qualify ("It's some sort of prepared food, isn't it?").

Copy for this item, in a catalog of cookware gadgets, reads:

Our new *VOL-AU-VENT CUTTERS* are such fun! Use on puff pastry (frozen works just fine) to make patty shells for creamed chicken, shrimp, or vegetables. So easy, it's a wonderful way to add elegance and excitement to a meal! Four great shapes, each approximately $4\frac{1}{4}''$ in diameter. Made in the USA.

The copy isn't bad; the picture does show the item. Defense might be, "If they don't know what it is they aren't our prospects anyway." Ah, but the catalog was addressed to "H. Lewis," who, even with a superficial knowledge of French and kitchens, couldn't pinpoint this. Are we mailing catalogs to those who don't understand the copy in the catalog?

Too, replacing the generic "So easy, it's a wonderful way to add elegance and excitement to a meal!" with a *specific* could only help clarity and salesmanship.

On to another question: what does "Fingerpaint" mean to you?

I tried this one on the same group, and answers without exception referred to kindergarten scrawls. So this headline—

FINGERPAINT MUGS

—didn't prepare any of us for the pleasant but mismatching descriptive copy:

Set of two prettily decorated earthenware mugs handpainted in bright springtime colors. A refreshing look. Set of two, 10 oz. each. Gift boxed.

#01265—two fingerpaint mugs $10.95

Looking at the mugs, I can see they're hand painted. But, at least *within my experiential background*, they aren't finger paintings. In no way could a finger, however well trained, create those designs.

Get those words: *within my experiential background*. It's inconsequential that the writer knows what he or she means. What matters is whether the *reader* knows.

If you think I'm being too harsh, consider: why should any catalog copywriter *ever* violate the Clarity Commandment? Whatever the writing style, whatever the admonition from on high, whatever is being sold to whomever, no one ever perished from an overdose of clarity.

What about those line breaks?

When you're writing text-type headlines, why not give the reader a break by breaking lines at logical points?

For example, which of these is easier to read?

_____

A Charming Pictorial Treasury of the Many Images of the
Jolly Gentleman with the Red Coat and White Beard

_____

Or . . .

_____

A Charming Pictorial Treasury
of the Many Images
of the Jolly Gentleman
with the Red Coat and the White Beard

_____

The second version does break the message into chewable bites; that's one step toward clarity. But if we have just two lines, we can add quick comprehension simply by changing the line break to eliminate an "of the" that leads nowhere:

_____

A Charming Pictorial Treasury of the Many Images
of the Jolly Gentleman with the Red Coat and White Beard

_____

Take a keyboard breath where you'd normally take a speaking breath and you're less likely to fluster the reader. A flustered reader is less likely to buy.

As I said, no one ever perished from an overdose of clarity.

Quilted Car Seat Covers keep hair and dirt off the seats (everything removes with a shake), and the durable black quilted nylon-poly keeps your pet comfortable—everyone is happy. Secure with elastic straps and hook closure. Fold to store. Machine wash/dry. Front seat cover is 28x48"; rear seat 48x56". Made in America.

307ALR Front Seat Cover **$24.98**

3539LR Rear Seat Cover, not shown. **$39.98**

Fig. 5.2:   Copy clarifies exactly what these seat covers are, what they do, how they attach, and what benefits you can expect . . . all in just six lines.

6

What's on Top of the Copy Block?

The Six Types of Headings

Analysis shows us two key families of headings:

- nominative
- descriptive

Nominative headings are simple categorizations such as "Dress," "Cordless Telephone," and "Radio."

Descriptive headings replace the name with what that name represents, such as "For an Evening Out," "Twirl as You Talk," and "AM/FM Cube."

Within each family we have three copy choices:

- basic
- romantic
- positioned

Basic headline copy is a no-nonsense, unassailable approach: "Red Jersey Dress." Romantic headline copy attempts to superimpose an emotional reaction: "The Paris Salon Look." Positioned copy replaces product with product-in-use: "Perfect for Office or for Evening Out."

So actually, we can choose from six headline types:

1. basic nominative
2. romantic nominative
3. positioned nominative
4. basic descriptive
5. romantic descriptive
6. positioned descriptive

So what? So this . . .

Match headings to your readers.

By matching headings to your readers you're more likely to get an order. Why? For two reasons:

First, it's possible to promise too much, just as it's possible to promise too little. Either way, you've disconnected the thin line of rapport you're hoping for as the recipient flips through the first few pages of your catalog.

Second, business-to-business catalogs take a calculated risk when they depart from basic nominative. That risk can pay off, by either adding enough romance to generate an impulse buy or by positioning the item so the reader becomes an unwitting convert; or the risk can turn off the energy flow. That's the challenge of this business!

Is it profitable to romanticize the headline so much that readers have to stop, reconnoiter, then check the picture again to be sure they have understood what you're selling? Headline copy becomes a game of Russian roulette.

Contemporary catalog writing leans toward romanticization without touching either a nominative or descriptive base. This is a bleedover from the most upper-crust catalogs, and it seems to have filtered down to all levels. Sometimes it's a way for the writer to show off, and that's when it gets dangerous because the reader just can't follow the writer into the byzantine maze of nondescriptive words.

(The whole issue doesn't exist in catalogs that don't use headings at all. They have to grab with the first few words of body copy . . . or with an overpowering illustration.)

A catalog headline says:

Strike it Rich!

The picture shows a miniature replica of an oil derrick (positioned, for some reason, against a venetian blind, which makes the derrick hard to see). Body copy doesn't implement the heading or follow through on the "Strike it Rich" romance:

These 18K gold-plated oil derricks are perfect conversation pieces for home or office. . . .

Sure, we know the phrase "Strike it Rich"—we'd also either capitalize "it" or remove the caps from "Rich"—can relate to an oil strike. But if we're romanticizing *without* a nominative or descriptive base, do we intrigue or confuse?

An indication of how the heading affects the tone of the whole copy block is this description of a necklace:

Rondo a la turquoise: neo-classic variations on a theme of silver circles, with a touch of the blues. Counterpoints by Jay Feinberg. Faux turquoise necklace of antique-looking silver discs in a jazzy progression of sizes.

Interesting. *After* Jay Feinberg we have a solid description of what the item really is.

Safe isn't always best.

You don't really need a catalog writer for basic nominative headings. In fact, catalog houses whose copy stems from product managers defend this type of heading on grounds of "descriptive integrity." They have a point: it's hard to exaggerate or make a phony claim in a basic nominative heading.

But safe isn't always best. A powerful writer can bring a mundane item to life with a bright headline that romanticizes or positions.

Can you intermix heading types? You bet. Try doing it. At worst, you'll stretch some rusty creative muscles. At best, you'll add wallop to some rusty descriptions.

We're all victims of neatness complexes. We set a pattern for description headings, and then we're stuck with that pattern throughout the catalog.

Our theory is sound—the catalog gains coherence—but our execution of the theory may cost us some orders.

Fig. 6.1:   The heading says "Oster Mixer." That's what it is. Had the heading been enhanced with even a few generics, such as "State of the Art Oster Mixer," would reader appeal and an accompanying buying impulse have been enhanced?

Leave it to Harley-Davidson to combine vintage '40s styling with today's technology.

Authentically detailed right down to its tractor-style seat and spokes, this true-scaled miniature of the brand new 1997 FLSTS™ Heritage Springer Softail captivates with classic appeal. One look at the 1940s-style fenders and classic horn design will tell you this is definitely not just any motorcycle. Displayed on the rear fender is a replica of the Heritage Springer's DOT-approved, retro-'40s tombstone tail light commonplace on Harley's decades ago. Fishtail mufflers and whitewall tires further enhance the vintage styling. Resembling a 1948 Harley-Davidson Panhead, this brand new design returns to yesteryear in honor of a bygone era of motorcycling. All we can say is, "This machine was born to be wild!" 1:10 scale. 7" long.

660018 Harley-Davidson FLSTS™ Heritage Springer Model $49

Fig. 6.2: Romancing the product is a totally valid selling technique for an item whose appeal is emotional rather than functional. Suppose the heading had been "Harley-Davidson miniature model." How much appeal would have been lost?

Your warm, fluffy towel is ready.

Until now, towel warmer bars have been indigenous to luxurious European hotels and spas. But when a convenience is this cozy and inexpensive, there's no reason it shouldn't be in everyone's bathroom. The rack's four warming bars will heat even the thickest towels with a flick of the On/Off switch. Freestanding rack includes brackets for optional wall mounting. Long 5½' cord.

410014 Towel Warmer $99 ✈

✈ *Additional charge for air delivery.*

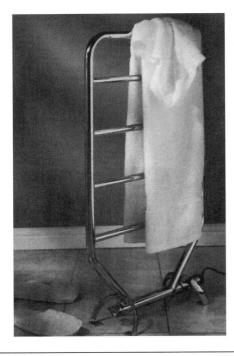

Fig. 6.3:   Here is a perfect example of product romanticizing. The average catalog copywriter would have written a headline such as "European-style towel warmer bars." If you can create a headline such as this, combining elegance with economy of words, you're a master copywriter.

CARRY POWERFUL PROTECTION WITH A CLEAR CONSCIENCE.

You're returning to your car from the mall or fumbling for your keys at your door when you are grabbed from behind!

Thanks to the device hidden in the palm of your hand, a life-threatening situation is avoided! As reported in U.S. News and World Report, the Pulse Wave Myotron is a whole new level of nonlethal protection that "really works." Developed for the FBI and used by law enforcement officers all over the world, Pulse Wave Myotron is saving lives every day. Advertised on national TV for $229.95, it is now available to you through Lifestyle Fascination for just $149.95!

Personal protection without violence! The Pulse Wave Myotron isn't fired like a stun gun. In fact, it's less than half as big and five times more powerful than the best police stun gun. It works by emitting pulse waves that intercept brainwaves controlling aggression and the voluntary muscles. [In order to tell you about the Pulse Wave Myotron, this writer watched a demonstration videotaped in front of CIA, FBI, and Justice Department representatives. They broke out in applause after a female volunteer used the Pulse Wave Myotron on a career criminal volunteer. (He instantly fell back, collapsed, and remained incapacitated for over 15 minutes. Yet he recovered completely within 30 minutes.)] Because it does not cause serious bodily harm, the U.S. Bureau of Alcohol, Tobacco and Firearms does NOT classify the Pulse Wave Myotron as a weapon, so you can carry it legally. Attach it to your key ring, so you'll have it with you wherever you go. You've got nothing to lose (it has an unconditional lifetime warranty). Order it today. Tomorrow it may save your life! Totally maintenance-free; 20-year lithium battery never needs to be charged or changed! (Not sold in New Jersey.)

Protect yourself with the most potent, nonlethal weapon developed by the U.S. Army. Knocks an assailant out cold, yet you can carry it legally! Not a stun gun!

Pulse Wave Myotron (black)	#AMY007	List price $229.95	Our price $149.95
Pulse Wave Myotron (white)	#AMY008	List price $229.95	Our price $149.95

"…A quantum leap forward in effective personal protection."
David C. Eaton, Past President of Colt Firearms

Fig. 6.4:   This is a positioning headline that emphasizes *use* rather than product name. The decision is simple enough: that the product is called "Pulse Wave Myotron" is inconsequential; that it offers personal protection is as significant as any claim could be. This makes it a natural for a positioning headline.

7

Let Me Make This Absolutely Clear.

First, *You* Try It!

Your assignment . . .

You supervise the copy department at a catalog house. You sell sports, diving, and upscale automobile equipment. One of your writers, a recent college graduate, has handed you a piece of copy containing these words:

> *turgid*
>
> *minimal*
>
> *incongruity*
>
> *bifurcated*
>
> *maturation*
>
> *plethora*
>
> *utilize*
>
> *haut monde*
>
> *pulchritudinous*

You decide: Which of these words belong in catalog copy? Which don't?
Take thirty seconds. No longer than that.

I hope your decision is that *none* of these words belong in catalog copy. We're supposed to be communicators. The catalog writer who practices vocabulary *suppression* is the professional communicator. Save your massive vocabulary for the crossword puzzle.

(What's wrong with *utilize*? It's pompous. Why utilize *utilize* when you can use *use*? If you're hiring writers and an applicant uses *utilize*, beware!)

"Yipes!"

I was in the less-than-fortunate position of moderator at one of those panel discussions on copywriting. Instead of being able to assume the anticipated role of mentor and kindly dean, I found myself defending what seems to be an increasingly uncommon (and even unpopular) approach to copywriting.

One of my fellow panelists had made this brave conjecture:

"The copywriter's role is to teach, to instruct. We aren't just parrots. We're leaders. The reader has a responsibility, just as we do. If we write on an eighth-grade level, that's as far as our readers' learning level will reach."

The other panelist agreed:

"Yes, that's the only hope we have if we want others in marketing to take us seriously. We can't just use the words everybody knows without looking up if we want to justify our profession."

My own reaction—"Yipes!"—was drowned in a sea of acceptance by those present. The sentiment was unmistakable: this group, at least, sees the copywriter's role in a different light from the rose-colored lamp I've been shining on my keyboard.

I long have preached: one key to successful copywriting is vocabulary *suppression*. My "Yipes!" reaction stemmed from my ongoing fight to clarify what we have to say by using as many one and two syllable words as possible. Then the flashes of color come from *colorful* words, not from such words as *incongruity* and *plethora*.

When I challenged the logic of assuming the casual reader would stay with us through an exercise in intellectualized terminology, one of the attending group answered, "Readers appreciate learning something new. They have dictionaries, just as we do. If we use a word they don't know, they'll look it up."

Will they, now? My keyboard has a lot of scar tissue that says otherwise. So my conclusion that afternoon, philosopher that I am, was . . . okay. Until the mob leads those copywriters to the rhetorical gallows, let them eat cake.

Why the Reader's Dictionary Won't Budge Off the Shelf

We have every right to expect our catalog recipients to know the word *cat* and the word *free*. But how about these words, each of which was thrown at me in hit-and-run copy within the pages of three catalogs addressed to an anonymous me:

tumid
zonal
disparity
optimal
bifurcated
nonpareil
brachial
dulcet
potpouries
umbels
tractable
cavalier

As it turns out, I know the meanings of all the words except *umbels*. (Want to know what it means? Look it up, as I did. Hate the writer, as I did.) In fact, I'm literate enough to see that *potpourris* (plural of *potpourri*) is misspelled. And what does that prove?

As a catalog browser, I'm not going to jump into the arena and engage in a battle of wits with the copywriter. For heaven's sake, by what divine edict does a writer arrogate the right to *demand* the reader's parallel knowledge?

Don't *you* resent someone you don't know (and don't care about) testing your knowledge? Wouldn't you sidle away from a dinner guest who used *brachial* and *zonal* in conversation?

The reader's dictionary will stay on the shelf and your description won't generate any reaction other than annoyance . . . *unless* the illustration is such a barn burner the reader feels a driving need to know more about what you're selling. But consider: is the writer who uses illustrations as a crutch a true professional?

But if you *have* to use an unfamiliar word . . . let's be charitable.

Let's embrace this supposition: you *have* to use a big word. The manufacturer has said, "If you don't tell them this is *aqueous-nonadhering* canvas you don't get any co-op money."

How do you handle it?

Simple: your description incorporates what the manufacturer wants you to say . . . *and* what the reader's eye accepts. Your copy would open something like this:

NEW! Aqueous-Nonadhering Canvas

Aqueous-nonadhering means water won't penetrate. No matter how wet and blustery the weather, this haystack cover will. . . .

Key "tie terms" such as *means*, *is named for*, or *our way of telling you that*, or even a definition within parentheses will help the reader through the maze.

We're in their ballpark.

Maybe we'll reach a dim day when (a) all printed and on-line catalogs except one have gone out of business, and if you want to read catalog copy it's this one or nothing; or (b) some goofball offers a test-plus-prize for being able to define all the bizarre words in the catalog. Until that day, I'll stick with my belief that somebody whose catalog readership is casual, not forced, doesn't give a hoot how big a vocabulary *we* have.

The ability to simplify—what a lovely, useful talent! Those with that talent can write catalog copy without ever developing a case of foot-in-mouth disease. Their copy won't win the William F. Buckley lexicographer's award. But they're true communicators, operating inside the reader's experiential background instead of their own.

An unswerving opinion: catalog copywriters who say smugly to the victims reading their words, "I know something you don't," are in the wrong profession, marking time until Scrabble becomes a career instead of a game.

Dress Covert Trouser

The material of these pants was also made by the same people who make the Papal vestments. No surprise. Only the Italians could produce a worsted wool that is light enough for summer in Palermo, yet has the textural dimension reminiscent of slacks worn on grouse hunts in Tuscany. They share with the finest slacks in the world full dress-pant construction: full curtain, french fly, anti-roll waistband, and belt loops that are wrapped around the waistband before being sewn. The seat has a generous 2½" let out – the siren song of cannoli, sfudgetelle, and tiramisu can only be resisted so long. Specify length. Made in U.S.A. Dry clean.

#4236-78G   Light Lichen   Even sizes 32-44   ¹169

Fig. 7.1:   Look up *covert* in your dictionary. Do *any* of the definitions clarify what this heading means? While we're on the attack, what is "also" doing in the first sentence of body copy? As we read this description, we recognize a valiant try . . . possibly too hard a try . . . at creativity.

B. Keep Your Priorities In Meticulous Order
With The Novel Aluminum Agenda.

Bright, lightweight, brushed aluminum cover protects your planner pages and contact information perfectly. Stylishly embossed for a truly modern look, the spine conceals a clever penholder. Convenient color-coded tabs file everything in sections for quick access. Six-ring binder is compatible with many available forms and fillers. If you use a daily organization system, the Aluminum Agenda is the compact, cool metal way to go.

Aluminum Agenda   **#11-210 $58**

Fig. 7.2:   Read the headline just once. Without going into the text, what is this for? If you're puzzled, so will be many catalog readers who respond to clarity and benefit . . . but not to puzzles they regard as inconsequential.

8

Should Catalog Writers Have to Take Literacy Tests?

First, *You* Try It!

Your assignment . . .

You're the proofreader at a catalog house. A copywriter delivers this description:

> *AN HISTORIC FIRST!!*
>
> *There's many kinds of rainware for ladies. But not one of them are like* Miladie's Coat-ture! *This coat feels like silk but actually breaths, you won't feel hot and uncomfortable. It's velcro fasteners let you zip up quick and easy. S-M-L, $49.95*

Clean up this copy.

Take thirty seconds. No longer than that.

If your first move wasn't to change "An Historic" to "A Historic," your background has some phony pomposity in it. And did you get rid of the second exclamation point? Good for you, because two exclamation points are weaker than one.

Now to the serious stuff. Let's list the problems:

1. The writer always has a stronger way to start a sales argument than "There is . . ." or "There are . . ."

2. The first sentence has a singular verb (*is*) and a plural subject (*kinds*).

3. *Rainwear* is misspelled.

4. The next sentence has a singular subject (*one*) and plural verb (*are*).

5. "Miladie's" has the apostrophe in the wrong place, but because this is a trade name we might pass responsibility for this illiteracy on to the manufacturer.

6. The word *breathes* is misspelled.

7. Two sentences are hooked together with a comma ("This coat feels like silk but actually breaths, you won't feel hot and uncomfortable.")

8. *Its* as a possessive never has an apostrophe. Terrible!

9. The final qualifiers should be adverbs, not adjectives—*quickly* and *easily*.

Did you get them all? You can be my proofreader. Did you miss some? Uh-oh. Don't write catalog copy until you brush up on spelling and grammar.

Yes, Writers Should Be Literate

Back in the antediluvian days when the Sears catalog was the standard training ground for catalog copywriters, the question of writer literacy didn't exist.

Why? Implicit in being a writer was being literate. Plumbers had their tools; writers had their literacy.

Here we are, into the supposedly advanced twenty-first century, and many plumbers don't carry tools. They're consultants, making a disgustingly stratospheric living by charging for estimates.

A lot of catalog writers seem to have an empty tool chest, too. Is it because their background isn't formalized? What a wonderful society! Anyone can proclaim: "I'm a writer." Voila! He's a writer. She's an author. They're poets. Ready or not, here we come.

And what's wrong with that?

When a catalog marketer asks me to share my usual set of cynical comments about copy, the company is forewarned: I take a hard look.

So I welcomed the opportunity to sail into an assemblage of the eight-person creative staff, plus a dozen assorted executives, of a giftware cataloger. It wasn't my fault that right there on the inside cover was this copy:

AN HISTORIC ISSUE

I thought my chiding was mild. *Everyone* knows it's "A historic . . ."—or *does* everyone know it? Apparently not. The columnist William Safire doesn't. The preening TV newscasters don't. (Do they say, "An history book"?)

"What's wrong with that?" The question came from the copy chief. No damage below the waterline yet.

But then the head of the company piled on. "Yes, what's wrong with that?"

The questions were edged, almost triumphant. Had they caught me in a wrongful accusation?

Now, here's the point of all this mini-hullabaloo:

I had two backups with me—books on grammar by respected authorities. Both said flatly: no such construction as "An historic." It's "A historic."

Only because the consultation day was just starting out did I join this battle. And you know what? Nobody in the room was even mildly interested in what the books—or I—had to say about this construction.

Trying to save the day with a little humor, I quipped, "I guess everyone had 'their' say on that point."

Blank. So what? We've stumbled so far down the grammatical ladder that singulars and plurals line up together like salt and sugar in the same bowl.

"Those kind" didn't move them either.

So I scrapped grammar as a topic of discussion and went on to safer lands, such as omission of size in product description.

Okay, I stamp "borderline literate" on a bunch of foreheads. But are they wrong in ignoring the venerable rules of grammar?

Partly. Only partly.

"What we got here is . . ."

I've given up on "have got." I was there when *impact* and *access* became transsexual, switching from nouns to verbs. I no longer cringe openly when thirty-nine-year-old teenagers use *party* as a verb, now that on several occasions I've heard, "He architected the decision."

It isn't that my own standards lie flat on the ground. I'm not Strunk & White, the *Harbrace Handbook*, or the *Associated Press Stylebook*. I'm just another guy, toiling in the weedy fields of professional copywriting.

And because our job is to communicate, not educate—with the gap between those two words getting wider by the hour—I offer the Rule of Effective Communication:

> ✏ The target reader's comfort is the paramount consideration in word choice.

This isn't Miss Norwalk's second-grade English class. She'd never let her charges end a sentence with a preposition. I not only don't mind this minor gaffe, I embrace it because of a great big overriding factor, crazy-glued to the underbelly of the Rule of Effective Communication: that's the way people talk.

As communicators, we *should* write the way people talk. This isn't inconsistent with basic literacy.

So we writers walk a tightrope. Sure, we have so much latitude the tightrope is the size of an aircraft carrier's hawser, and sure, it's only a few feet above the ground. But it's there, that rope, giving us an uneasy footing above the grammatical abyss; when we lose awareness of it we cease to be professional writers at all.

Let's use the flaw-seeking loupe on ourselves.

I'm bothered that catalogs can be award winners from one point of view and totally unacceptable from another.

What's unacceptable? Consistently poor grammar, for one thing. The same cataloger who suffers for hours over product positioning on a page doesn't seem to give a hoot that the headline on that same page strings two sentences together, tied by a comma.

I'm looking at a winner of a major catalog awards competition, judged by a panel of experts. It's as gorgeous a catalog as modern European production techniques can make it. But here's a typical headline:

Each skin type has specific herbal needs, that's why Active Care is such an effective skin care program.

It doesn't matter, you say? It won't hurt response? I'm afraid you're right . . . and our profession is in trouble. The word *writer* always has had class and dignity, even with the soul-soiling prefix "copy" attached to its front end.

The Internet seems to have inflicted serious damage on our credentials. Anybody and everybody has a website . . . and as the base spreads, outlanders flock in like the Oklahoma Land Rush, claiming chunks of territory whether they know how to drive the corner stakes or not. Mistakes in grammar and spelling become so commonplace the reader or visitor becomes desensitized.

If we're spawning a generation of catalog writers who neither know nor care about learning rules of communication because they concern themselves only with what they call the "visual experience" of each page, then *glut* is too easy a word for the catalog world. *Rut* would be more apt.

Maybe we should have our own stylebook.

If I didn't know as well as you do that we never can get any two people in the catalog business to agree on anything, I'd suggest assembling a catalog stylebook.

This stylebook would differ from the one developed by the *New York Times* and the one circulated by the Associated Press.

For example, my ideal stylebook wouldn't adhere slavishly to the stringent rules of grammar we learned in the third grade. Oh, I'm not backing away from my insistence that any writer with passable literacy should be able to separate two sentences with a period, not a comma. I *am* backing away from the antique notion of never ending a sentence with a preposition.

Heck, if we couldn't end sentences with prepositions we'd have to put on the outside of a mailing envelope the antique and forceless legend "This is the catalog you requested" instead of the twice-as-powerful "This is the catalog you asked for."

And I'd allow paragraphs to begin with "And," as this one just did. Perfectly acceptable: the King James Bible has lots of paragraphs starting with "And."

But I'd shoot through the sloping forehead the writer who uses *for* when he, she, or it means *because*. Why? It's a pomposity born of insecurity, that's why. And I'd handcuff to the next atomic-bomb test a writer who in any seriousness uses *etc.*

A Broad Boulevard, Not a Tightrope

If your reaction is, "This guy has us walking a tightrope," my answer is: "It's a broad boulevard, not a tightrope. Catalog writers are supposed to be communicators, and all we have to do is follow the easiest, least stringent, and most logical rule of force-communication—the Whose Message Is It Anyway? Rule already mentioned in this text. Just in case you've forgotten:

> ✏ Your message should operate within the experiential background of the message recipient, not within your own experiential background.

Does the typical reader of your catalog say, "I turned on the lights, for it was growing dark" or "I turned on the lights because it was growing dark"? Does that reader ever use (as some order forms do) the phrase *referenced items*? Does that reader use *architect* as a verb?

How about *impact* and *access*? The world of computers has standardized *impact* and *access* as verbs. (I do draw the line at *window* as a verb.) If you're writing for any group, within that group's experiential background, readers won't be cowed or outraged or puzzled by the terminology.

On the other hand, can you write a whole forty-eight-page catalog of computer accessories and peripherals without once using *impact* or *access* as verbs? You bet. This gives hope to the broadly educated writer who doesn't have mastery of in-terms but does know how to communicate.

About a year after video players began offering DVD and Divx components, a survey asked *owners* what "Divx" stood for. Zero knew. (I still don't.)

Poets beware!

Poets revel in inside-out descriptions, in "conceits" tying two unlike thoughts together, and in abstruse literary references.

So unless they can switch off their afterburners, poets aren't good catalog copywriters. Still, sometimes a benevolent or desperate cataloger hires a poet, who stays in practice by peppering catalog copy with inside-out descriptions, conceits, and abstruse literary references.

I assume it was an unsuccessful poet who wrote:

DRINK TO ME ONLY WITH THINE EYES . . .

. . . and I'll drink in, with my own orbs, your romantically elegant and relevant knit.

Crumple? Perhaps in rhapsody, never in the midst of revel. At witching hour, this Fairyland Black comes into its own, but Cinderella needs only glass slippers to claim her prince.

Like one of those puzzle contests in which twenty thousand winners get a new set of puzzles, this copy leads into itself. Let's see: Ben Jonson wrote "Drink to me only with thine eyes," but so what? He's been hit and run over by the rest of this copy. Cinderella—ah, there's a recognizable name. At midnight, did she turn into a pumpkin? No, that isn't right. Let's start somewhere else: "witching hour" is midnight. The knit dress is black.

Whee! Solved one. But "Fairyland" wouldn't have witches, would it? It wouldn't be black, would it? And why the capitalization? Is "Fairyland Black" a name, like Morgan Fairchild?

Let's look at this copy through less jaundiced eyes. We realize that high-fashion copy can invent its own set of rules. Depending on the ambience—*Bloomingdale's*, for example—the reader *expects* unconventional copy.

A quick look at a Bloomie's catalog gives us evidence. Some headings for fashion descriptions:

- Your message to the world: Keep an eye on this body

- Reversing or traversing

- The statement is you, pure and simple

- Carole Little explores the color/shape equation

- An undemanding delivery

- Gloria Vanderbilt's weekend joys

(To a male who stumbles onto this catalog, that last one is brutally uninviting.)

But that's Bloomingdale's. Their catalogs are of a piece. Consistency overrides the Clarity Commandment, especially since, after the headings, copy settles down to hard-boiled, Windex-clear descriptions.

(With an occasional exception: copy for a blazer refers to "creamy black suede with tuxedo-like lapels of ostrich lamb." No one I know can identify "ostrich lamb," and if it's supposed to mean "ostrich-*grained* lamb-*skin*" the young woman who called this copy to my attention would appreciate the clarification.)

Why Not Have an Outsider Read It?

Let's not get too inbred. Inbreeding brought hemophilia to the royal houses of Europe. Inbreeding weakens the bloodlines of racehorses. Inbreeding of humans is outlawed in most states.

So why not bring in outsiders—fresh genes—to proofread catalog copy?

If you really want to avoid the witching hour at Fairyland, go a little overboard in your instructions to the proofreader. Ask for red stars next to copy carrying the seeds of obscurity. Then, after the outside proofreader has gone back to Conehead Corners for the night, make dispassionate

executive decisions. (You want a detective for this one, not your ombudsman, and proofreaders are guides, not gods.)

Don't just get anybody to read proofs. Look for a demographic-psycho-
graphic match. The closer an outsider parallels your target group, the more
likely your copy will follow the Whose Message Is It Anyway? Rule.
Matching message to recipient won't win a prize for poetry, but it's a good
way to stay in business.

Aw, what's the big deal?

My plea: don't plant more weeds in our grammatical garden. Let those
other guys debase the language. We'll be there as aerial observers, and
when their linguistic atrocities become slang and then general usage we'll
alertly adapt.

But let's not lead the way to perdition by following the lead of whoever
wrote, in an upscale fashion catalog:

A richer, heavier silk is styled with fully stitched front pleats that always lay flat. . . .

Now, let's suppose your reaction is, "So what? Who knows or cares that
the word is *lie*, not *lay*? What's the big deal?"

The big deal parallels finding a tiny rivulet of blood trickling down
your face. Where did it come from? Are you quietly bleeding to death?

Nothing so dramatic. But writers—even copywriters—still carry a
reflected glory, a patina rubbed off from Shakespeare and Aldous Huxley.
Over the last five years or so, with the help of Internet parvenus, we've
seen *The Invasion of the Grammar Snatchers*, and Brasso has replaced
silver polish.

Too obscure? A handful of specifics, then . . .

Let's not use these terms.

If your own grammar is a little shaky, how about this: between now and
one month from today use this starter kit to avoid minor errors in English.
Just avoid *these*. Then, every month, add one or two more.

DON'T SAY "The pearl necklace *compliments* the worsted suit."
INSTEAD, SAY "The pearl necklace *complements* the worsted suit."

DON'T SAY "You'll feel *badly* if . . ."
INSTEAD, SAY "You'll feel *bad* if . . ."

DON'T SAY "*Irregardless* of what you've used before . . ."
INSTEAD, SAY "*Regardless* of what you've used before . . ."

DON'T SAY "It's *different than* any other high-density disk."
INSTEAD, SAY "It's *different from* any other high-density disk." (Anglican countries: *different to*.)

DON'T SAY "We *might of* used a looser weave."
INSTEAD, SAY "We *might have* used a looser weave."

DON'T SAY "We'll *try and* get your order out the same day."
INSTEAD, SAY "We'll *try to* get your order out the same day."

DON'T SAY "We'll *appraise* you of the shipping date."
INSTEAD, SAY "We'll *apprise* you of the shipping date."

DON'T SAY "This *luxuriant* set of furniture . . ."
INSTEAD, SAY "This *luxurious* set of furniture . . ."

DON'T SAY "The cassettes will *learn* you to speak French."
INSTEAD, SAY "The cassettes will *teach* you to speak French."

DON'T SAY "You'll know where *it's at*."
INSTEAD, SAY "You'll know where *it is*."

If you're unconvinced that grammar and effective catalog copywriting are related, I'm not chagrined. This mini-list won't affect (not *effect*) you, but it makes me feel better!

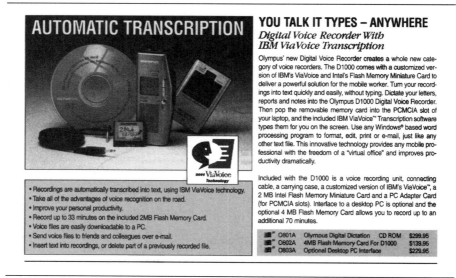

Fig. 8.1: "You talk it types." No. It should be either "You talk, it types" or "You talk. It types." Is this significant? To the catalog copywriter dedicated to clarity and literacy, it certainly is.

Fig. 8.2: In a vain search for *lensatic*, the frustrated reader gets this message: "Lensatic is not in the dictionary. No alternate spellings are available." What unquestionably happened: the copywriter picked up the word from a fact sheet. But the copywriter is selling, not buying, and this cavalier technique of regurgitating in-terms is poor salesmanship.

9

Catalog Copy for the Web

Eyeless in Gaza

What's your opinion of this, the total copy on a catalog's Internet home page? (See page 109.)

Savanna Jones
The Company for SUV Enthusiasts

Home | Company Info | Ordering Info | Accessories | Parts Bin | Specials

JEEP
Chevy
Dodge
Ford
Geo
GMC
Honda
Isuzu
Land Rover
Mercury
Nissan
Oldsmobile
Suzuki
Toyota

New Products!

Welcome to **Savanna Jones**:
The Company for Sport Utility Vehicle Enthusiasts

For years, Savanna Jones has been a leading catalog company specializing in replacement parts and accessories for Jeep vehicles. Our reputation for offering a wide variety of quality accessories at competitive prices has been translated over to the SUV market with the introduction of:

OFF-ROADSTORE.COM....Our Online Catalog!!

Although we are in the midst of programming a direct-ordering system, you can currently order via phone or fax 24 hours a day, 7 days a week! Please see Ordering Info for more information on ordering, including our Order Form, as well as our Company Policy.

Check Out our NEW PRODUCTS!!!
Check out our New Jeep Clothing!!

For easier and faster viewing, please allow pages to fully load.

Q. Do you have "printed" catalogs available?
A. The only "printed" catalog that we produce is for the Jeep CJ and Wrangler; we print and mail a limited number each year. For all other SUV's, including Jeep Cherokees and Grand Cherokees, our Online Catalog is it; but, it will consistently reflect our product lines, which are currently available, as well as ever-changing specials and promotions.

Q. Do you ship orders outside the United States?
A. Presently, we are not shipping orders outside the United States. However, we do ship to APO/FPO addresses.
Note on Specials:
Until our direct-ordering system is available, we can only accept Specials pricing via Fax orders, not via phone orders. Just print out our Order Form

http://www.savannajones.com/

Fig. 9.1:   This well-constructed home page provides links for fourteen different sport utility vehicles, plus a "New Products!" link. This enables the visitor to bypass corporate folderol and click directly on the subject of interest. The text makes several references to specials, but none appear on this page.

Into the Wind Kite Catalog

Choose from over 200 of the world's finest kites, from radical hi-tech sports kites to traditional lazy-day-in-the-meadow kites, plus boomerangs, flying toys, windsocks, and kitemaking supplies. Fast, friendly service with your sky-high satisfaction guaranteed. (Only available in the United States.)

Yeah, that's my opinion, too. This cataloger is unaware of the First Rule of Website Copy:

> ✐ **Stop surfers in their tracks.**

Where's the stopper here? "The world's finest kites" is as standard a cliché as any catalog copywriter could unearth. Nuggets are here, left buried in the soil. What *are* "hi-tech sports kites"? Leading with even a nominal description would save the page.

(I never did get to find out what the hi-tech sports kites might be because the only "link" on this page is "Send for Free Catalog." So, really, this is more a banner than a home page . . . which makes the not-so-stirring copy even more derelict.)

Can conventional print copy work on the Web?

Sure, a cataloger can transfer print copy "whole" onto a website . . . if the copy is Net material to start with.

For example, a well-known catalog of kitchen items accompanies a big, colorful picture with this text:

No more soggy foods or messy spatters!

Imagine roasts, chops, chicken, and stir fries moist and juicy on the inside, yet crispy and browned to perfection on the outside. The secret? The unique cone-shaped glass cover trimmed with stainless steel traps condensation . . . keeps food from becoming soggy. Sauteed foods brown to perfection with minimal fat, while the stove top stays clean. Fits most standard cookware $9\frac{1}{2}$ to 11" in diameter. Stovetop, oven and dishwasher safe. Made in Germany.

Brilliant copy? Nah. It's workmanlike copy, which often pulls better than brilliant copy. The picture shows the cover and all is well. Here we have a photo-copy matchup that fits any medium. So special Web treatment isn't necessary. (I do object to the read-through: the typical reader scans together "trimmed with stainless steel traps.")

A catalog such as *Lands' End* has an automatic advantage in the twenty-first-century Internet ambience: the company's print catalog copy already is breezy, matching the biggest group of Net surfers. Converting those surfers to visitors and then to buyers isn't as difficult as it is for more sedate catalogs that have to decide: should we adapt our image to the "Gotta go! Gotta go!" mentality of the skimmer-surfer?

On one occasion this catalog's home page had a cleverly worded legend (spot the cleverness):

Where in the world can you find first-quality classic clothing and soft luggage at Direct Merchant prices?

What's clever is the "Direct Merchant" reference that somehow suggests discount without saying so. The page has two links: "Out our way" and "The Goods."

"Out our way" becomes the real home page, and that's another clever touch. The spartan first home page downloads in a flash, a spur to moving along. This second page is loaded with links. Click on "Women's Casual," then "Sleepwear," and this site delivers a single item: "Women's Sleep T." Here I disagree with whoever set up this page because opposite the photograph is the price "From $18.00." Uh-uh. Far down the page (actually on another page if one prints it out) is the explanation of "from"—short-sleeved T-shirts are $18, long-sleeved T-shirts are $22. The photo shows the short-sleeved T-shirt, which indicates how easy it would have been to dump "From $18.00"—not an effective Web pricing ploy—and replace it with "Short-sleeved as shown, $18. Also available in long-sleeved model, $22."

I'm picking nits here, but the Web has matured, and copywriters either adapt their craft to the medium or go back to writing obituaries (perhaps for catalogs that haven't recognized the Web as its own medium). Nit-picking will be more common than finding huge mistakes, as copywriters discover *and implement* techniques of Web salesmanship.

Make a deal.

Ignoring the obvious physical contrast, analyze the differences between a mailed catalog and a Web catalog.

A mailed catalog, even to an existing customer, is *intrusive*. The sender performs an active role; the recipient is passive. Interaction comes when the recipient decides to contact the sender.

On the Web, the roles are equal. The customer comes looking for you. That's the beginning of an *interactive* relationship. And it's also why flat descriptive copy, lifted whole from the pages of a printed catalog, often doesn't compete with dynamic Web-sensitive copy that strengthens the fragile thread connecting visitor and site.

So even though no cataloger can be sure of competitive victory, a sound philosophy is the Web Exploitation Rule:

> ✏️ Make a deal. Make visitors feel rewarded for having tapped and clicked and paid for the time.

That means special offers, limited to Web visitors . . . which in turn means you can't lift all your copy in one piece from the printed catalog, even if the catalog also offers special deals.

And that in turn means . . .

Change that offer! Capture that name!

I'm shaking my head in bewilderment at the number of catalog sites I visited in 1999, looking for grist for this chapter. One of my favorite catalogs, a Canadian award winner, still said, "Welcome to our 1998 catalogue." A fashion catalog still had Christmas offers from the previous year, as did a candy catalog and a flower catalog. The year before, nearing Mother's Day, that candy catalog still had Valentine's Day specials.

How many surfers will revisit those sites? Letting a site go unchanged for a lengthy period of time is a game of Russian roulette, and you'll lose. Far better is to have a single item—a "Daily Special"—to entice the visitor over and over again.

And to let a visitor escape without capturing the name is criminal. Offer a monthly prize and visitors will register. Award the prize, publish the winner's name to validate your offer, and award discount coupons to the runners-up. Meanwhile, you have names.

E-Mail: A Not-So-Trivial Benefit of Capturing Names

Depending on who's commenting, E-mail is a blessing or a curse.

Here's another example of blaming the medium instead of those who use it. E-mail can be the fastest moving, least expensive, most productive medium ever made available to the perceptive marketer who knows how to use it.

What has so many commentators (and competitors) exercised is a glut of E-mail messages to individuals with whom the marketer has no relationship. Okay, that's a totally valid objection, parallel to telemarketing cold names.

Ah, but if individuals have given you their on-line names by registering for something or acknowledging a willingness to look at "special private offers" or . . . whee! . . . actually entering into a transaction, you can and should use E-mail to keep them active.

Start with a "thank-you" note, including congratulations on being one of the elite who will see specials *never* made available to the general public. Then E-mail offers at whatever interval you have something that qualifies.

"Member-get-a-member" works with E-mail, especially since you're dealing with on-line names in which people can feel secure, not disclosing their real names until they're ready.

Don't snicker at E-mail. It works.

(By the time you read this, various state and federal governmental agencies may have placed stringent rules on E-mail. Not to worry. The rules shouldn't apply to messages sent to those with whom you have a relationship.)

Be a "happy camper" at your own risk.

A parenthetical comment: the Internet is international. If you want business from other countries, include a box on your home page enabling the passerby to choose a country . . . and have text in that country's language. The results not only will far outweigh the cost of translations, but international customers often display a loyalty factor unknown within this country.

If international business represents a considerable segment of your enterprise, be careful about using jargon and argot. A Web advertiser headed his offer "You'll be a happy camper when you . . ." confounding Web visitors from Europe and Asia.

Nail 'em. THEN get lavish with words.

The Internet has a huge advantage in its ability to offer options. Suppose you're selling gardening equipment. Once the visitor has clicked on Garden Tractors, you can offer page after page after page, each one with a link to an order form. Visitors can glut themselves with descriptive fact or read just enough to convince them to go directly to the order form or back to the home page. What an edge over printed catalogs!

If you haven't yet concluded that the Web's characteristics differ from other media and require a distinct copy philosophy, spend more time looking at what other catalogers are doing.

The days when the medium is also the message are waning. Catalogers are abandoning the Net even as replacements are pouring in. To those who leave, three questions hang in the air:

1. Did you really use the Web with recognition of what it is?
2. Did surfers and visitors have an easy time finding you, and once they did, did your home page set up fast?
3. Did you offer them a deal and change it often?

Chances are, if the answer to any of these three questions is "No," you might have had better luck with messages tailored to this amazing, grotesquely overblown, overhyped, super-competitive, frustrating, still evolving marketplace.

But we've come a long way, baby.

Some of the journey has crossed the wasteland and found a smooth, pleasant highway. Some has been a long walk on a short pier.

Catalogers can draw any of three conclusions, surveying their own websites (or plans for websites) and those of other catalog companies:

1. What nonsense—it's all hype and no sales.
2. This is a niche medium and I'd better start talking to printers again.
3. Wow! What a bonanza.

It can be exhilarating . . . and frustrating.

On any given day, if you take an electronic spin around the Web you're bound to absorb a curious mixture of exhilaration and frustration.

Catalogers spend a ton of money finding and massaging lists of potential buyers to whom they'll mail printed catalogs. How to get them to the Web? How much does a Web catalog have to spend in conventional media, advertising its site, to generate traffic? The laws of economics are stringent and brutal.

Figure 9.2 is a typical space ad touting a website. This ad appeared in the *Wall Street Journal*. (The site itself is shown as figures 9.3a to 9.3h.)

The recipient of a catalog, finding that catalog uninteresting, tosses it away. The visitor to a website who finds the site dull or flat or difficult to navigate will draw a cosmic conclusion about catalog websites altogether. We're all injured by shrapnel from the fallout.

So to protect the Web against misuse we have the Law of Web Romance:

> ☞ The smart website says to a visitor: "You love me . . . and this is why."

Note the two halves of the law. "You love me" alone won't carry the day. We're lurching through the Age of Skepticism, and without the second half of that equation the visitor says, "You're blowing smoke."

Fig. 9.2:   Incentives are here: "World's best values," "America's 1ˢᵗ discounter," the major brand names in fine watches. Using other media to drive potential buyers to a website is an insurance policy against having a surfer type the word *watches* . . . and be exposed to thousands of competitors.

So if you have both printed and on-line catalogs, you *may* mirror the printed catalog on your website . . . or you may require a separate approach.

For example, in a printed catalog, spartan copy can succeed because of the ambience. You have a digest-size page and four items on the page. The situation is self-limiting. On the Web, each page needs its own dose of romance. So think where you are and who is skimming past.

But what if it isn't their fault? So what?

The technical difference between print and electronic media is stupendous. We can attend a press start-up and tell the press operator, "Pump some more magenta into this." Then we mail our catalogs and start lighting candles once they're in the hands of the post office.

With the Web, a glitch can be anybody's fault. A "Site not found" message pops up. Maybe your Webmaster (an evil term) is blameless. Maybe the surfer hit the site just as your server died or was overloaded or blew a fuse and couldn't deliver the proper pages.

Or maybe visitors signed in and were hung up in a bunch of stuff they regarded as useless nonsense. Maybe a more direct way into actual *selling* pages exists but wasn't publicized. That's a potential killer, and you can't beg off saying it's beyond your control.

Here's another modest proposal.

Think this through: the competitive ambience increases geometrically, not arithmetically, because if we're looking for hiking shoes or electric toothbrushes or vitamins our search engine can give us six hundred sources . . . only one of which is the one we started out to see.

But worse: we can be derailed along the way by a siren song we hadn't expected. A cunning competitor may have the word *sex* in a link. Another might use the word *free*. A third might say, "Lucky you! Everything listed here is half off, this week only" . . . and actually show the prices. Farewell, original target.

A modest proposal for all catalogers who are on the Web, alternately preening over having a site and wondering where the orders are: think like a *marketer*, not a technician.

If technical expertise could outsell intelligent marketing, no catalog printed in fewer than six colors on less than one-hundred-pound stock with less than two-hundred-line screens could exist; and the beginning car salesperson who knows how many CCs are in the engine and what the gear ratios are could outsell the old pro who says, "Settle in behind the wheel and take her for a spin."

It's as simple as this: if you'd rather announce than sell, I hope you're my competitor.

Fig. 9.3a: This is the home page one encounters after clicking on the company's URL. The page contains little information that might urge a visitor to go forward, but it isn't hard to read. Will the visitor click on the link icon at the right? What is the incentive to do so?

Welcome First Time Visitors

Lest we brag, we are America's first mail-order discounter of precious jewelry and fine Swiss watches.

For over thirty years, our reputation has been based on knowledge, integrity, service and value. This philosophy has earned us the respect and continued patronage of thousands of clients worldwide.

We trust that your experience with us will be as satisfying as they have been for Dr. Richard Koch, our very first mail order client. His sentiments are expressed in the following letter:

Newcomers SCROLL DOWN **Return Guests** CLICK HERE

DR. RICHARD A. KOCH, MD
PHYSICIAN AND SURGEON
PILOT ROCK, OREGON 97868

```
June 27

Ken Marcus
3340 Peachtree Rd. NE
Atlanta, GA 30326

Dear Ken,

I have just learned that our relationship goes back over thirty
years.

To refresh your memory, I have purchased Rolexes for each member
of the family as well as recommending you to my friends who
successfully bought from you. I still have the Patek Philippe
that was the first purchase I made from you. I have purchased
diamonds from you, fortunately in the larger sizes, before
inflation took over. Thanks to you, I ordered two, three, and
four carat stones that, if I'd sell, would be a great return on
my investment.

I still consider you my personal jeweler, everything you sold me
was as stated, and you provided G.I.A. certificates if
requested.
```

Fig. 9.3b: Opening with a testimonial *the visitor hasn't expected to see* is a dangerous ploy because the visitor's interest is blunted. This letter opens in low gear and stays in low gear. Unquestionably, many potential customers drop out right here. We'll click on "Next page" to see figure 9.3c.

```
With all the great deals you have made, I fault you only for not
insisting that I buy the Rolex King Midas, the nine carat
emerald-cut diamond, and that beautiful eight carat Burmese
sapphire that would have been great buys at today's prices.

I wholeheartedly recommend you to any one, my old friend, and
thank you for the close personal relationship over the years.
You have been a big factor in my family's happiness at holidays
and birthdays throughout the years.


Affectionately,

Rich


P.S. Do you have anything that I cannot live without?
```

NEXT PAGE

Fig. 9.3b (continued)

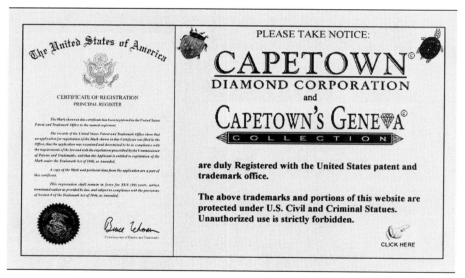

Fig. 9.3c: We're well into the site and the company is still presenting its credentials. Suppose the visitor says, "Enough! Let's get to the merchandise." It isn't possible because we have only one option, other than leaving the site altogether: "Click here." We do, to see the screen shown as figure 9.3d.

Click icon for a message from the Marcus Family. (14.4 RA 2.0)

Click icon to download Real Audio.

Capetown... A Special Company For Special People

After 25 years, we're still the wiser choice. September 1969 witnessed the birth of America's first mail-order watch and diamond discounter. Starting from our kitchen table in Tustin, California, our family changed forever the way thousands of consumers would buy expensive jewelry and timepieces. Our plan was simple and forthright. We would drastically discount laboratory certified diamonds, as well as new and used upscale watches, via a no frills, low overhead, mail-order format.

Now, a quarter of a century later, as the jeweler of choice for thousands of America's best and brightest, we know that in order to prevail in today's marketplace, we are not allowed to rest on our laurels. The last decade has brought major changes to American retailing. Where discounting was once unique, now it is the norm. A low price is simply not enough. Today, security, superior warranties, reliable after-sales service, and knowledgeable guidance are de rigueur.

Remaining #1 is a full time job. To that end we faithfully remain sensitive to the changing needs of our clients and of the marketplace. It's this attitude that sets us apart. In all modesty, when it comes to knowledge, price, integrity, length of warranty, customer service, and depth of inventory, we are confident that no one can beat Capetown.

As we enter the 21st century, the commitment to our philosophy remains steadfast: to give our clients true value, real service, and to always be the wiser choice.

The Marcus Family & Assoc.

CLICK HERE

Fig. 9.3d: Where is a specific? Where is an offer? This, the fourth screen, is indicative of the difference between what the seller wants to show and what the buyer wants to see.

Fig. 9.3e: This partial frame (one has to move the arrow to see the right edge) is the fifth screen. Here we have solid links, such as "Competition Killers" and "Private Party Specials." Sophisticated jewelry buyers know what "Private Party Specials" are; others might not know. We click on "Competition Killers" and see figure 9.3f.

Please note:

The special promotions found in this section are one-of-a-kind or very limited quantities of new watches & fine jewelry. To facilitate their liquidation we offer them at greater than normal discounts.
THESE ITEMS CONSTITUTE ONLY A SMALL PORTION OF OUR MULTI-MILLION DOLLAR INVENTORY.

Besides these "Competition Busters", *we also discount thousands of other fine watch and jewelry items.* If the item you are looking for is not represented in this section, you may wish to:

1. View our "Private Party Specials" section, which offers items consigned by private parties.(To access click on main menu below)

2. **Can't find exactly what you want??** Phone or Fax our Atlanta Mail Order Center with specific needs. Mail Order hours M-F 10:30-6:00pm EST. Phone:(404) 365-9503 Fax:(404) 365-0176

Mᴀɪɴ MENU

CLICK HERE TO VIEW

Fig. 9.3f: Even though we've clicked on "Competition Killers," we now need to click on "Click here to view Competition Busters." The visitor still has seen no solid offer, nor has the visitor had the opportunity to enter "Rolex" or "Breitling" or "Under $2,000" or any brand or price range.

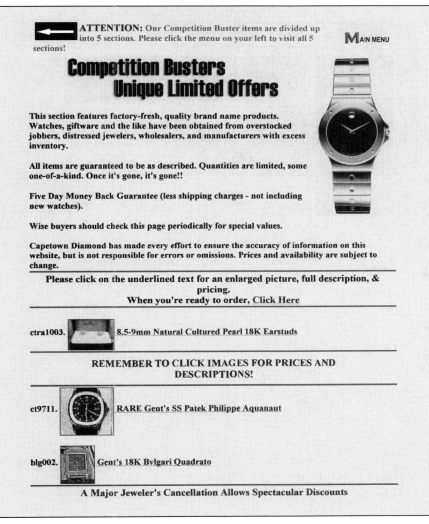

ATTENTION: Our Competition Buster items are divided up into 5 sections. Please click the menu on your left to visit all 5 sections!

MAIN MENU

Competition Busters
Unique Limited Offers

This section features factory-fresh, quality brand name products. Watches, giftware and the like have been obtained from overstocked jobbers, distressed jewelers, wholesalers, and manufacturers with excess inventory.

All items are guaranteed to be as described. Quantities are limited, some one-of-a-kind. Once it's gone, it's gone!!

Five Day Money Back Guarantee (less shipping charges - not including new watches).

Wise buyers should check this page periodically for special values.

Capetown Diamond has made every effort to ensure the accuracy of information on this website, but is not responsible for errors or omissions. Prices and availability are subject to change.

Please click on the underlined text for an enlarged picture, full description, & pricing.
When you're ready to order, Click Here

ctra1003.   8.5-9mm Natural Cultured Pearl 18K Earstuds

REMEMBER TO CLICK IMAGES FOR PRICES AND DESCRIPTIONS!

ct9711.   RARE Gent's SS Patek Philippe Aquanaut

blg002.   Gent's 18K Bvlgari Quadrato

A Major Jeweler's Cancellation Allows Spectacular Discounts

Fig. 9.3g: At last the visitor is inside the bazaar. Here is the first of eight pages—just the first group—of "Competition Busters." Note the line in the middle of this page: "Please click on the underlined text for an enlarged picture, full description, & pricing. When you're ready to order, *Click Here*." This suggests the customer has to abandon the page with description and price to order . . . which, as figure 9.3h shows, really isn't necessary. We'll click on "Gent's 18K Baume & Mercier Wristwatch."

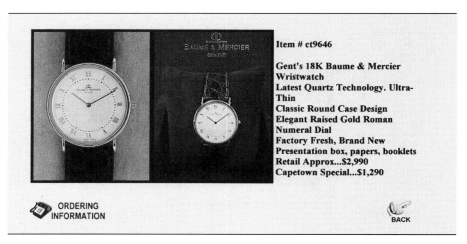

Fig. 9.3h: We have gone through many screens to reach this offer. Once here, we have specificity. Altogether, this huge and professional website seems to lack just one key component: a direct link from the mention of an item the visitor wants to see to the actual item.

10

Why Not Tell 'Em What It's For?

First, *You* Try It!

Your assignment . . .

You're teaching Catalog Writing 101. A student hands in this description of an automobile seat cover:

> *RICH, THICK LAMB'S-WOOL SEAT COVER gives you high style and high comfort.*
> *Fits every domestic and imported car (specify make and model).*

"Nope," you say. "You've left out the key ingredient."

"What's that?" your student asks. So you tell your student what *you'd* have included, which is . . .

Take thirty seconds. No longer than that.

Okay, what did you change or add? Right! Your student didn't realize that many catalog readers don't know why they should install a lamb's-wool seat cover. Telling them what it *is* and what it *does* interests the seller; telling them what it will do *for them* interests the readers.

So you add "You'll be cooler in summer, warmer in winter." As a parallel, you add "You won't need to run your air conditioner as much." You add "Genuine lamb's-wool seat cover helps circulation of your blood by equalizing weight distribution." You add "It protects the upholstery."

Lord knows *what* you add. But as a professional copywriter you know the difference between what the vendor cares about—what it is—and what I as buyer care about—what it will do for me.

Phrases with a Promise

What do these phrases have in common?

- This will enable you to . . .
- Now you can . . .
- Ideal for . . .
- For the first time you'll . . .
- Wear it to the . . .
- This not only will . . .
- When you need . . .

It doesn't require a heavyweight guess to give us the answer. Each of these is a promise: the copy that follows will tell us what it's for.

What could be easier?

A primitive function of the copywriter is to swap places with the reader. The copywriter, in the reader's position, asks, "What's it for?"—and then answers the question.

Sometimes we forget: the reader's experiential background doesn't parallel ours. We assume a knowledge base that doesn't exist.

(I wonder how many millions of sales dollars are lost in computer software, peripherals, and supplies because the writer doesn't swap places with the reader. The writer blithely uses initials and in-terms the digitheads know but the typical user doesn't know. Unwittingly the catalog aims itself at a coterie instead of the broadest base of potential buyers.)

What could be easier than telling us what it's for? Sure, a hammer doesn't need a ton of description—unless it differs from standard hammers. But how about a knife? Haven't you seen copy glorifying by *label* the type of steel and the type of handle, with no space allocated to *use*?

A key benefit of telling the reader what it's for: you help justify the price.

What brought this to mind is a copy block I saw in a catalog I much admire. The first sentence is useless. The second sentence specifies uses, within a narrow range outside my fields of interest. It's a weak "covering" sentence (actually, two sentences hooked together with a comma). Once the copy gets into gear, do I as reader begin to salivate? By the time the writer completes the description, has he or she diddled my imagination so the relatively high price justifies itself?

It's the copywriter's call because space is adequate and plenty of information exists. The description:

Here's everything you ever wanted in a pocketknife—and more! Ideal for hunting or fishing, with 29 implements it's also the perfect general purpose knife. Features include: large blade, small blade, corkscrew, can opener with small screwdriver, cap lifter with screwdriver and wire stripper, reamer/awl with sewing eye, scissors, Phillips screwdriver, magnifying glass, wood saw, fish scaler with hook disgorger and ruler (cm & inches), nailfile with metal file/metal saw and nail cleaner, fine screwdriver, keyring, tweezers, toothpick, chisel, pliers with wire cutter, mini-screwdriver, ballpoint pen. Crafted in Switzerland of first quality stainless steel by Victorinox. $3\frac{1}{2}''$ closed. Weighs just 6.5 oz. 2691T Swiss Champ Knife $72.00

All right, you're the copy chief and this crosses your desk. What's your comment?

Obviously the copy chief for this company said, "Okay, get started on the next item." Would you have made a few suggestions to broaden the appeal? For example:

1. We say, "Ideal for hunting and fishing" and suggest no other uses. Are these all the possibilities? How are all those screwdrivers pertinent to hunting and fishing? Mightn't we say, "A whole tool chest in your pocket, no matter where you are. Ideal for hunting and fishing"? We no longer exclude logical buyers.

2. How about that ballpoint pen? When has anybody seen a knife with a built-in pen? Can't we make something of this?

3. The laundry list of features seems to be copied off the manufacturer's spec sheet. Why not combine the screwdrivers ("Five different screwdrivers!") and list the blades by use groups?

I'm beating this about the head and shoulders unnecessarily because, except for that first sentence, we have a completely acceptable piece of copy. What we don't have is recognition of the total marketplace: (a) I don't hunt and I don't fish; (b) This isn't an outdoor sports catalog; (c) What's in this knife for me?

A couple of words will do it.

If you can see the difference between benefit-oriented figures 10.1 and 10.2, and flatly descriptive figures 10.3 and 10.4, you can just as easily see the difference in power, appeal, and salesmanship.

If you have the feel of it, take a look at this copy block and imagine how much weaker it would be if "without using a stove" weren't there:

Imagine being able to have a *hot meal* in your car, office, dorm and even in bed *without using a stove!* Our soft, vinyl pouch container with its automatic thermostat that's set at 170°, will steadily warm and hold any cooked food put inside! It safely heats unopened canned goods, thaws and warms frozen dinners or boil-in-bag entrees. Keeps them *piping hot for up to 10 hours*, without loss of taste, texture or quality . . . ready to eat when you are. Plug it into standard household current or into cigarette lighter of your car, boat, or recreational vehicle! (adapter included). Interior is insulated, so the pouch always stays cool to the touch. Measures $9'' \times 12'' \times 1\frac{1}{2}''$. UL listed. Brown. P.S. It's great for shut-ins!

Even without the *stove* reference, it's a superior piece of descriptive copy because it tells the reader what it's for in three different ways. The *stove* reference adds another evaluation level—a touchstone. We know going in, this isn't just warm; it's really hot.

And when they obviously know what it's for . . .

We all knew when we started this chapter what those lamb's-wool automobile seat covers do: they cover car seats.

But now we know a little more. We know we should look at those seat covers and that knife and *everything* we sell and ask: is that really what they're *for*?

Covering the car seats is what seat covers *do*, not what they're *for*. To unearth their purpose we dig into the magical world of *benefit*. If you expound on benefit you implicitly tell the reader what it's for.

That's how we answered our thirty-second question about lamb's-wool seat covers. Are they for covering the car seats?

No.

They're for a whole bunch of benefits—physical, aesthetic, financial, status. When you describe benefits, you tell the reader what it's for.

Here's yet another modest proposal.

Knives, meal heaters, lamb's-skin seat covers—these are easy and obvious examples.

When you're writing copy for men's or women's fashions, for luxury accessories, for flowers, for exotic foods, for office supplies—that's when you should hurl down the gauntlet at your copy.

Ask yourself, "Have I told 'em what it's for?" If you haven't, delete some of the puffery, some of the surplus adjectives such as *beautiful* and *attractive* (for that matter, deep-six the word *useful* unexplained), and even some of the historical base if it takes up space you need for reader benefit.

Use the space you've picked up to increase the pulling power of your description by telling the reader what it's for.

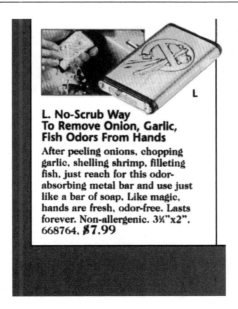

L. No-Scrub Way To Remove Onion, Garlic, Fish Odors From Hands

After peeling onions, chopping garlic, shelling shrimp, filleting fish, just reach for this odor-absorbing metal bar and use just like a bar of soap. Like magic, hands are fresh, odor-free. Lasts forever. Non-allergenic. 3¾"x2". 668764, $7.99

Fig. 10.1: How simple . . . and how elegant. This is a pure "benefit" heading. The name of the product isn't mentioned at all. Both the casual catalog reader and the reader looking for a product react more strongly to what it does than to its name.

FITNESS

Burn big calories (and fat) with the mini stepper!

This compact, yet rugged "stair climber" lets you reap all the benefits of stepping as you would on full-size gym equipment, but takes up a fraction of the space. Tone your waist, calves, hips and thighs while you get a high intensity, low impact cardiovascular workout.

Don't be fooled by its size, this stepper offers a unique pulley system with 2 hydraulic cylinders—one under each foot—for incredibly smooth, even operation. Count your progress with a built in computer that measures elapsed time and number of steps. Professional quality construction with a low center of gravity for safety. Ideal if space is a problem because it folds for easy storage. Uses 2 AA batteries (included).

Mini Stepper
KL0100 $89.95

Sold elsewhere for $99

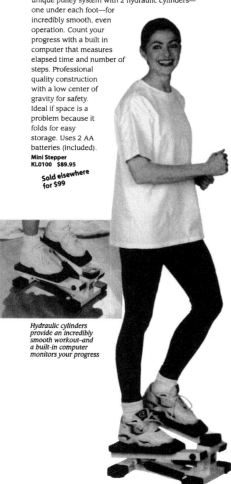

Hydraulic cylinders provide an incredibly smooth workout–and a built-in computer monitors your progress

24 InteliHealth Healthy Home®
Lifetime Money Back Guarantee

Fig. 10.2:   Suppose the heading had been just "The mini stepper"? The point of its value would have been buried in the text.

Extra-stable TV Pedestal
swivels 360°

This sleek pedestal's full-swivel platform positions
the TV at a 31" height for optimum viewing from your bed or easy chair.
Engineered to the most exacting safety standards, it's made from powder-coated
cold-rolled steel with a sturdy platform and extra-wide 22" base for utmost
stability. A removable safety strap secures the set in place, and two power
cords can be concealed inside the curvilinear upright. An optional bracket can
be mounted beneath the platform to hold your VCR. Lifetime warranty. USA.
8276A TV Pedestal for 19"-20" TV (19 lbs.) $179.00
8283A TV Pedestal for 25"-27" TV (21 lbs.) $199.00
8291A VCR Bracket, not shown (7 lbs.) $39.00
Please specify black or white

Fig. 10.3:   Okay, so the pedestal swivels 360 degrees. What's the benefit of that? Whatever answer to that question comes to mind, it's superior to the heading shown here.

World's most powerful linear shaver is now faster and smoother. Our exclusive upgrade model!

Panasonic's latest and best wet/dry linear shaver delivers an incredible 13,000 strokes per minute — 1,000 strokes faster than before — for more power, greater smoothness, and less vibration. Triple 3-D independently floating heads glide gently over your skin, helping avoid irritation. For a much closer cut, the outer edge is now angled a sharper 45° and the ultra-hard stainless foil is even thinner. Twin-gate slit blades introduce 156% more hairs. A pop-up trimmer touches up your sideburns, mustache, or beard.

Do not confuse this top-of-the-line linear shaver with Panasonic's less expensive, look-alike model sold elsewhere. Our durable, lightweight metal body is fully immersible — use wet or dry, with or without foam. Recharges automatically in the included stand with the latest induction-charging system. LED meter shows battery status. Converts automatically to international voltage. Made in Japan. Comes with a soft case. One-year warranty.

Panasonic® Linear Float Shaver
$299 #PA803

Angled edge-shaped blades cut closer. *Floating triple heads are gentle to your skin.* *Induction-charges in just one hour.*

Order by phone **1-800-344-4444** 24 hours every day

Fig. 10.4:   Do you think the lengthy headline projects a benefit? If so, what is it? What is the *benefit* of being the world's most powerful linear shaver? What is the significance of being linear? "Faster and smoother" are too loose to draw a word image. Look to the body copy for actual benefits. They're in there.

11

Give Them a Reason to Buy.

The Difference Between a Clerk and a Salesperson

Let's suppose I have a retail store.

I also run newspaper ads, in both the main news section and the classified section. I mail catalogs four or six times a year. And I have a Web catalog.

Quick, now: in which marketing media should I most carefully consider giving my prospective customers a *reason* to buy what I'm displaying—whether that display is an array of the actual merchandise, a photograph of the merchandise, or merely words describing the merchandise?

If you answer quickly, "All of them," you've given a knee-jerk response based on the differential between a salesclerk and a salesperson, without considering the buyer's state of mind when entering the arena.

Roltronic Pro Avantgarde Shaver

Acclaimed "The World's Greatest Shaver" by a
European consumer magazine, the Roltronic Pro gives
the closest, fastest, most comfortable shave ever. The
first shaver to use both horizontal and rotary cutting
action to reduce shave time and increase comfort, it
also reduces vibration so your shave is whisper quiet.
An ultra-thin micron screen allows for a blade-close
shave and is platinum coated to protect skin. Used as
a cordless, the Roltronic Pro recharges in less than
60 minutes anywhere
in the world and gives
you about two weeks
of clean, close shaves.
Icing on the cake:
built-in retractable head
protector; pop-up
two-position trimmer.
5½" x 2½". x 1½".
Made in Austria.
4222A Roltronic Pro Shaver
　$249.00
4223A Replacement Cutter
　$24.00
4225A Replacement Foil $24.00

Fig. 11.1:　The headline proclaims it's a "Roltronic Pro Avantgarde Shaver." So what? The first sentence of body copy
says it was "Acclaimed 'The World's Greatest Shaver' by a European consumer magazine." Uh . . . do we dare ask whether
the magazine has any import or influence? Reading the entire copy, does anything convince you the claim is valid?

Are buyers aware? Or unaware?

In three of the four instances, the buyer enters the arena *aware*. When customers walk into my store, unless they're "mall browsers" they know what I sell. The desire to upgrade awareness to buying impulse depends on whether my merchandise is well displayed, whether my price and ambience match the buying mood, and (for impulse buys) whether I'm able to generate instant excitement.

(Only that last area—a big one, I'll admit—suggests a point-of-sale piece, a striking mannequin, or an actual demonstration to create a reason to buy. Why? Because the customer has come to me. I'm the host. Our encounter isn't accidental.)

Even more clear-cut is my advertising in the classified section. Classified ads aren't (or at least shouldn't be) parallel to display ads because the marketplace isn't the same. Once again, the prospective buyers plowing through the classified ads are *aware*. They may not have sought *me* out, but they've sought out my category.

So my classified ad should be competitive with what I expect the reader to find in the ads atop and beneath mine. I don't have to emphasize a *generic* reason to buy; I have to emphasize a reason to buy *from me*.

In that respect, my Web catalog more closely parallels a group of classified ads than it does my printed catalog. We re-identify a minor difference between a printed catalog and a Web catalog. No serious prospect stumbles into your Web store unaware. Generic sell—reason to buy a category—has to give way to specific sell—reason to buy from me.

Now consider R.O.P. (run-of-paper—can be anywhere in the publication) newspaper ads, magazine ads, and the catalogs I mail. In these instances I catch the reader *unaware*. The generic desire to buy may preexist in embryo or dormant form, but it hasn't been triggered. That's my job. I have to give the reader a reason to buy.

So the half-trained clerk in my retail store may not damage the sale by limiting the pitch to a naked description. The counter clerk at the newspaper may not ruin my ad's chances by writing a bare-bones classified ad whose copy limits itself to an announcement of product for sale.

Sure, my cup runneth over if either of those individuals has some knowledge of salesmanship, but the significance of their words isn't as critical as the descriptions in my catalog.

So why doesn't everybody do this?

Why doesn't every copy block in every printed catalog include a reason to buy?

Four possibilities:

1. The catalog writer or instigator doesn't agree with the concept.
2. The catalog is from a source so well-known, so thoroughly established, or so dominant that the catalog itself becomes a reason to buy.
3. Space is too tight.
4. The writer doesn't think in terms of buyer benefit.

I yield graciously to the second reason, and I sadly acknowledge the third, warning that in many cases it's an argumentative crutch. (Web catalogs, rejoice! The second possibility need not exist at all for you, as figure 9.2 showed.)

To those who subscribe to the first and fourth reasons, I'll point out that the "hot" printed catalogs of the last five years almost universally pitch reason to buy in their copy, sometimes allocating this facet of the marketing mix double the space allocated to what it is.

Figure 11.2 is a typical description from a business-to-business catalog that consistently excels in injecting a reason to buy, not only in the headline but also in the descriptive copy that follows.

We might add a fifth reason: "We're doing very well, thank you." No argument, except: how about testing copy with a "reason to buy" thrust?

An example: the catalog that has this description of a group of travel accessory cases could very well claim, "We're doing very well, thank you." Yes, they are, but the pages of this magazine offer us a laboratory setting. Random selection of this copy doesn't mean it's defective, but rather that it's typical:

Personalized Packs are trimmed in tan genuine leather—handsome in textured black vinyl with 22K Gold initials, smart snap-flap closings. Toiletry pack hangs $15\frac{3}{4}''$ long on brass-plated ring for easy access to 3 nylon zip sections—one $9\frac{1}{2} \times 5\frac{1}{2} \times 2\frac{1}{2}''$ deep for bulky essentials. Super-slim tie pack holds up to 8 neat and crease-free on sturdy brass-plated rods.

Description is satisfactory. But I, as a casual page-flipper, read a few words and keep flipping. Unless I've been looking for a "Personalized Pack" (is this the best "grabber" description?) I'm left outside the copy. The writer hasn't given me a reason to buy.

Leaning on the Everlasting Crutch

From the first day I sank my fangs into the neck of this so-called profession I've heard the weary cliché "We don't have enough space." No, we never do, and I used to lean on that crutch myself.

Fig. 11.2: Near-perfect descriptions such as this prove it's possible to present a business product in a no-nonsense way and still load the copy with a reason to buy.

The reason I now attack where I once sympathized isn't because the statement is flawed; no, it's universally true. It parallels somebody saying, "The reason I'm ugly is because I have two ears" or "The reason I'm slow is because I only have two legs." Hey, there—*everybody* has two ears and two legs. Find a more logical excuse. *Everybody* has too little descriptive space, even those fellows who use two solid pages to describe an exercise machine.

An excellent catalog, one from which invariably I buy something I didn't think I wanted when I picked up the catalog (ah, what a triumph for the copywriter!), packs reason to buy into tiny copy blocks.

An example, in a block $1\frac{1}{4}''$ wide × $1\frac{1}{2}''$ high (I'm ignoring the heading because that's grist for another chapter):

Here's a cutting board that isn't hard on finely-sharpened knives, won't absorb food flavors, and won't harbor bacteria. What's more, it won't develop low spots over the years. It's made of a space age thermoplastic, easy to clean, and perfect for rolling pastry with just the lightest dusting of flour. It's huge—24" by $17\frac{3}{4}''$ by $\frac{1}{2}''$!

What could be more pedestrian than a description of a cutting board? But look at the motivators crammed into that little copy block! Why they used one of my least favorite phrases ("What's more") I'll never know, but I forgive them because they loaded the copy with reasons to buy.

Think for a moment: the product manager gives you a sample cutting board and asks you to write a quick description of the item. Misled by the word *description* you do describe. Unless the product manager spoon-feeds you some reasons to buy, you don't emphasize reasons to buy.

Your catalog writing is forty years out of date.

What's your opinion of this description?

LEATHER BRASS ACCESSORY CASE from Spain has brass fittings for an exquisite look that is perfect for any man or woman. Velvet lined $8'' \times 6\frac{1}{2}'' \times 4''$.

"For an exquisite look that is perfect for any man or woman" is awkward, but that isn't the major problem. Rather, it's the *substitution* of this cumbersome phrase for a reason to buy. Professional catalog copy-writers should know how to mask puffery within the reason-to-buy cloak. "An exquisite look" smacks of desperation, not inspiration.

Wordsmithy in Business-to-Business Catalogs

I think writers of business-to-business catalog copy are more likely to think automatically of benefit, and this is strange.

It's strange because the catalog itself is more likely to parallel a classified ad than a consumer product description. (That's why so many business-catalog websites are direct "lifts" from the company's printed catalog.) Business-to-business catalogs implicitly are aimed at a "vertical" marketplace where seller says to buyer: "What's in these pages matches what you use or need."

Answering the Question "Why?"

The reader knows we want to make a sale. As long as we're pitching, why don't we carry our sales argument to a logical conclusion?

We say to the reader, "Buy this."

The reader says, "Why?"

If we can answer, "Because . . ." we enter the Kingdom of Heaven by adding the magic password—a reason to buy.

New! Widen snug jeans, slacks and skirts to fit comfortably again

Whether your favorite jeans feel tight after they've been washed, or you've gained a few pounds, our Easy Fit Waistband Stretcher is the safe and easy answer to temporarily stretch your waistband. Simply moisten jeans, slacks or skirt, insert Easy-Fit into the waist area, and extend to desired size... stretches up to 5". When the garment dries, it retains the new size until the next washing. Constructed of lightweight, sturdy plastic, Easy-Fit works up to a size 50 waist.

Easy-Fit Waistband Stretcher   BQ0100 $29.95

Fig. 11.3:   This description is shot through with reason to buy. Had the headline been "Easy Fit Waistband Stretcher"—which many copywriters would have used as a knee-jerk approach—effectiveness would have been fractional.

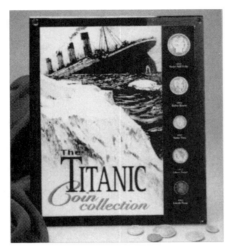

Titanic Coin Collection

Few events of the Twentieth Century are as vividly remembered as the sinking of the Titanic. On April 14, 1912, over 1500 people lost their lives when the British luxury liner struck an iceberg and, in less than three hours sank to the bottom of the Atlantic. These five coins, all minted in 1912, are the same as those that went down in the pockets and purses of the ship's passengers. Like the Titanic, these coins are pieces of history. The Lincoln Penny was in only its third year of issue, and the Liberty Nickel was minted for the last time the following year. The classic Barber Liberty Head Dime, Quarter and Half Dollar were all struck from .900 Fine Silver from the mines of the Western frontier.

#3528A $49.95

Fig. 11.4: Because this appeared in a catalog aimed at collectors, the headline isn't as flat as it would have been in a general-interest catalog. Notice how the copy takes form: before trying to sell the coins, the writer tells the story of the *Titanic*. Without that clever reason to buy, who would want coins just because they're dated 1912?

12

Lovely? Useful? Unique? Prove It!

First, *You* Try It!

Your assignment . . .

You've written a description of a golf-instruction videotape. This is your copy:

> *"Arnie's Army of Tips" is as useful as it is practical. Packed with great and important golf tips, this is the ultimate golfer's video.*

Your copy chief hands it back to you, commenting, "You haven't said anything."

"Yes, I have. I've called it useful, practical, packed with great and important tips, and the ultimate."

"I know. You haven't said anything. Do it over."

Take thirty seconds. No longer than that.

Okay, did you replace all those nonspecifics with specifics? Did you write a line similar to "Watch the great Arnold Palmer in slow-motion show you how to cock your wrists on the backswing and get an extra 40 yards on your drive"? Did you write "When (if ever) should you use a 2-wood? How far apart should your feet be when you putt with a flat-bladed putter? How about a knob-headed putter?" Did you insert some guts into your description? Getting rid of *useful*, *great*, *important*, and *ultimate* is a wonderful way to start beefing up your copy.

You Call Yourself a Writer?

Let's sit in the boss's chair. Now it's *our* turn to squat on our perch atop Mount Olympus and throw thunderbolts at those other guys whose catalog copy wasn't as inspirational-motivational as ours.

See this catalog? The writer describes a dress and doesn't even use the word *lovely*. What kind of writer is she, leaving out that word? We use it all the time.

And how about this one? This guy writes about a silver-plating solution and doesn't even use the word *different*. He ought to be drummed out of the corps for leaving out that word. We use it all the time.

Here's a floating flashlight. The photograph shows a hand pulling it out of the water, but copy just tells us it's waterproof and doesn't even give us the word *useful*. What kind of catalog writing is that, leaving out the favorite word we use all the time?

We live in the era of generalized encomiums.

Sometimes, reading product descriptions—especially in consumer catalogs—I get the feeling copy was written by the same person who writes boilerplate eulogies.

You know what I mean if you've ever been to a funeral and heard a clergyman, who never met the fellow in life, lauding the dearly departed. Dignity in death demands a degree of extolment and verbal tribute, but lack of familiarity limits the encomium to generalities.

What might the clergyman say? "He led a useful life"? Gee, that man of the cloth might be just the person to write our next catalog.

This is the era of generalized encomiums (for purists: *encomia*). We take the low road. The clergyman sees an address and a fur-clad widow and is safe in using the word *useful* to describe a life. We see a tool with a bunch of gadgets and are safe in using the word *useful* to describe what we're selling.

In neither case do we cut through the gauzy separator between message sender and message recipient. In both cases we step off the word-trail before we've reached and opened the psychological gate.

Watch for these words . . .

Generic words, used as substitutes for specifics, create copy that marks time. It runs in place. An example is: *feature-packed*. This term is okay as a space filler . . . provided the writer follows up with a solid description of what some of the features are.

But if you've been thinking of complaining you don't have enough space to mount a valid description, take a look at a hunk of your copy before marching into the boss's office. Has your own copy degenerated into a group of generalized encomiums?

Here are some words to look for. Hit the "Search" key and see how many of these you find:

add a special dimension
beautiful
the best
decorative
easy to use
effortless
feature-packed
finest
great
important
incredible (a ruined word)
a must
oh-so-wearable
practical
pretty
revolutionary
sensational
special
timeless
ultimate (a ruined word)
useful

Figure 12.1 shows three adjacent descriptions from the same catalog. One is "best," one is "superb," one is "finest." Do *any* of these three words supply anything beyond puffery, especially since this is a catalog of gourmet foods?

Understand, please: these words deserve attack when they substitute for specifics. When they're a prelude to specifics, they're safe, protected by the Live Encomium Rule:

> ✏ A generic description becomes dead puffery unless ongoing copy justifies it.

The Live Encomium Rule is the protector of those who use generalized encomiums as the alpha of an alpha-to-omega—or at least alpha-to-gamma—sales argument.

Sure, they'll call a traveler's first-aid kit "useful," but then they'll explain *why* it's useful. Sure, they'll call a fashion "timeless," but then they'll give us a comparison explaining *how* it's timeless.

Call Free On-Board ★759   **SkyMall** presents   *www.skymall.com*

Balducci's
CATALOGO DEL BUONGUSTAIO
THE SHOP-FROM-HOME CATALOG FOR THE GOURMET

Each chocolate is handmade and handpacked into one of these elegant boxes.

SMOKED MAINE SALMON FILLET (FILET FUMÉ)
America's best smoked salmon

This Prized Piece comes from salmon farmed off the Maine coast, which boasts the country's best farmed salmon. Filet Fumé is lightly smoked over a blend of four different woods and minimally salted at a small artisan smokery in the heart of Maine's fishing community. This filet is meant to be cut into thick strips rather than thin slices like other smoked salmons.
Approximately 1 lb., serves 8 to 10.
  Order #4659A$50.00

BALDUCCI'S GOURMET CAVIAR
Indulge yourself with one of nature's finest creations

  Imperial Beluga—Taken from the world's largest sturgeon, these are the most delicately flavored eggs. Their color ranges from pearl gray to charcoal gray; they separate easily and are uniform in size.
  Sevruga—These eggs are light gray to charcoal gray in color and have a smaller grain than Beluga. Their flavor is clean and briny-fresh.
  Salmon—Salmon eggs are large, bright orange pearls that pop pleasantly in your mouth with a mildly briny juice.
Each sampler includes a 1 oz. jar of Beluga, a 1 oz. jar of Sevruga and a 2 oz. jar of salmon caviar packed in an insulated tote.
  Order #4569A **$75.00**

PYRAMID OF FINE CHOCOLATES
Superb handmade chocolates

Our Gold Box is filled with wonderfully tempting bonbons. Inside the silver box is a fabulous array of truffles (hand-rolled with rich chocolate, natural fruit and tasty liqueurs). The bronze box is bulging with Fudge Love (a buttery mousse of rich, dark fudge coated with hazelnuts). *Three boxes.*
  Order #4136A$28.00

Fig. 12.1: Unquestionably these are gourmet treats. Unquestionably, too, they deserve a less hackneyed encomium than "best," "superb," and "nature's finest." (If the Maine coast "boasts the country's best farmed salmon," what about *farmed* salmon makes it superior?)

Some words are exempt from the rule. *Heavy-duty* and *classic*, for example, lift themselves out of the morass of generalization by drawing a word image for the reader.

Careful, now! Don't lean on these exempt words too hard. Remember what happened to words such as *quality* and *value*. They went to that Great Lexicon in the Sky, killed off by overuse. (Should we hold a service for them, larded with encomiums?)

Other words, such as *stylish*, *luxurious*, *exclusive*, and *deluxe*, are borderline. They *almost* draw a word image.

I mentioned *incredible* and *ultimate* as ruined words. Here we have once powerful words that, mildly tarnished, were downgraded to respectable. Now, beaten about the head and shoulders by thoughtless wordsmiths, they've become spongy, of such dubious worth that most copy is more successful when a sad but realistic editor blue-lines them.

(To complete the attack on *ultimate* and its confrères, see chapter 13.)

Are these thoughts of caution making you gun-shy of your keyboard? One golden ray: if catalog copywriting didn't involve word-selection discipline, we couldn't justify what we do as a profession, could we? And we couldn't get, from all the readers we inspire, such encomiums.

IGIÁ® ULTRA CLEAR
Amazing European
Blemish Remover

Made for
Men & Women

A battery operated blemish remover is a beauty system scientifically designed in Europe for the removal of skin blemishes. It uses a non-invasive process to destroy bacteria from the skin and enables the natural healing process through the pores. Proven effective for skin problems such as pimples, blemishes, blackheads and ingrown hairs. IGIÁ Ultra Clear System safely removes the appearance of unsightly-skin spots without needles squeezing the skin. It can also be used safely in conjunction with cleansers, lotions, anti-oxidant creams. IGIÁ Ultra Clear has been clinically tested and proven effective in having a 28% decrease in the number of blemishes. **FREE** IGIÁ Pre & Post Treatment Lotions.
SMCL1A $99.95

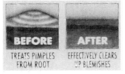

BEFORE   AFTER
TREATS PIMPLES   EFFECTIVELY CLEARS
FROM ROOT   UP BLEMISHES

Fig. 12.2: *Amazing* is exempt from the group of generalized encomiums because the word does spark an emotional response. The description is solid, but how does one pronounce the product name? Probably some telephone orders are lost because individuals are unsure of the pronunciation.

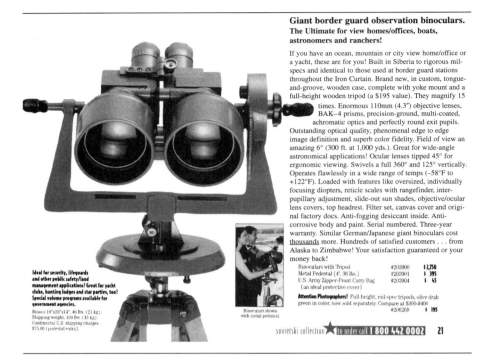

Giant border guard observation binoculars.
The Ultimate for view homes/offices, boats,
astronomers and ranchers!

If you have an ocean, mountain or city view home/office or
a yacht, these are for you! Built in Siberia to rigorous mil-
specs and identical to those used at border guard stations
throughout the Iron Curtain. Brand new, in custom, tongue-
and-groove, wooden case, complete with yoke mount and a
full-height wooden tripod (a $195 value). They magnify 15
times. Enormous 110mm (4.3″) objective lenses,
BAK–4 prisms, precision-ground, multi-coated,
achromatic optics and perfectly round exit pupils.
Outstanding optical quality, phenomenal edge to edge
image definition and superb color fidelity. Field of view an
amazing 6° (300 ft. at 1,000 yds.). Great for wide-angle
astronomical applications! Ocular lenses tipped 45° for
ergonomic viewing. Swivels a full 360° and 125° vertically.
Operates flawlessly in a wide range of temps (–58°F to
+122°F). Loaded with features like oversized, individually
focusing diopters, reticle scales with rangefinder, inter-
pupillary adjustment, slide-out sun shades, objective/ocular
lens covers, top headrest. Filter set, canvas cover and original factory docs. Anti-fogging desiccant inside. Anti-
corrosive body and paint. Serial numbered. Three-year
warranty. Similar German/Japanese giant binoculars cost
thousands more. Hundreds of satisfied customers . . . from
Alaska to Zimbabwe! Your satisfaction guaranteed or your
money back!

Binoculars with Tripod	#203900	$2,750
Metal Pedestal (4′, 36 lbs.)	#203901	$ 395
U.S. Army Zipper-Front Carry Bag	#203904	$ 45
(an ideal protective cover)		

Attention Photographers! Full-height, mil-spec tripods, olive drab
green in color, now sold separately. Compare at $300–$400
| | #206268 | $ 195 |

Ideal for security, lifeguards
and other public safety/land
management applications! Great for yacht
clubs, hunting lodges and star parties, too!
Special volume programs available for
government agencies.

Binocs 16″x28″x14″, 46 lbs. (21 kg).
Shipping weight, 100 lbs. (45 kg).
Continental U.S. shipping charges
$75.00 (pedestal extra).

Binoculars shown
with metal pedestal.

sovietski collection ▶ to order call **1 800 442 0002**   21

Fig. 12.3:   What about these binoculars justifies the word *ultimate*? The word may be misused here because the line
"The Ultimate for view homes/offices, boats, astronomers and ranchers" doesn't compute. For a $2,750 price, "ultimate"
should give way to "next-generation" or "state-of-the-art" or "The one chosen by governments for border surveillance."

13

The Ultimate Explosive . . . and Other Overused Oddities

First, *You* Try It!

Your assignment . . .

You've written a catalog description of a telephone headset. Your copy begins with this headline:

The ultimate executive headset—works like a handset!

You realize you've used the word *ultimate* in headlines for other descriptions. This becomes one time too many. Looking through the product sheet, you see benefits: lifting it activates it; putting it down hangs up the phone. It weighs $\frac{1}{2}$ ounce and has an adjustable volume control.

Change the headline to get rid of *ultimate*, replacing the word with a descriptive term. Take thirty seconds. No longer than that.

What's your solution? "The half-ounce headset that thinks it's a full-size phone"? Not bad. "At last! The headset you can hang up like a regular phone"? Not bad, but not as good because "hang up" without a prior reference has too many peripheral meanings. "The best handset phone . . . in one super-comfortable feather-light headset"? Pretty good except that it isn't true because the best handset phone has a lot of buttons you won't find on a headset.

Whatever your solution, replacing nondescriptive hyperbole with selling fact is a step forward.

Loose Superlatives Don't Hack It

The Good Book says: "Wisdom crieth aloud in the streets," or something like that.

No, no, I'm not the guy who wakes up just before dawn each morning, says, "Let there be light," and confidently settles back under a blanket of golden clouds. I'm just a catalog reader who wonders, month after month, why copywriters think they've perfected product description by plastering the same nondescriptive superlatives onto one product description after another.

What's a little thoughtless underscoring?

You've seen this argumentative ploy before: the person who's losing an argument—or worse, an audience—gets shrill. The way to grab attention is to shout, not to caress or convince. So here goes that inevitable lapse into nondescriptive shouting adjectives.

This is thoughtless underscoring, the "Wow! Gee Whiz!" effect. The writer's brain is out of gear and, idling at high speed, it spits out words to keep the flow going until the reader turns the page.

If you're an inveterate catalog reader you know two of the words catalog writers use and abuse as crutches. We exploded those two words in the previous chapter: *important* and *ultimate*. Damn these writers anyway. They've made me so gun-shy of those two once-proud words I've begun to use them less frequently than they deserve in my own copy.

Check out some new candidates.

A catalog I once admired went out of business. The copy just didn't pull the way it once did. Looking through a vintage issue of that catalog, I may have discovered the reason, and it's given some new candidates for my list of crutch words. Leading the pack is the once explosive word *explosive*.

The inside cover of this catalog explodes with the headline:

EXPLOSIVE CD AUTOMATION

Were we supposed to ignore the obvious mismatch between those two words, concentrating instead on what must have been the writer's intent—to stop and grab the reader? Okay with me, but the cataloger should have known and heeded this WARNING: *explosive* is a far more mnemonic word than *ultimate*. You've used it. Keep it in your hip pocket for the rest of the catalog.

Not this writer. The secondary headline begins:

Your stereo system's sound will explode with life. And, you'll thrill to the ultimate in CD automation.

If the word *ultimate* weren't in there and if the statement made some sense, the doubled use of *explode* would be within the bounds of logical copywriting. (Hold that word *thrill* for a moment.) But in the very first paragraph of body copy we read:

. . . this new . . . oversampling CD player will explode any perception of sound quality . . .

We still aren't done, because on this same page we have, as a subhead in the copy:

UNLEASH EXPLOSIVE AUTOMATION RISK FREE

Not only is this too many explosions, but I as reader still am unconvinced the words make sense. Instead, I get the feeling the writer is in love with the word—a dangerous rhetorical game.

Let's add some more words to this arsenal of terms. Overused, they're blanks in the communication gun.

First, we have *thrill*. We've already seen it once, and like *explosive*, it's a word we can't keep popping away with, as we might with *a*, *an*, or *the*. But here's what we find, on this same page:

You'll thrill to a signal-to-noise ratio of 96db . . .

And, you'll thrill to every musical nuance in a stunning new way . . .

The next candidate for overuse becomes the runaway leader in this catalog: *incredible*.

Before we explore the incredible sound you'll hear . . .

Because of the incredibly low price of this awesome 6-CD changer . . .

We're in a word game, where one clue leads to another. *Incredible* leads to *awesome*. Before we struggle out of this page we stumble over:

_____

From the awesome digital sound . . .

AWESOME AUTOMATION [a subhead] . . .

_____

And we bring back an explosion to make the description incredibly awesome:

_____

I wish I could be there to see the expression on your face the first time you hear the awesome CD sound explode around you.

_____

These words still aren't burned up. A few pages down the line we have a radar detector: "X and K band sounds explode into action"; we have an "automated" cassette deck: ". . . you'll have the incredible vibrance of 105db dynamic range." (Vibrancy, isn't it?)

For a software program: ". . . an incredibly sophisticated integrated word processing and graphics program."

Next page, same item: "This program is incredibly powerful . . ." and "Make your ideas explode in front of your readers." (Huh?) Last sentence on the page: "And oh, it's so incredibly easy to use."

You get the idea. Within seven lines of each other we encounter "these incredible systems" and "you get an incredible deal." Page 11 brings the words even closer together: "This typewriter represents an incredible value for your investment and an incredible savings of typing time."

Champion is the page that has—

- "an incredible breakthrough price"
- "an incredible wail for help"
- "They're incredibly rugged"
- "this incredible safety/entertainment device"
- "this incredible system"
- "just count the incredible number of entertainment and emergency features"

We aren't finished with *explode* either. The copy block for a jet printer begins "Let your ideas explode in front of your readers." At that point I put the tired old catalog down, convinced that if I wanted to wander through more pages of this golden realm I'd enjoy additional incredible explosions. They'd be thrilling and awesome, I knew, because those words kept popping up, too.

The Rule of Word Re-Use

Sometimes it does pay to re-use a word. Just in case you aren't sure whether your next try does or doesn't fit the mold, here's a working example:

You may think you own a great CB. But I'm talking about a *really* great CB.

That's the Rule of Word Re-Use:

> ✏ If you have to re-use a word, emphasize the key word before its second use to show the reader the repeat is intentional.

This rule won't do much for your writing finesse. (In fact, if your descriptive power is limited to the word *great,* you have big problems in this profession.) The rule does have the potential of adding pep to flat copy. And, oh yes, another benefit: you tell cynical readers like me you *meant* to reuse that word or phrase.

A couple of computer programs, some of them built right into word-processing software programs such as WordPerfect and MSWord, have the capability of counting the number of times you've used the same word in one piece of copy. If you're plagued by the falling-in-love-with-a-word affliction, one of those programs might be an eye-opener—and a salvation—for you.

Does all this nonsense thrill you? It should. It's incredibly explosive.

Fig. 13.1: This catalog likes the word *blowout* and often uses it on the cover, as well as repeatedly within its pages. (*Blowout* is a rather excitingly descriptive word if not overused.) This is the first of four examples from the same catalog.

Fig. 13.2: Here we have a "Scanner Blowout!" The highly exclamatory word usually is accompanied by an exclamation point.

Fig. 13.3: The catalog continues with "Blowout pricing!" on a UPS.

Fig. 13.4: "Blowout Prices!" apply to a modem. Other blowouts may occur in the pages of this catalog, but you get the idea . . . and the contagion this word causes, exemplified by the cover of a competing company's catalog, figure 13.5.

Fig. 13.5: Notice any similarity? The word *blowout* seems to have considerable impact both on copywriters and on customers in the world of computer-products catalogs.

14

Why Should I Pay You That Much?

First, *You* Try It!

Your assignment . . .

You're editing copy for a catalog of expensive gadgets. This copy for a global positioning system crosses your desk:

> GPS III
>
> *This handheld, waterproof GPS (Global Positioning System) gives you an accurate map of your surroundings. The base map is built in. It gives you a detailed picture of cities, roads, highways, railroads, rivers, lakes, and coastlines. A dozen parallel receivers pinpoint your location. $349.*

You hand the copy back to the writer with this comment: "You've left out something." What did the writer leave out? Think about it.

Take thirty seconds. No longer than that.

Actually, you shouldn't have needed more than ten seconds if you read the title of this chapter. The writer left out a *reason* for charging $349.

Assuming typical readers haven't previously recognized any need or value for a GPS, why would they consider paying $349 for this one?

So you probably added phrases such as "You'll never be lost again" or "You'll never have to stop to ask for directions." Whatever you did, you justified the cost—an apparently high amount without the justification. (The actual description for the GPS is in figure 14.1.)

With GPS III, you always have a map in hand that says "You are here."

Imagine, never being lost again. Always knowing where you are and how to get where you want to go. And being able to retrace any route on your way home, without manually storing waypoints (electronic markers). That's just the beginning of what this hand-held, waterproof global positioning system can do for you. Twelve parallel channel receivers constantly determine where you are on planet Earth and provide you with an accurate map of your surroundings. The built-in basemap gives you detailed pictures of cities, roads, U.S. state/interstate highways, state/county boundaries, railroads, rivers, lakes and coastlines. You can view the maps either vertically or horizontally to best view the areas you're looking for. The Tracback feature lets you quickly navigate your way back home. It also features user-selectable icons for map

zoom/enhancement, a selectable compass pointer screen and a resettable trip odometer. All of this in a hand-held device that can withstand having soda spilled on it—or being dropped in a lake. It's a great comfort and timesaver for road trips, backpacking, weekend adventures and daily travels about town. Best of all, you'll never have to admit you're lost or stop to ask for directions again.

    810015 Garmin GPS III $349
    810031 Auto Adapter $24.95

Waterproof to 20 meters.
Protect your GPS, cell phone or cash from fresh or salt water, spray, sand or snow. Buoyant PVC case with crystal-clear reception you can hear and see through. Quick-release Aquaclip for fast access, neck cord, and a reflective strip that's easy to find if case is misplaced.

810023 AQ3 Waterproof Case $19.95

Field Trips 1-800-500-9266

Fig. 14.1:   The heading isn't particularly strong. "You'll never have to stop to ask for directions again" might have been more apt for a device selling for $349.

Ask—Because the Reader Will Ask

How much is a pair of tennis shoes?

The question isn't as blind as "How much is a house?" Typically, tennis shoes cost $25 to $60 a pair. Occasionally you'll see them on sale for less and occasionally you'll see a super-featured shoe for more.

I ask the question because, reading a product description in a current catalog, I wondered why these tennis shoes cost so much.

Here's the complete product description:

A. For Tennis. A man's performance tennis shoe that combines lightweight comfort with extraordinary support. Leather saddle over special urethane sole. Made in the U.S.A.   *$72.00*

Okay, suppose you're in the market for tennis shoes. You see ad after ad in your local newspaper. Every pair these days is said to combine lightweight comfort with extraordinary support. For a tennis shoe manufacturer that's like saying, "Good morning." Leather saddle and urethane sole? Standard. So what makes these shoes worth seventy-two bucks?

Fish for the answer . . . THEN write the copy.

I didn't call this catalog company to ask. First of all, whoever answers the toll-free number presumably doesn't have any more information than the ad imparts and probably would say to a fellow operator, "I have some nut on the phone. He's burning up our 877 phone charges to find out why the shoe costs $72."

Second, if the operator *does* know, then something is grotesquely awry within this company's internal lines of communication. How can the operator know and the copywriter *not* know?

It can't be the brand name or the catalog's upscale intention. A couple of pages away is "the favorite loafer, classic in every detail," for $54—considerably less than I'd expect to pay.

What happened, I think, is that the copywriter was hypnotized by a stack of shoe descriptions. The copywriter went at the stack doggedly, whittling it down by extruding workmanlike descriptions, neither adding nor subtracting any psychological impellers.

But somebody should have yelled, "Hold it! The description doesn't justify the price."

What if the copywriter had asked the buyer: "Hey, why are these tennis shoes so expensive? I can buy Adidas and Nikes and Pumas and Reeboks up the gazoo for $40 to $50, and every one of them has all the features we've named here."

The buyer then would *have to* open some hidden box of facts and give the writer what this product description needs: ammunition.

What justifies price?

1. A name brand justifies price.

    So if this were a "designer" shoe, *any* price would become logical. Sure, we've all prostituted the word *designer* so it has about 30 percent of the impact it had a single generation ago. But 30 percent is way, way above zero.

    "A genuine Bartolizzi design . . ." would have done it. Any shoe designer worth ten cents has an Italian name, right? Not necessarily. Take Calvin Klein, for example. A simple Calvin Klein deck shoe costs $79—considerably more than comparable shoes—but it has the name-brand justification:

Calvin Klein Sport designs a classic deck shoe of softest suede or napa leather with rust-toned rubber sole. Imported. White suede or coffee cream leather. Whole and half sizes. N $7\frac{1}{2}$–9. M $5\frac{1}{2}$–10. *8279A Calvin Klein Sport Shoes $79.00*

---

2. Strangely, a price reduction justifies price.

   A lot of people care less about the actual cost of an item than they do about what the price was reduced from. Another catalog shows a woman's ordinary-looking, low-heeled shoe with an ordinary description . . . plus the magic words "Made to sell for $169.95. Special price $99.95." The reduction justifies the price.

   Consider, too: this reduction is artificial, but it still works. "Made to sell for . . ." isn't a statement of fact; it's a statement of puffery. If this were a college course in logic, it would fade under the genuine sunlight of "Listed at $169.95 in our last catalog. Special price $99.95." Now the touchstone is factual. But so what? Casual catalog readers aren't that analytical.

3. Scarcity justifies price.

   This is a tough concept for shoes, but the "limited edition" notion works almost anywhere, so I suppose a limited-edition shoe isn't that outlandish an idea. Even if it is, we can justify scarcity by pointing out that these are handmade (or "handcrafted," a more generalized and less assailable term), one pair at a time.

4. Publicity justifies price.

   If these are the shoes Pete Sampras wears (not the same pair he just wore for that five-set match, but the same brand), some might think the magic of his arm might bleed off into every wearer of the shoe. If a celebrity wears these shoes they're lifted out of the gray milieu of sameness.

How About Just Words?

Words? Words can justify price if the words aren't transparent rhetoric with puffery substituting for fact.

But I suggest to catalog sellers who expect the copywriter to turn lead into gold: at least supply the makin's.

Let's form two tiny rules—two of the thousands hovering in the heavens—to guide us as we try to justify the last item in any description, the price. We'll call the first the Evidential Superiority Principle:

☞ Declaration isn't as convincing as evidence.

This means a *statement* of bargain . . . superiority . . . scarcity . . . no matter how well written, isn't as powerful as *evidence* of bargain, superiority, or scarcity.

While we're at it, let's tack on the second rule. We'll call this the Anti-B.S. Procedure because it explains why heavy production, full-bleed, printing in six colors, and sending forty people to Baluchistan to shoot photographs aren't, combined, as effective as an explanation of superiority:

☞ It's more logical to throw selling facts at the reader than to mask lack of facts in lavish production.

See the Anti-B.S. Procedure in action.

The Anti-B.S. Procedure apparently was unknown to one of the giant producers of collectibles . . . and was very much in the mind of a catalog house, which gave us a classic comparison.

B.S. isn't parallel to seasoning. Separating the two is one criterion of catalog copywriting professionalism. Adding B.S. parallels the adding of monosodium glutamate for just a touch of taste-bud vibration.

A cook sprinkles some Accent on a bland-tasting dish, and taste buds respond with delight. A catalog copywriter has the same opportunity . . . but not always the same inclination.

Sometimes the writer ignores the challenge to galvanize the reader's salivary glands into action. Sometimes the writer pours a whole can of rhetorical Accent onto the copy, smothering description with puffery. Sometimes the writer (usually a beginner who just has to be related to the owner to get away with such unprofessional writing) replaces description with puffery. Ugh.

Ah, but sometimes the writer realizes the need for romance and yet has discipline, tempering that inclination to drown information in a sea of romance. The wonderful balance should win awards—and would if awards weren't canted toward the cosmetic aspects of catalog production.

Enough already.

King Tut and Friends

Occasionally we see the same item advertised by several vendors. This gives us the opportunity to compare apples with apples.

The sample I'm looking at gives us the opportunity to compare pharaohs with pharaohs. It's a framed depiction of King Tutankhamen, prepared by (so help me) the Papyrus Institute in Cairo.

(An irreverent thought: can you imagine a parent's reaction if a high-school graduate said, "Dad, I want to continue my studies at the Papyrus Institute"?)

One version is a full page, with a restrained heading:

———————————

Until now, only museums owned original art like this.

———————————

Body copy gives us minimal information:

———————————

THE PAPYRUS INSTITUTE IN CAIRO REDISCOVERS A LOST ART FORM.

You have a rare opportunity to own a museum masterpiece created with the same painstaking techniques developed by the ancient Egyptians. Portraying the fabled boy king Tutankhamen and his lovely queen.

Rich symbolism. Timeless art. Glowing with gold and copper. Hand-painted on authentic Egyptian papyrus, hand-made by an art which has endured for 5,000 years. Preserved in a Far Eastern frame of black lacquered hardwood and gleaming brass. $275.

———————————

And that's it, except for a coupon, which has its own problems. I'll come to that in a couple of paragraphs.

No, this wasn't in a catalog; it was a full-page space ad, which has a greater impulse-buy responsibility. And that's exactly why it's a good example—because a better description *was* in a catalog.

I'm considerably less annoyed by partial sentences than I used to be, but I don't think I'll ever be able to take "Portraying the fabled boy king Tutankhamen and his lovely queen" as an acceptable nounless, verbless sentence. While I'm carping, who says the queen was lovely? From the art, she looks hydrocephalic.

(While we're in the neighborhood, if the art has been "rediscovered" it couldn't have "endured," could it?)

Now to the coupon . . .

What do the words "I wish to commission The Tutankhamen Papyrus" mean to you? Don't they mean the piece is made to order? Clever copy, perhaps—unless someone looks at a catalog that sells the same item.

It's the same item, different pitch.

A catalog shows this same art reproduction. It's one of five items on the catalog's page 11, so the amount of space certainly isn't greater than the competitor's description. The frame doesn't have brass corners, but the price is $75 less.

That isn't our concern as catalog copywriters. Compare the copy:

TUTANKHAMEN PAPYRUS

(left) The splendor of ancient Egypt casts its timeless spell. Glowing in rich oils and goldleaf paint, this masterpiece depicts the young King Tutankhamen and his wife, Queen Ankhesenamun, in a ritual hunting scene. Discovered in the tomb of "King Tut" in 1922. This faithful reproduction was painted on authentic Egyptian papyrus, handmade by 5000-year-old techniques at the Papyrus Institute in Cairo. It comes with a certificate detailing the making of a papyrus, and a full explanation of the scene. To show it to best effect, we offer a 24"h × 29.5"w black beveled frame with the papyrus suspended between see-through perfex. You will own an artwork of majestic beauty.

No ball game here. The catalog, which devotes about eighteen square inches of space to this art reproduction, gives us ten times the reason to buy we have from the full-page ad, which in seventy square inches transmits almost no specifics.

Can "Rich symbolism. Timeless art. Glowing with gold and copper" compete with "Glowing in rich oils and goldleaf paint, this masterpiece depicts the young King Tutankhamen and his wife, Queen Ankhesenamun, in a ritual hunting scene"? For that matter, can the nonsensical phrase "his lovely queen" compete with the queen's actual name?

The very inclusion in this catalog—might it be in other catalogs as well?—explodes the "I wish to commission" myth: obviously if the same art is shown in a catalog, the work already has been commissioned by a third commercial source.

What's the point?

The point of this harangue is the combination of two rules of force-communication:

1. The Puffery-Defeat Inevitability:

> No amount of puffery or self-applause can sell as effectively as a listing of specific benefits.

2. The Rule of Implied Importance:

> ✎ Importance should relate to the state of mind of the reader, not the writer.

That second rule comes clear when we read "Rich symbolism," unexplained; "Timeless art," unexplained; "Far Eastern frame," not only unexplained but out of key (the typical reader thinks at once of bamboo).

Did the writer of the space ad have access to the same information available to the catalog writer? Probably. Why didn't the space-ad writer use that information? Again, because the writer either didn't know or ignored two other rules of force-communication:

1. The Rule of Importance Determination:

> ✎ If you claim importance, prove it.

2. The First Rule of Weaseling:

> ✎ An effective weaseled claim is written so the reader slides past the weasel without realizing it.

Usually, a comparison of expensive space-ad copy and catalog copy leaves the catalog writer in the dust. What a pleasure it is to be on the winning side!

And that's the sermon for chapter 14. Much as we writers like to claim importance for our craft, we're firing blanks in a marketplace in which the target individual has some sense of values, unless whoever hires us gives us some bullets for our word-guns.

Pass the .44 Magnum, please. It's catalog-writing time!

SCAFFOLDING BED

This charming bed is great for the guest room, a beach house or a pared down, modern room. Made from actual, long-lasting and durable scaffolding material, its solid aluminum castings hold brushed aluminum tubing. Wheels with locks. Specify for use with box springs and mattress set or mattress only. 46"H headboard, 37"H footboard. Exclusively ours.

#6130 SCAFFOLDING BED

Twin . . . . ($150)	$1295.00
Double . . . . ($150)	$1595.00
Queen . . . . ($150)	$1795.00
King . . . . ($175)	$1995.00
Calif. King . . . . ($175)	$2195.00

Fig. 14.2:   Would you pay $2,195 for an aluminum-rod bed, based on a description that says it's "for the guest room, a beach house, or a pared down, modern room" . . . made of "scaffolding material"?

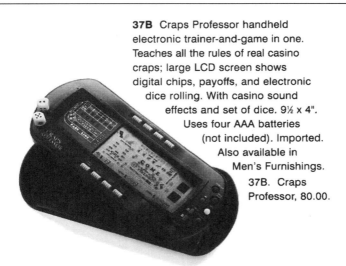

37B Craps Professor handheld electronic trainer-and-game in one. Teaches all the rules of real casino craps; large LCD screen shows digital chips, payoffs, and electronic dice rolling. With casino sound effects and set of dice. 9½ x 4". Uses four AAA batteries (not included). Imported. Also available in Men's Furnishings. 37B. Craps Professor, 80.00.

Fig. 14.3:   What about this description justifies an $80 price? Many similar electronic games retail for under $25. This one may be underdescribed because there is no explanation for the set of dice.

15

Positioning: A Key to Higher Response

First, *You* Try It!

Your assignment . . .

You've written this headline and first sentence of copy for a luggage cart:

STURDY LUGGAGE CART WITH 2 RETRACTABLE BACK WHEELS

Holds up to 175 pounds, folds compactly for storage.

The head of the company shakes his head. "No, no, we can't just *describe*. We have to *position* this cart. Everything we sell has to be unique. Make this the cart that holds more weight than any other."

"But others sell a cart that holds twice as much," you protest.

"That's their problem. Our job is to sell this one. Write me a headline and first line of copy proving our superiority."

Take thirty seconds. No longer than that.

What did you write? The headline is easy: just add the word *The*. The definite article is a *positioning* article. (Want proof? If I'd said, "The definite article is *the* positioning article," you'd interpret the statement to mean no other positioning article exists.)

The first sentence isn't so easy. You have to make a comparison, and—whether you or I agree with this sleazy philosophy or not—your boss demands it. So you probably wrote "This Hercules-tough cart holds 175 pounds, far more than most others."

Expect your boss to scratch the word *most*. Why? Because without "most" the statement is more likely to be true.

Making a Deal with the Devil

Discussing current results with catalogers, one begins to understand Dickens: "It was the best of times, it was the worst of times."

Gee, how I'd love to relate the pulling power of a catalog to the copywriter's talent. But not only would that be self-serving; it wouldn't reflect a professional attitude.

Oh, sure, good copy can boost—maybe even double—response. But mediocre copy won't kill an item if the other two elements—photograph and raw product description—are passably adequate.

Now, what if the copywriter goes one step beyond exciting description, into the precarious word-world of extravagant claims? It gives a synthetic boost to response. Do we pay a price? Have we made a deal with the devil?

Cataloger, position thyself.

Some of the murk clouding those catalogs that offer similar products and use similar themes seems to be clearing. Catalogs with "personality" are beginning to separate themselves from catalogs adhering to the traditional "Here's what it is" approach.

The key: positioning.

A statement of position makes a catalog super-competitive, *even if no competitor exists*. The reader actually believes, "This is the only place I can get this," even though it's a standard catalog item.

An example of this is a catalog that in almost every product description includes a flat statement of superiority. One simple trick is use of the word *the*—"The Hands-Free Personal Headlight," "The Self-Powered Wristwatch," "The Personal Bedside HDTV."

Visualize a heading without the definite article: "Programmable Electric Bathroom Heater" instead of "The Programmable Electric Bathroom Heater." See the difference? Without *the*, we imply the existence of competing electric bathroom heaters. The definite article suppresses them.

Are we setting a dangerous precedent?

One well-known catalog takes an editorial position by using an Olympian labeling system (see "I Am the Greatest" section in chapter 1):

- The Best Pants Presser
- The Best Cordless Phone
- The Only Travel Scale

- The Smallest Folding Guest Bed
- The Best Nose Hair Trimmer (No, I didn't make that up—see figure 15.6.)

Is this the best pants presser? Is this the best cordless phone? Might we find, on this planet, another travel scale? If we looked hard enough, could we find a smaller folding guest bed? (Is it the guest who folds?) Let's not even challenge the claim for the nose hair trimmer because the company might cross-challenge us to find another one.

At the moment, the answers are inconsequential because a reader who asks these questions isn't convinceable anyway.

What makes this a dangerous game is the possibility of abuse. The company's stated evidence parallels survey results crowing, "Preferred by four out of five people surveyed," when those polled were all from the same group.

I should clarify: I have to admire this procedure because this company knows the Rule of Preestablished Attitude, a tenet of primitive psychology:

> ✏ A product is what it is, plus what the buyer thinks it is.

So users *think* they are buying the best cordless phone. That this one transmits signals nine hundred feet and others transmit signals fifteen hundred feet is inconsequential. This one has been declared "best."

Figure 15.1 uses the word *this* as a positioner. Without that word, the layout still is eye-catching and the expense of the car is noteworthy, but *this* separates it from every other car.

Should we underline superiority?

The same catalog uses another technique well-known to anyone who ever wrote copy for computer software. It's the magic of four little words: *unlike other models which.* . . .

I use software as an example because as a veteran of these intramural wars, in which the difference between spreadsheets or word-processing programs isn't always clear . . . and the superiority of what we're selling isn't absolute . . . we know a sophisticated copywriting practice, the Law of Competitive Selectivity:

> ✏ Select only the vulnerable targets, and attack.

A: this Aston Martin has your name on it.

3 A numbered edition of ten Neiman Marcus Aston Martin DB7s will be hand made in England, exclusively for Neiman Marcus customers, allocated on a first-to-order basis. The Neiman Marcus edition features specially formulated jet black paint, a luxurious grey and black Connolly leather interior, carbon-fiber trim accents, polished alloy wheels, a chrome plated mesh grill, black leather luggage with chrome fittings, and a choice of manual or automatic transmission. Owners of the Neiman Marcus edition will have the opportunity to visit the Aston Martin factory and to drive the 335 horsepower supercharged Aston Martin DB7 at the Goodwood Motor Circuit, scene of Aston Martin racing success. For information and to place your order for an Aston Martin DB7 Neiman Marcus edition, please telephone 1-201-818-8351.

3. The Aston Martin DB7 Neiman Marcus Edition, 148,580.00 (X).

Fig. 15.1: Scarcity is underlined by the word *this* in the heading. Copy pounds the exclusivity theme as a factor far more important than the actual mechanical aspects of the automobile.

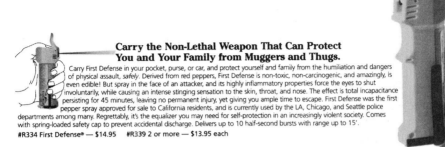

Carry the Non-Lethal Weapon That Can Protect You and Your Family from Muggers and Thugs.

Carry First Defense in your pocket, purse, or car, and protect yourself and family from the humiliation and dangers of physical assault, *safely*. Derived from red peppers, First Defense is non-toxic, non-carcinogenic, and amazingly, is even edible! But spray in the face of an attacker, and its highly inflammatory properties force the eyes to shut involuntarily, while causing an intense stinging sensation to the skin, throat, and nose. The effect is total incapacitance persisting for 45 minutes, leaving no permanent injury, yet giving you ample time to escape. First Defense was the first pepper spray approved for sale to California residents, and is currently used by the LA, Chicago, and Seattle police departments among many. Regrettably, it's the equalizer you may need for self-protection in an increasingly violent society. Comes with spring-loaded safety cap to prevent accidental discharge. Delivers up to 10 half-second bursts with range up to 15'.

#R334 First Defense® — $14.95   #R339 2 or more — $13.95 each

Fig. 15.2:   You can see how much weaker the position of "First Defense" would be without the often unnoticed but key word *the*. (A caps/lower case headline in today's marketplace places an unnecessary psychological barrier between vendor and reader.)

So copy that reads "Unlike other models with one or two channels, it has 10 FCC-approved channels to eliminate interference from other cordless phones" suggests *all* other models have one or two channels. But read it again. No, no, that isn't what it says. It's just what the writer wants us to think it says.

Therein lies the brightness of the writer—and the danger of the game. Catalog copy has been curiously exempt from this pre-flavoring.

We balance the benefit of cleverly constructed claims of superiority against the detriment of having others bring hopeless confusion into the marketplace by establishing their own "institutes" (see figure 15.6). We see uncontrolled private, arrogant, coldly unscientific testing designed to prove a preconceived copy point. And we see—what?

Not pretty, is it?

A Happy Middle Ground

Is this the only way to claim superiority? I'm unconvinced.

What gives me hope for a future of copywriting that isn't so baldly self-serving is copy such as the description of a sweater in figure 15.3. Headline:

Three cheers for chenille

Copy glorifies the fabric, as it should. The reader concludes there just ain't no sweater like this one, as the reader should. The effect is there without the danger. What if this heading had been "The Only 'Toasty-Warm' Sweater" or "The Best Chenille Sweater"? Would that sell more sweaters?

(Parenthetically, I endorse a headline that isn't all caps and lower case as in figure 15.3.)

I hope you're thumping the table and saying, "Whether an 'I Am the Greatest' headline pulls better or not isn't the question."

No, it isn't. The question is subtly double-faced.

The obverse face: are catalogs, in the struggle for survival through positioning, beginning to build a dependence on cunning?

The reverse face: isn't it logical for the copywriter to use every ounce of ingenuity to keep the catalog's bottom line healthy?

As a catalog lover with a predetermined viewpoint—part of my income depends on them—I lean, emotionally, toward survival at any legal price. As curmudgeon-in-residence I lean, intellectually, toward exhausting our brainpower in a more responsible direction before teetering toward duplicity . . . or, just as bad for the world of catalogs, the accusation of duplicity.

That's probably the Kingdom of Heaven, and I suspect few of us, with our cynicism and hard-boiled business attitudes, ever will get a set of keys to that Kingdom. But we'll enjoy the battle of wits before we disappear into limbo, won't we?

Three cheers for chenille

Evening winds whip through the stadium, urging you to turn up your collar against the chill. You're in your element with this plush chenille pullover. And warm as toast, yelling your heart out from the stands. Here is a welcome touch of plush for any wardrobe. A meltingly soft blending of rayon and Lycra® spandex, in three stop-the-clock colors: berry, black and tan. Sumptuous. Spirited. Absolutely sensational. With a high crossover neckline and slimming shape that skims yours to a mid-hip length. USA-made; dry clean. Sizes XS-S-M-L-XL. Specify berry, black or tan chenille. [MR1-2543] **$98 each**

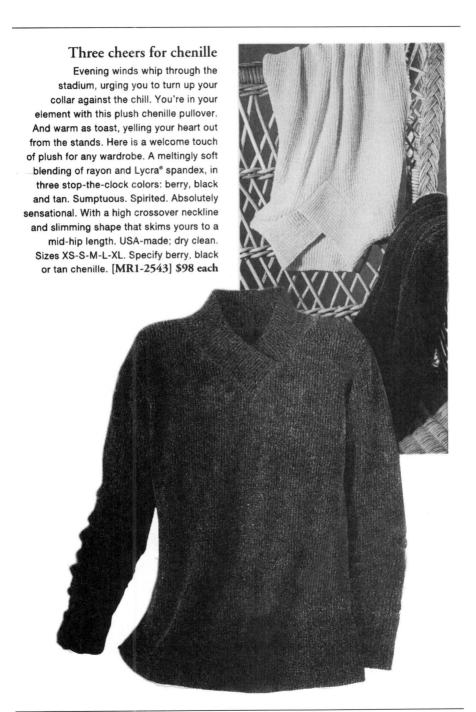

Fig. 15.3: "Three cheers for chenille" . . . and for the copywriter who created this way of ennobling this fabric. Copy touches on the word *cheers* through references to a cold outdoor stadium, where one can cheer without chill.

TEHĀMA

F. GETTING NOTICED CAN MEAN EVERYTHING

It really started with a chance encounter in a hallway. Clint was a struggling bit actor when he happened to bump into an executive at CBS. The executive noticed Eastwood's rugged good looks and asked him if he was an actor. Getting noticed landed him the role of Rowdy Yates, which, of course was the springboard for one of the most remarkable careers in entertainment history. This signature pullover may not launch you into stardom, but it <u>will</u> get you noticed. It's made from 80/20 cotton-polyester fleece blend. Luxury-rib knit for a soft, comfortable fit. The zipper front features a TEHĀMA logo pull. TEHĀMA is embroidered in tonal colors on the chest to match the body. In navy, sizes M to XXL.
T1067 TEHĀMA Signature Pullover $79

G. MORE THAN A CAP

This TEHĀMA Cap is hard to miss. It is made from 100% chino twill and features a low profile, soft front with the longer "fisherman's bill". The leather backstrap is adjustable with a brass buckle so one size fits most. In black only.
T1076 TEHĀMA Cap $19

Fig. 15.4:   Celebrity endorsement is a standard (but sometimes expensive) positioning technique. Notice that the wry headline in a golf-products catalog doesn't mention the actor's name. Many writers automatically would write something such as "Clint Eastwood's favorite pullover, and yours too" . . . which might have been an even more effective eye-catcher.

Bobby Jones®

SIGNS OF GREATNESS

No one will ever forget the Grand Slam in 1930, but Bobby Jones would still be remembered for his integrity, his strength of character, had he never won a tournament. The Bobby Jones solid signature polo is crafted with those same values in mind. Design integrity, strong construction and the highest quality materials make this polo an exceptional value. The taped, 3-button placket features detailed embroidery of the Bobby Jones logo on the inside surfaces. Made in Italy of 100% double-mercerized Egyptian cotton. Machine wash in cold water. Specify royal, white, pine, black or red in sizes M to XXL.

**T1085 Bobby Jones
Solid Signatuare Polo $109**

In the 1925 US Open, Bobby Jones was penalized a stroke, a stroke that ended up costing him the title. At address, his iron touched the grass, causing the ball to move slightly. That is the rule. The thing was, no one saw it. Not his caddie, not his fellow golfers, not even the tournament officials. But Bobby Jones saw it.

Honesty and integrity were clearly defining values for Robert Tyre Jones.

More importantly, perhaps, was his enduring love for the game of golf. For him, not taking that penalty, no matter how invisible the infraction, would have irreparably harmed the sport he loved.

Bobby Jones won the club championship at his home course, the East Lake Golf Club, in 1916, at the age of 13. He won his first major tournament in 1923, as an amateur. Eight years later, at the peak of his career and one year after capturing the Grand Slam, Bobby Jones retired, still an amateur. During that all-too-brief time, he won 13 major titles—5 U.S. Amateurs, 4 U.S. opens, 3 British Opens, and 1 British Amateur.

It's hard to argue that anyone has had more impact on golf than this quiet, unassuming amateur. Bobby Jones will always be remembered for the Grand Slam and for founding Augusta National and the Masters, but more, he'll be remembered for his integrity of character, his casual elegance and his love for the game.

1 • 888 • 713 • 8687

Fig. 15.5:   From the same golf-products catalog as figure 15.4, the vintage photograph seizes the eye. Bobby Jones is long gone, but his name on a sweater has great impact on golf enthusiasts.

BEST NOSE HAIR TRIMMER. Chosen Best by the Hammacher Schlemmer Institute over other models for its precision trimming capability, comfort of operation, ease of cleaning and quality design, this trimmer cuts unsightly hairs from the nose and ears. Its high-speed stainless steel blades rotate inside the unit's cutting head assembly to quickly and painlessly trim unwanted hair. The 4-ounce trimmer has a barrel shape that makes it easy to handle and it is compact enough to fit into almost any shaving bag. Rust-resistant blades can be rinsed clean under running water. Comes with a plastic blade cover. Sturdy plastic housing. Runs on one AA battery (included). 4¼" H x 1¼" W

62138J.......................$24.95

Fig. 15.6:   Just what is the "Hammacher Schlemmer Institute"? Is it parallel to Underwriters Laboratory? Or is it a promotional ploy? A small copy block on the inside cover says, "A 'Best' designation (for example, our Best Carry-On Luggage) means that it has been independently evaluated and tested by the Hammacher Schlemmer Institute. The Institute regularly conducts side-by-side tests of the newest products in a category before awarding 'Best' ratings."

How many readers of this catalog will penetrate this disclaimer? And how many will wonder who volunteered for side-by-side tests of nose hair trimmers?

16

Turning on the Reader's Toggle Switch: Building Rapport with Copy and Guarantees

First, *You* Try It!

Your assignment . . .

Visualize how you'd describe a sterling-silver art nouveau rectangular pin with artistic cutouts and a leaf-and-berry effect at two corners. It's an eye-catching accent for a tailored outfit but too understated to compete with a floral print. Reread the assignment twice more before you start . . . no excuses that you aren't a fashion writer because a professional writer can handle *any* description.

Take thirty seconds. No longer than that.

Did you ignore "an eye-catching accent for a tailored outfit but too understated to compete with a floral print"? I'd have ignored it, too, not only because it's too abstruse a concept to transmit in brief catalog copy but also because it's reasonable to assume the illustration will make this point.

Did you build romance around the art nouveau aspect rather than the sterling silver? That's what I'd have done because it's the only unique handle to grab.

Whatever you wrote, I guarantee it's superior to the copy which actually ran. (I've buried it in the text to enhance the possibility of your reading this chapter.)

Keeping Our Heads Clear

Anyone reading these words isn't a typical catalog recipient. We're in the business—probably competing with the catalog we're reading tonight—and our reactions are analytical rather than emotional.

No problem. That's how we keep our heads clear.

But when our target readers slowly transmute their attitudes from emotional to analytical, we've lost that bronze word—*neutrality*—or worse, that silver word—*interest*—or heaven help us, that golden word—*rapport*.

The Seven Basic Reactions of Catalog Recipients

The recipient sees your catalog and has one of seven reactions:

1. disgust
2. annoyance
3. neutrality
4. faint interest
5. moderate interest
6. strong interest
7. rapport

The seventh reaction usually is reserved for those who are already multi-buyers. I greet the catalogs from Sporty's and Viking Office Supply as old friends; my wife is so tuned to *Gardener's Eden* and *Levenger* she's begun to point out (very rare) typos.

But how does a catalog, mailed to a "cold list" name, achieve this magic seventh stage?

Let's accept as a fact of business that X-percent of recipients greet your catalog with annoyance or disgust. If that percentage is higher than, say, 10 percent, it's time to question lists, copy, or both. You have a mismatch: the people you're reaching don't want what you're selling or don't respond to your type of pitch; you're projecting arrogance; your layout screams, "Schlock!" while your copy murmurs, "Class"—*something* is wrong.

At the very least, go back to chapter 1 and reexamine the list of approaches. Can you, with your most cold-blooded analytical attitude firmly in place, find a mismatch between what you're writing and your best prospects? Might an experiment—not with your whole list but with a segment—lead you into a more profitable marketing avenue?

Recognition that one person's meat is another person's poison sometimes leads catalogers to start up an entirely new catalog with different copy, layout, and even pricing, to appeal to the market the original catalog missed.

Nobody bats a thousand, but . . .

Converting the first stage to the third is possible through a powerful match of product to recipient-psychographics, probably on pages 2 to 3 of your catalog. (If the cover achieves this match, you probably won't be cast into the first- or second-stage dungeon to start with.)

Converting the third to the seventh is possible if your copy generates an "I like these guys" reaction from the reader.

Can you lift a recipient from the first stage all the way to the seventh, in one catalog? Not likely.

Sure, you can attract a first-time buyer with a sweepstakes or a bunch of discount coupons or a wild offer or photograph on the cover, but you aren't then working up from the first stage. At the very least, you have a fourth-stage running jump—for that reader.

Figure 16.1 is the inside back cover of a handbag and accessory catalog. As an opinion, it's overly art-directed because rapport-building copy is set in tiny type.

Oh, by the way: it's a lot easier to fall quickly *down* those golden stairs than it is to climb them tortuously. That's the potential problem all of us should mount sentries to detect: Rome wasn't built in a day, but it burned in a day.

For example: I'm looking at a catalog photograph and description of a garden hose. Copy is certainly adequate, although the name of the hose—Flexogen—suffers from an epidemic of registered trademark symbols (®), which destroys the reading rhythm.

That problem won't transform a seventh-stage reaction all the way down to stage 1. But another factor will: the photograph shows a $3 cash-rebate certificate attached to the hose package. The last line in the copy block: "Rebate is no longer in effect."

Hold it, fellows. This isn't a case of The Hose giveth and the Hose taketh away. I hadn't even thought about a rebate. *You're* the ones who brought it up. If the rebate is no longer in effect, couldn't you have replaced the illustration?

Or, if deadline was on your neck, couldn't you have raised the price $3 and then sent the rebate yourselves, explaining that the manufacturer's rebate has expired but you're the good guys?

Cast this copy back into the pit of stage 1.

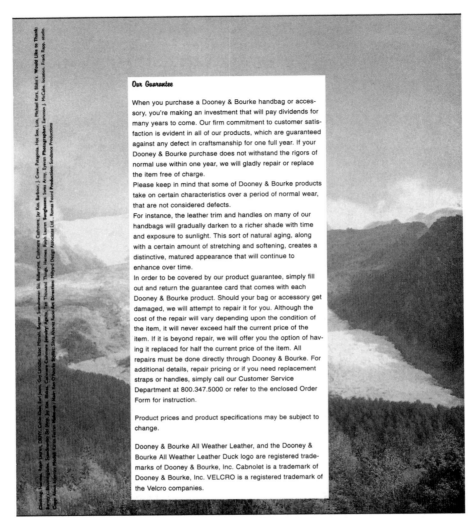

Our Guarantee

When you purchase a Dooney & Bourke handbag or accessory, you're making an investment that will pay dividends for many years to come. Our firm commitment to customer satisfaction is evident in all of our products, which are guaranteed against any defect in craftsmanship for one full year. If your Dooney & Bourke purchase does not withstand the rigors of normal use within one year, we will gladly repair or replace the item free of charge.

Please keep in mind that some of Dooney & Bourke products take on certain characteristics over a period of normal wear, that are not considered defects.

For instance, the leather trim and handles on many of our handbags will gradually darken to a richer shade with time and exposure to sunlight. This sort of natural aging, along with a certain amount of stretching and softening, creates a distinctive, matured appearance that will continue to enhance over time.

In order to be covered by our product guarantee, simply fill out and return the guarantee card that comes with each Dooney & Bourke product. Should your bag or accessory get damaged, we will attempt to repair it for you. Although the cost of the repair will vary depending upon the condition of the item, it will never exceed half the current price of the item. If it is beyond repair, we will offer you the option of having it replaced for half the current price of the item. All repairs must be done directly through Dooney & Bourke. For additional details, repair pricing or if you need replacement straps or handles, simply call our Customer Service Department at 800.347.5000 or refer to the enclosed Order Form for instruction.

Product prices and product specifications may be subject to change.

Dooney & Bourke All Weather Leather, and the Dooney & Bourke All Weather Leather Duck logo are registered trademarks of Dooney & Bourke, Inc. Cabnolet is a trademark of Dooney & Bourke, Inc. VELCRO is a registered trademark of the Velcro companies.

Fig. 16.1: "Our guarantee" seems to be equivocal, not because of any lack of integrity but because of incomplete explanation that seems to be a hedge, but isn't. The handbags are guaranteed "against any defect in craftsmanship for one full year"; if an item "does not withstand the rigors of normal use within one year, we will gladly repair or replace the item free of charge." Deeper copy says, "Should your bag or accessory get damaged, we will attempt to repair it for you. Although the cost of the repair will vary depending on the condition of the item, it will never exceed half the current price of the item." Had the explanation clarified that this exception refers to damage not related to manufacture, it would seem less harsh. Two words—*such as*—followed by a few examples of outside damage would soften the statement and transform a possible negative reaction into heightened rapport.

On the other hand ...

The very same catalog won my heart with its description of an insect killer that has the wonderful name "Big Stinky."

In the description of Big Stinky, we see this parenthetical phrase:

(not recommended for inside homes because of it's smell)

Huge flaw in the copy—"*it's* smell"—is the universal symbol of border-line literacy. I'm violating my own rule of never giving a positive comment to copy misusing *its* and *it's*; in this case sincerity wins out over education.

Here's the actual copy from the "First, *You* Try It!" exercise that began this chapter (and which undoubtedly ate up considerably more than thirty seconds of copywriting time). Would you buy from a catalog description that downgrades interest from stage 5 to stage 2 with a too-lean description of the silver pin?

Our new 2" sterling silver pin is a proper finishing touch to so many outfits (164Z) $56

We're back to the old saw, the Specifics Superiority Principle:

> ✏️ Specifics sell; generalities don't sell.

My guess: the writer never saw the pin. Neither did you—but you know better than to fill even minimal space with generic unmotivating copy.

Who Is Reading This?

The catalog writer has a big edge over the writer who creates a solo mailing—a generalized profile knowledge of customers who have bought before.

Our job, then, isn't to be all things to all people. Our industry has come too far from the good old Sears catalog of the 1930s.

In an era of hyperspecialization, we're supposed to hold prior buyers firm at stage 7 . . . lift non-buyers from stage 3 to at least stage 6 . . . and hope no misstep on either our part or the list selector's part will result in any copies lying dead in the cemetery of stages 1 and 2.

Do "Guarantees" Mean Anything?

Do catalog customers pay any attention to a guarantee?

The answer is the standard reply to any question related to a bulk response: some do and some don't.

For a cataloger whose customers don't, the very inclusion of a guarantee can be a waste of space. A cataloger whose customers *do* sacrifices a tactical advantage by burying the guarantee on the order form—which more than half the catalogs (both business and consumer) seem to do.

Catalogs that include a "president's letter" on the inside cover usually include a "We want you to be satisfied" homily in that letter. Great. But "We want you to be satisfied" without explaining how we'll assure your satisfaction isn't a guarantee. A guarantee is an official statement of position, which is why so many catalogs quite properly encase it in an official-looking border.

Once they've spotted the word *guarantee*, do catalog customers actually read the text?

Same answer: some do and some don't.

For those who don't, the three ingredients of a successful guarantee are inconsequential. For those who do, leaving out one of those ingredients can mean a lost sale.

The three ingredients:

1. sincerity—the customer believes you really are telling the truth
2. rapport—the customer believes your guarantee is designed to generate an ongoing relationship
3. totality—the customer believes your guarantee is complete and not equivocal

Coming upon these criteria unaware, how would you rate your guarantee? If you sense any caviling, any hedging, ask yourself *why* you haven't gone flat out. If a customer returns something, you'll offer a refund or replacement, won't you? Why let halfhearted wording rob you of a potential sale?

Figure 16.2 is a next-to-order-form page that inspires confidence, not because it offers a specific guarantee but because it lists toll-free numbers for every circumstance, *including* twenty-four-hour customer service. Missing is a toll-free fax number, which many catalogers are recognizing as a major marketing tool.

ORVIS® *Guide to Ordering, Services,*
CLOTHING & GIFTS *and America's Best Guarantee!*

For over 100 years, we have offered the strongest return policy in the business. We will refund your money on any purchase that isn't 100% satisfactory. Anytime. For any reason. It's that simple.

- **Call 1-800-541-3541 anytime . . .**
Our professional sales representatives are always ready for your phone order. That's 24 hours a day, 7 days a week.
(Hearing impaired—TTP 800-828-1120)

    . . . or fax us at 1-540-343-7053.

Fax your order form to us and we will process it as fast as a phone order. (If retransmitting a fax, please write "duplicate" on the second try.) You may place or track orders on-line at:
www.orvis.com
Para Español 888-680-5680* (M–F 8 a.m.-midnight-MST)

- **Like to know the status of an order or return?**
Just call 1-800-444-6330.
Our new automatic answering system can access this information swiftly and easily using the latest communications technology, and you won't ever be put on hold. (Requires touch tone.)
Other questions for customer service?
Call 1-800-635-7635.
We're staffed with trained, friendly people 24 hours a day! Our customer service professionals have yet to meet a problem they can't solve!

- **Shipping and Delivery**
Standard Delivery
In-stock items normally leave our warehouse within 24 hours. Our charge for standard service is only $6.50—whether your order totals $25 or $2,500 (corporate orders excluded).
Orvis Express Service
Your in-stock order will normally be delivered within 3 business days after we receive it. (Excluding personalized or altered items). This service is $7.00 in addition to our standard delivery charge of $6.50.
Next-Day Service
Orders placed by 5pm EST, Monday through Friday will be delivered *the next business day*. Please ask our representative for merchandise availability and our best rate to your address.

- **Oversized Items Delivery**
Oversized items may also require a shipping charge (amount listed in parentheses after price) in addition to standard delivery charges. Applies only to delivery in the 48 contiguous states. (Please call for freight charges abroad.) Gift wrap and express delivery is not available on these items.

White Glove Delivery
We offer a white glove delivery service for specially designated items. White Glove deliveries are brought into your home, placed where you choose, uncrated, assembled and inspected. all packaging is then removed. Delivery is available by appointment Monday through Friday. We'll call to arrange the day. Service available in the 48 contiguous states (call for other destinations). Please call for more information.

- **Personalize Your purchase**
We offer **four different types** of personalization on many of our catalog items: watch engraving, embroidery, brass plate, and leather embossing. Please ask our telephone representative to determine whether personalizing is available and which style is most appropriate for your item.
When ordering by mail, we will select the style most appropriate. Please use the area specified on the order form and print the initials or the name exactly as you wish it to appear. $5 per item (except where specified in description).
Please allow 2 days extra delivery.
<u>Watch engraving:</u> Maximum of three lines. No more than six characters on first line; twelve on second line; six on third.
<u>Embroidery:</u> Initials—upper case block. Short Names—upper & lower case script. Names may be up to six characters.
<u>Brass plate (or direct etching on metal item):</u>
Maximum four upper case letters (plus periods), as shown at right (unless specified otherwise in description).
<u>Leather Embossing:</u> Maximum four upper case letters (no periods used), as shown at right.

Watch Engraving

Mary
Embroidery

Brass Plate

Leather Embossing

Fig. 16.2: This company offers separate toll-free numbers, not just for orders but for checking the status of an order and for customer service. Note the clarity of explanations.

Mr. Alpha, meet Mr. Omega.

Two catalogs exemplify the diversity of guarantees. Read both guarantees, then decide which company would be your source, product selection being equal. Both are in small boxes on a panel backing up the combination envelope-order form.

Catalog A:

100% Guarantee

All of our products are guaranteed to give 100% satisfaction. Return anything purchased from us at any time if you are not pleased with our products. We will replace the item, refund your purchase price or credit your credit card. We want you to be completely satisfied with anything you buy from this catalog.

(Farther down this panel are "5 Reasons to buy from us." The first reason: "Our guarantee extends for the life of the product—not limited to 30 days.")

Catalog B:

Our Guarantee

If you are not satisfied with your purchase, please return it promptly in its original condition, and we will gladly exchange the item or refund your money. Custom or personalized items are not returnable.

Catalog A might have dropped the awkward "with our products" after "if you are not pleased" and written "credit your charge card" instead of repeating "credit." But our three key ingredients shine through these minor word scratches.

Catalog B has logic on its side, but the wording defeats rapport. How would you have worded this second guarantee to transmit the same message . . . with warmth? Here's one suggestion:

If you aren't delighted with your purchase, just return it and we'll gladly exchange it or send you a refund. (Much as we'd like to, we can't accept returns of personalized items, because they're custom-made for you and we can't restock them.)

Same information, light-years of difference in rapport. Adding contractions, replacing "satisfied" with "delighted," dropping "in its original condition," which can daunt a would-be customer, and adding a reason for refusing custom and personalized items—these aren't changes; they're happy dust sprinkled on the message.

A refund on shipping costs? Benevolence isn't universal.

The word *sorry* goes a long way in holding rapport together under shaky conditions. A catalog of photo frames and albums has this copy block on its order form:

RETURN POLICY

Follow the instructions on the back side of your packing slip. (Sorry, I can't accept C.O.D. shipments or refund original or return shipping costs.)

It's a little obscure because of word pileup toward the end; dropping "original or return" might lose a little specificity and a lot of confusion. But can you see how *sorry* and one other word eat into potential exasperation? Okay, what's the other word?

You spotted it, of course: *I. I* connect with you one-to-one; *We* can't connect as thoroughly because you're dealing with an anonymous group.

Another catalog decides to be totally reader-friendly. Right under the president's message is:

MONEY BACK GUARANTEE

If you are not happy with your purchase for any reason, return it within 90 days for a full refund of the purchase price, including your original shipping charges.

I said this catalog *decided* to be totally reader-friendly; I didn't say it succeeded. What would *you* have done to warm up the message, again without changing the thrust? Here's my candidate:

100%-*PLUS* MONEY-BACK GUARANTEE

If *for any reason* you aren't delighted with any item you get from us, just send it back (within three months, please) for a 100% refund of every cent you paid for it—including your original shipping charges.

A third catalog covers shipping only if they've made a mistake. This might be a happy middle ground for catalogers who (regrettably, often with justification) fear user abuse:

RETURN INFORMATION

Satisfaction is fully guaranteed. If less than satisfied, please return your purchase for replacement, credit or refund. Follow the instructions on the enclosed packing slip. Should your order be filled incorrectly, we will be glad to offer full reimbursement for shipping charges incurred.

A bit arm's length, what? Inclusion of passive voice and words such as *incurred* are standoffish devices, but mitigation comes from the realization that this is a high-fashion catalog whose first three words under "DELIVERY" are "Please be advised." Hauteur is the right arm of fashion, isn't it?

In for a penny, in for a pound.

I see nothing wrong with flaunting a total guarantee—"ABSOLUTE 100% MONEY-BACK GUARANTEE" doesn't differ in fact from "GUAR-ANTEE," but fact isn't one of the three key ingredients.

Some guarantees are so generalized they become mushy. A catalog of imported selections includes a standard guarantee on the order form and this wording within the president's letter:

We guarantee you quality, value and service, and we promise you will not be disappointed.

One catalog has a box following a strong guarantee. First, the guarantee:

WE GUARANTEE SATISFACTION

If for any reason you would like to return your purchase, send it back for a full refund or exchange.

Then, immediately following, this boxed message:

WE BELIEVE

1. That our customers must be given the best possible service.

2. That we must keep our operating costs as low as possible—to keep our savings as high as possible.

3. That our business ethics must be consistent with the faith of the owner in Jesus Christ and His teachings.

This is both charming and disarming, but obviously a procedure that might confound some recipients. Incidentally, I'd change "our savings" to "your savings" in point 2.

An old-line catalog prints its guarantee on the face of the bound-in order envelope and also includes heavy text under a "Billing Rights" heading—total disclosure of who does what and who owes what if the company or you screw up on charge billing. I question including "If you fail to pay the amount that we think you owe, we may report you as delinquent" on the combination order form–credit application. Such matters are best left to private correspondence, such as a returnable agreement enclosed with a "Welcome" letter accepting the individual as a charge customer.

Does it really make a difference?

Would a catalog perish if it didn't print a guarantee on its order form or with its president's letter?

Probably not . . . because the best catalog buyers have become so used to standard guarantees they take them for granted and don't even look for them.

The great stature builders of our world are pioneers such as *L.L. Bean* who set a tradition of accepting—without question—returns submitted years after an item left the warehouse. All of us ride on the coattails of this established reputation.

All of us, too, should uphold it. Otherwise, the next generation of buyers might start looking for an ironclad guarantee before lifting pen or phone.

17

Describing the Complicated Item . . . Explaining the Deception Perception . . . and Other Matters

First, *You* Try It!

Your assignment . . .

Your overseas buyer hands you a sheaf of descriptive information on a "Digital Diary." He tells you, "I want a headline telling our buyers of electronic gadgets what this is. For example, 'Latest business success team: You and "The Boss."'"

You ask, "'The Boss'?"

"Sure. Boss. B.O.S.S. Business Organizer Scheduling System. Oh, and tell them it has double the memory."

"Of what?"

But he's gone.

You look at the photograph. It appears to be a tiny computer the size of a large wallet. It has a keyboard and an LCD screen, and it has "64K Super Memory" emblazoned on its face. A fact sheet tells you it can store thousands of phone numbers and notes, up to 384 characters each. "B.O.S.S.?" you muse. "Double the memory?" You decide to write your own headline. What is it?

Take thirty seconds. No longer than that.

Is your headline "Carry this powerful computer . . . in your suit pocket"? Not bad. Is it "An electronic secretary with more than 64,000 bytes of memory—in your suit pocket"? Pretty good.

Believe it or not, one of the world's best-known marketers of electronic gadgets used this unappealing headline:

> *Latest business success team: You and "The Boss." Top-of-the-line Digital Diary has double the memory. And more.*

Whatever headline you wrote, I'll bet it was more communicative than the one which appeared in the catalog.

The Rule of Absolute Communication Connection

One of the stiffest tests of catalog-writer professionalism is the ability to describe a complicated item to readers whose technical knowledge is—or may be—nonexistent.

Note the hedge: the difference between "is" and "may be" in this instance doesn't exist. If it's "may be," it's "is." I justify this appeal for primitivism in descriptive copy with solid fact, the Rule of Absolute Communication Connection:

> ✏ Simplifying the description won't alienate those who have the same background you do; showing off your product knowledge with terminology and "Level II" description positively does alienate those who don't have the same background you do.

What a universe of difference in reader reaction between "The writer is telling me something I didn't know before" and "The writer is telling me he knows something I don't." Want to have the opportunity to sell whatever it is to *all* your catalog readers? Swallow your arrogance.

So I admire whoever wrote this description of "Nike's Training Monitor":

NIKE'S training monitor coaches your workout—in English

You simply strap on the NIKE Monitor and take off on your run, walk or hike. It automatically keeps track of your speed, pace, mileage and heart rate and reports them to you on command—with its digitized voice—so you can custom-tailor your workout.

Note the terminology. It "keeps track of," not "registers." It "reports them to you," not "discloses" or "apprises." You can "custom-tailor" your workout," not "adapt" or "modify."

Deeper in the copy, the writer unlooses "Doppler Effect ultrasound," but by then we're buddies.

And that's one of the keys to effective catalog copywriting, whether consumer or business: don't lead off with a display of encyclopedic terminology. Save it for later. Bury the castor oil in a chocolate soda.

Another example—a painting on Egyptian papyrus (not the same one we discussed in chapter 14). The undisciplined writer would pick up a pedantic description of papyrus and regurgitate it onto the copy sheet. This writer gets off to a rocky start with the standoffish word *rendition* and a meaningless puffery reference about rarity and value, but overall the copy succeeds because the writer wasn't afraid to communicate on the reader's level:

King Tut's legacy lives on.

As bold as the Pharaoh himself and unlike any other rendition, *The Funeral Mask of King Tut*, an Egyptian painting on *papyrus*, is a rare—and valuable—find. The bright colors you see in this picture are paints made from the natural pigments of plants, rocks, and vegetables. Pressing the papyrus paper is an art in itself—stemming from a 3000-year-old process. Stocks of the papyrus plant are cut, pressed and woven by hand. . . .

Escape *sensational* and all those nondescriptions.

In earlier chapters I've registered a reader objection to overuse of key words. Remember the not-so-dearly departed cataloger who used *explodes* or *explosive* a dozen times in each catalog (chapter 13)?

Writers have that option, assuming they're aware of their infatuation with the word. But when a major catalog hits us with an unbacked *sensational*, it's time to pound the "Delete" key.

Copy says:

_____

Vaneli pairs comfort and style in these sensational new leather sandals. They're made in Italy with open toed, woven strapped fronts, closed backs, and side buckles. Allow four to six weeks for delivery.

_____

Okay, what about this description makes the shoes sensational? Made in Italy? Every pair of shoes my wife owns comes from Italy. Open-toed, woven-strapped fronts? A pair of huaraches qualifies.

I'm not attacking the worth of the shoes. I'm attacking the laziness that excreted the word _sensational_ without justification. (For that matter, _any_ use of _sensational_ in catalog copy is suspect.)

I'll tell you what else bothers me: carelessness.

So I was surprised to see, in a catalog I admire enough to be a customer, the same illustration used for two different products. One was on page 6; the other was on page 30.

Let's suppose the two products are allied. The first is to cover fever blisters cosmetically; the other is to control those blisters. A professional way to handle this is to have one illustration serve both masters, with copy blocks adjacent. Using the photograph twice seems to be a mistake even if it isn't a mistake because the person interested in one implicitly is interested in the other.

The Deception Perception

Catalogs traditionally have been free of an occasional ailment afflicting some solo mailings. I call this ailment the Deception Perception:

> ✏ When a reader penetrates a statement whose intention is to mislead, getting an order drops to a likelihood of near zero or less.

So we have two options:

1. Don't give the reader any ammunition to strengthen preconceived skepticism.
2. Couch misleading wording so cleverly or positively that the reader doesn't penetrate the rhetoric.

Does this copy, from a "membership"-type catalog, qualify for either option?

No Risk Membership!

Cancel at any time and the balance of your membership dues will be refunded.

Sorry, buddy, I don't regard a refund for the "balance of my membership" as a no-risk membership. *No* risk doesn't mean *some* risk. If I sign up and decide after seeing one or two copies of your *Insider's Hotline* it isn't for me, I still owe you for those issues. I'm at risk. Why not borrow a page from subscription promotions and actually make it *no* risk? That way, you won't have to hedge.

Can tight description still sell?

Some catalog writers complain about space restraint: "I don't have enough space to describe *and* sell. The only solution is to describe."

Right, if it's that tight. But we've all seen tight descriptive copy that still sizzles. Consider this example that's a cut above the pile of standardized fashion copy:

Sizzle . . . this dress does. Cut high on top and short on the bottom with contrasting/contouring white taping and front zipper completing the sultry appearance. Acid-washed blue cotton denim with polyester/cotton trim. Machine wash. Made in U.S.A.

Without those first four words and the wonderfully descriptive *sultry*, it's just another piece of journeyman copy. Here, somebody was thinking: how do I add *sell* without larding up the copy with a bunch of synonyms for *beautiful*?

Do you love it or hate it?

When you hit the "Enter" key, if you're a professional writer you're always a little dissatisfied . . . but your dissatisfaction is vague, not specific. You don't *know* you've oozed out a bunch of words instead of grabbing and shaking the reader. Why? Simple: if you do know, and you don't rewrite, you aren't a professional writer.

An Ingenious Solution to the Dripping Infuser

Fishing a tea infuser out of your tea pot and dripping it over to a saucer is an inelegant operation, at best. This cute-as-a-button tea pot has an easy-clean infuser built into the lid, so you can enjoy your favorite loose tea without ruining table linens. A simple twist removes the infuser for filling or cleaning. Crystal-clear tempered glass lets you see exactly when the tea is ready to pour, and a quick tug on the lid knob lifts the infuser up out of the tea for serving. The feet and lid are polished chrome, with a cool-touch plastic handle. 16 oz. capacity; 6" H x 4¹/₂" Dia. Taiwan.

51-146   Tea Maker $29⁹⁵

Fig. 17.1:   Wait a second: when copy opens with "Fishing a tea infuser out of your tea pot and dripping it over to a saucer," we tend to envision a metallic tea bag. But an infuser isn't parallel to a tea bag, as ongoing copy explains. An inset shot of the "infuser" would clarify quickly.

BEDROOM FURNISHINGS

9A-E. The French have always had a flair for design, and these pieces prove it magnificently. Made of New Zealand pine solids and veneers, each is finished with carved details and lightly honed metal accents with antique patinas. The bed has insets of double cane to lighten the overall look. Chest of drawers (shown left) has four large drawers, with a jewelry tray in the top drawer. Armoire has 34"W x 22½"D x 30"T TV compartment behind doors that open 150°, two adjustable shelves, four removable shirt partitions, one interior tray drawer, vented and removable back panel with cord exit hole, and two drawers. Measures 52½"W x 28¼"D x 91"T overall. Queen bed: 68½"W x 88"D x 89"T. King bed, 84½"W x 88"D x 89"T. Nightstand with one drawer and two doors, 40"W x 18"D x 29"T. Chest, 55"W x 24"D x 47"T. Imported. Allow 6-8 weeks. See order form for delivery information. *Save on shipping and handling charges when you buy two or more pieces from this collection. Ask your Sales Representative for more details.*

9A. Chest   2,649.00 (260.00)
9B. Armoire   4,699.00 (370.00)
9C. Queen Bed   3,799.00 (285.00)
9D. King Bed   3,999.00 (290.00)
9E. Nightstand   1,299.00 (185.00)

Fig. 17.2:   "The French have always had a flair for design." Fair enough . . . except that copy goes on to say these pieces are made of New Zealand pine, with the relationship unexplained. Don't add confusion where none might exist had you not opened Pandora's box.

Get pain relief where you "Kneed-It" — Now with magnets!

New magnetic Kneed-It™ XM combines the great shock absorption of the original design, enhanced by strategically-placed magnets. Designed for rough and tough activities on the knees, like basketball, running, in-line skating, tennis, volleyball and weightlifting, the Kneed-It relieves minor knee pain by absorbing shock and pumping soreness away. Also effective for knee pain associated with arthritis and tendonitis. One size fits all.

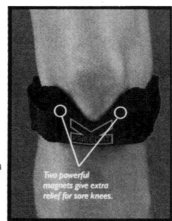

Two powerful magnets give extra relief for sore knees.

Magnetic Kneed-It XM...#MG520-A $39.95 each

Fig. 17.3:   Does the play on the word *knee* help sell this item? Or does it turn what might be a benefit into a joke?

Let there be light, anywhere you want it!

GE's® Ultra Thin Line™ fluorescent fixtures are inexpensive alternatives to custom-built lighting. They're fully assembled, easy to install, and ready to use anywhere. Built-in outlet lets you plug a tool or appliance directly into them. On top of cabinets or tall furniture, the warm white, pleasing light creates interesting decorative effects on walls, ceilings. Barely 5" wide and 1" high with a light-diffusing acrylic lens, energy-saving 13-watt bulb, 6' power cord. UL listed. For replacement fluorescent tubes, see below.

#10212 12" Thin Line™ $24.98
#10213 21" Thin Line™ $39.98
#10214 24" Thin Line™ $44.98
#10215 33" Thin Line™ $59.98
#10216 42" Thin Line™ $74.98
#10226 12" Fluorescent Tube $9.98
#10227 21" Fluorescent Tube $10.98

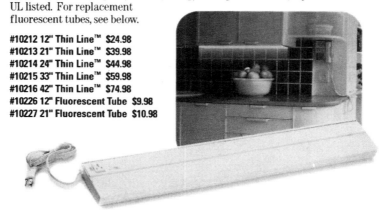

Fig. 17.4:   All right, these fluorescent fixtures are "easy to install." In what way? With screws? Velcro? Magnets? A do-it-yourself item needs this explicit information.

18

The More You Know . . . the More You Can Say

First, *You* Try It!

Your assignment . . .

You're writing copy for a home products catalog. Copy blocks are small—about fifty to sixty words, maximum.

Here's a pastry fork. You wonder if people still use pastry forks to make pie crusts and stuff like that. What can you say that will use up even fifty to sixty words? After all, it's just a pastry fork. Think of a grabber first sentence.

Take thirty seconds. No longer than that.

Did you use that first sentence to *glorify* the fact that a pastry fork is old-fashioned, so you've made it impossible for the reader to think of old-fashioned as a negative? Good for you! If you injected a little benefit in that same sentence, you're a big-league catalog copywriter, as is whoever wrote the actual copy shown as figure 18.1.

The Catalog Writer's Hair Shirt

The relationship between underdescribed copy and merchandise returned because of buyer dissatisfaction is one of the more obvious hair shirts catalogers wear.

Pastry Blending Fork

This old-fashioned aluminum *Pastry Fork* makes short work of cutting flour and shortening together to make pie crust, biscuits or pastry. It's nice and light, short enough (8 1/2 inches) to allow you to get the power of your wrist right down into the bowl, and just plain feels good in your hand. A kitchen classic.
4565 Pastry Fork, *1/4 lb.* $3.95

Fig. 18.1:   Nostalgia is a strong selling weapon. The deliberate use of "old-fashioned" adds an image of stability and dependability.

More subtle, statistically, is the number of sales lost because a writer *over*described an item, introducing fact-puff-trivia weakeners more damaging than helpful.

And last is the reason copywriters exist: to generate a buying impulse through the raw power of copy.

If you don't tell us, we can't tell them.

I'm looking at a copy block for a home pinball machine. As I read it, I'm reminded of Tom Wolfe. Adrenalin starts to flow. Rhetorical pheromones beckon. I don't want a home pinball machine, but I'm tempted—not because of the item but because of the writer. A sampler:

Slam! You flip the ball up and it crashes into a kick-out crater, setting off an explosion of sounds and spinning scoring drums. *Whoosh.* The ball shoots out of the crater, and your perfectly timed flip blasts it up the hyperspace channel, where it disappears into a black hole.

Now, the whole galaxy erupts. . . .

Save a Rainy Day for Your Garden

Pure, chemical-free rainwater is the very best water for your garden. Unfortunately, rain doesn't always fall when it's needed. Our Deluxe Rain Barrel collects and stores up to 75 gallons of cool, pure rainwater to refresh your plants whenever they're thirsty. It comes complete with lots of great accessories that you'd usually pay extra for: a 4' hose with an on/off thumb valve; an overflow hose that diverts excess water away from your house; a safety grid to prevent children from falling in; and a removable debris screen to keep sticks and leaves out of your water supply. Hose stores neatly in a slot in the top of the barrel. Hunter Green. 36" H x 28" dia. Sorry no shipments to AK, HI, PR, or VI. **EXCLUSIVE**

#06-323 Deluxe Rain Barrel $99.95
Buy 2 or more $90.00 ea

- Handy thumb valve
- Safety grid
- Hose notch
- Overflow protection
- Debris screen

Fig. 18.2: If you had the assignment of selling a rain barrel . . . and what is more old-fashioned than a rain barrel? . . . could you have sold the product the way this description does?

You get the idea.

This copy tells me: the writer actually played this pinball machine. The writer wrote from experience, not a fact sheet. The writer had an advantage over most of us who get a photograph and description—and can't match the vivid "You are there!" quality of this description.

Compare this with a description of Picasso prints:

_____

Pablo Picasso's overwhelming creativity, versatility and energy place him among the greatest masters of all time. By special arrangement, we are able to bring you these limited edition prints *Femme au Chapeau*. . . .

_____

My conclusion: the catalog writer has little idea who Picasso was, why his paintings "place him among the greatest masters of all time" (ugh), or really, what's being sold here. And please don't think I'm suggesting we have an art teacher write this copy. I'm suggesting copy that both creates and justifies a desire to buy.

As catalogs evolve from the general to the specific and from the specific to the hyperspecific, successful descriptive copy will lean more and more on writer experience.

I'll point out a danger in this: specialization.

Writers who want to sell anything to anybody have to communicate on the experiential level of the message recipient. That's why an art teacher, describing a Picasso print, probably would communicate on the wrong level with casual catalog browsers. Even in business-to-business catalogs aimed at vertical interest groups, we have to be careful not to overuse private terminology.

Don't duck the negatives.

Fear of killing the sale causes catalog copy to slide off center and go awry.

Sometimes it's as simple as tiptoeing over negatives such as "requires assembly" or "batteries not included." The unwary buyer—who may be eighty-five years old and arthritic—gets the exercise bike in what seems to be a thousand pieces. The single line "Some assembly required" might have killed off the order but also would have prevented an automatic return. ("A child can assemble this in 12 minutes" might make the point and get an order without generating the return.)

Sometimes the copywriter doesn't have enough information to euphemize around a negative—or, for that matter, to include it. But negatives can actually have a *positive* value as preventives: the phrase "Not for use in . . ." has prevented not just returns, but lawsuits.

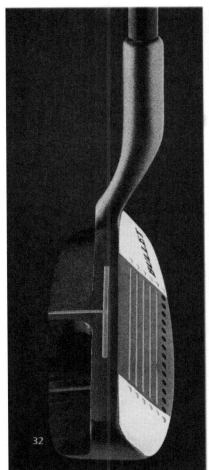

Chip Straighter, With Better Touch, And No Sculled Shots!

If a 7-iron were meant for chipping, it wouldn't be so long, and the lie would be more upright! But that's the club most of us use around the greens, even if we do have to choke down, and struggle to get the club face square. Now Bullet has perfected a better scoring weapon.— the Bullet Chipping Iron. Set up like a putter, the Chipping Iron has an upright lie and a putter's length (35"), but with a 7-iron's loft, and a radius sole that prevents stubbing your chips. Stroked just like a putt, the Chipping Iron lifts your ball gently onto the green with plenty of roll. You'll chip more accurately, thanks to a deep sole that automatically squares up the clubface. Bullet's T-sighting system makes it easy to see the line right into the hole. And a sharply offset hosel keeps your hands ahead for clean contact. Steel shaft (RH only). *Specify men's or ladies'.*

#GS589 Bullet Chipping Iron — $49.95

Fig. 18.3:   The writer obviously is describing from experience. A golfer has far greater confidence when a description seems to have been written by a fellow golfer. Mutual familiarity by writer and reader, for anything being sold, is a prime key to acceptance.

Safe, rubber-tipped arrows

Our Child-Safe Version of Olympic Archery
Bring the thrill of Olympic sport to your own backyard! Our archery set includes an unbreakable 39" flexible nylon bow with a durable bow string, three 23"-long arrows with all-weather feathers and rubber safety suction tips, a quiver to store arrows and a weather-resistant, durable plastic target with three-legged tripod. Parental guidance is recommended.
Size: Target measures 20"W x 33 1/2"L.

Archery —
Item #2206 $39.95   5+

Fig. 18.4:   After describing the archery set as "Child-Safe," the writer cautiously adds "Parental guidance is recommended." Will this damage sales? Probably it will help sales, since thoughtful parents will nod in agreement.

Breathe Pure, Clean Air Wherever You Go

Ever notice how the stale air in airplanes and office buildings makes you feel headachey and listless? That's because recirculated air contains high amounts of bacteria, dust and pollen, which stress your respiratory system and sap your energy and vitality. Our Personal Air Purifier uses charged grid technology to draw in and destroy airborne contaminants, and then directs ultra-pure air up to your face at a normal breathing rate. Smaller than a beeper and weighing just 8 oz, the Purifier is hardly noticeable — but you will notice how energized, alert, and healthy you feel! Excellent for allergy sufferers. Operates up to 35 hours on one 9v battery (not incl). Includes A/C and car adapters. Pacemaker users should consult a physician before using.

#31-080 Personal Air Purifier $99.95

Fig. 18.5:   Note the final sentence: "Pacemaker users should consult a physician before using." The writer is showing more than medical responsibility; he or she is preventing both returns and lawsuits.

It may be attention-getting, but . . .

Let's suppose you sell lingerie with a secret compartment designed to hold a passport or credit cards. How would you describe it and how would you show it?

I'm looking at a catalog that shows a striking female model (un)dressed in a camisole. The illustration carries our eye far past the passport pouch, down her shapely legs to spike-heel shoes that don't quite fit. As attractive as she is, she isn't what they're selling. Product ends at the hips; the rest is for dramatic effect. Ancient curmudgeon that I am, even as I admire the ma'am's gams I wonder if this isn't a scam—the cataloger preventing me from turning the page by the most ancient of attractions.

Okay, the cataloger wins. I do stop and read the copy. But this item is 100 percent female, and the suggestion is more seductive than salesworthy. Did it justify the space? Why didn't the catalog show less of the model and more of the product? I've learned not to ask these questions without having a bodyguard at my side.

Use Product Knowledge to Sell

Magalogs—catalogs masquerading as magazines, in magazine format—have sold merchandise where straightforward, descriptive catalogs haven't. Describing what something does, not tightly tied to a bunch of selling adjectives, often cracks the apathy barrier, justifying the dedication of page space.

I once had the happy experience of including a four-step diagram of how to tie a bow tie, adjacent to a group of bow ties. The cataloger actually had letters of thanks from people whose old bow ties had been stuck deep in a closet for want of tying know-how. That's no way to keep score; we aren't altruists in this business. BUT most of those letters accompanied an order for bow ties, and inch for inch, this segment was successful.

Think of one article in your catalog whose use, installation, or variations might—just might—not be clear to every reader. In an adjacent tint-block, describe what may be obvious to you but not to the reader. You might attract buyers who otherwise think, "That isn't for me" or "What would I do with it?"

Polished copywriting suggests transmitting product knowledge easily and simply enough to attract moths who may not have seen the flame before . . . or even recognized it as a flame.

19

The Law of Absolute Confusion

Your assignment . . .

You love portable CD players, so when you have the opportunity to describe a $189 CD clock radio you don't have to think twice. Your headline: "Sony CD Clock Radio folds to an astonishing $1\frac{3}{4}$ inches."

Your copy chief *doesn't* love portable CD players the way you do. She fires the copy back at you with this comment: "So it folds to a small size. Is that the best way to sell this $189 item? Try another headline that might better convince someone to buy it."

You may not agree, but she's the copy chief, so you rewrite the headline, aiming the copy thrust at the combination: a CD player plus a clock radio.

Take thirty seconds. No longer than that.

Did you consider what was in your copy chief's mind? The benefit of the *combination*? If you romanced the reason for having a portable clock radio with the pleasure of having a CD player, you could have written the heading that actually ran. The actual ad is figure 19.1. It's not a masterpiece of American poetry, but somebody paid a professional to write it . . . and got her money's worth.

You Have to Kill in Five Words

We know what we meant. But are "those people" out there reading it the way we wrote it?

It may have been a while since you read chapter 2. The cornerstone of that chapter, this book, and your career as a communicator, should be the Clarity Commandment.

Catalog writers, far more than any direct-response communicators, should be slavish worshipers at the shrine of this commandment:

> ✏ In force-communication, clarity is paramount. Don't let any other component of the communication mix interfere with it.

The editorial writer has a luxury we don't have—the reader's willingness to accept a subtle or oblique opening shot, reinterpreted as text develops. The creator of a solo mailing has another luxury we don't have—multiplicity of components, so raw product description never stands alone.

So you can't write rotten copy if you hammer the Clarity Commandment onto the Five-Word Nail Admonition:

> ✏ Catalog copy nails readers within the first five words or loses them forever.

One exception: the top-end catalog, which may allocate a whole page to one item. The reader knows from its *format* this isn't a direct, condensed description.

So why do they . . . ?

I'm looking at a successful discount catalog. The page has five items, not just one, so it doesn't qualify for the exception. Two copy blocks strike me as examples of reader misdirection. One begins:

Listen Carefully . . . you can almost hear the thunder of the rails and smell the rich aroma of gourmet food every time you look at this authentic replica. . . .

What does this copy describe? A lamp. "Listen Carefully" throws the reader offtrack. "If you listen carefully . . ." might have made the reference less obscure because it would become a condition, not a command. Even this change is a Band-Aid because the next sense reference is "smell," which doesn't involve the ears.

The writer is trying to set a mood. It doesn't work because the reader isn't prepared to jump headfirst into the mood. Lyrical copy is out of key with most copy in this catalog, but that isn't a major problem; who says

The Sony CD Clock Radio folds to a mere 1¼"and includes stereo headphones for private listening.

Wake up to your favorite CD anywhere in the world

On any given day, you can enjoy this portable Sony CD clock radio in your hotel room, on the plane, at the pool—anywhere you go. The compact take-me-anywhere package houses two full-range speakers and Sony's Mega Bass® sound system for full, deep tones. Wake up to CD, radio, or buzzer alarms, then press snooze to doze a few minutes more. Local and world time are displayed in precise 24 hour military time. Also includes radio sleep timer, clock battery backup, telescoping antenna, and global time/zone map. Operates on AC adapter provided or four AA batteries.
6½"W x 6½"D x 1¾"H.
9894 Sony CD Clock Radio $189.00

Fig. 19.1:   The headline is deceptively simple. In a few words, it describes clearly and completely what this is, what it does, and what one of its major benefits can be.

catalog copy should be a one-string fiddle? No, the major problem is one of *connection*.

If I were writing this one and an exalted creative director demanded "You are there" copy, I'd have started off:

Turn on this lamp, an authentic replica from the Orient Express. You can almost hear the thunder of the rails and smell the rich aroma. . . .

I'm not suggesting mine is superior copy. No, I'm suggesting it's *digestible* copy because it connects the writer's intention to the reader's awareness.

The second copy block on this same page has as its heading:

Keep an Eye on Baby with the Mobile Monitor

Suppose you read this heading to your spouse. Wouldn't the logical interpretation be "Oh, a video monitor." That's what "Keep an eye on" suggests. It isn't; it monitors sounds.

No, these aren't ghastly transgressions. They don't destroy comprehension; they just hinder it a little. So does using them as examples become an unreasonable attack?

I don't know about you, but I don't think so. Copy calling for eyes-closed imagination runs a dangerous course, not because the concept is unsound—in radio copy it's standard operating procedure—but because of the gap potential between what the writer thinks the reader understands and what the reader actually does understand.

Is Nairobi in Australia?

The catalog description of a man's hat:

The Aussie Hat. A laundered Nairobi™ hat with a leather band and poplin lining. . . .

I've been to Australia many times and to Nairobi a couple of times. A relationship between the types of hats doesn't exist, and this hat looks like . . . well, like a hat.

Let's assume Nairobi, because of the "TM," is a trade name. Do recipients of the catalog know this? Or are they confused by an apparent mismatch? The writer should have known, and heeded, the Law of Absolute Confusion:

> ✏️ Buying interest decreases in exact ratio to an increase in confusion.

One more. I'm looking at a catalog of men's wear. Here's a photograph of a typical male model with the fashionable Don Johnson five o'clock shadow. He's wearing a herringbone sport coat. Just one problem, one we see too often when we relate copy to illustration: the product description for this picture includes the sport coat (which I see), the necktie (which I see), and the trousers (which I don't see). Copy is no help, because this is all it says:

Bombay Trousers. #J710 $59. Specially priced for you! Sophisticated midweight wool allows for limitless year 'round wear. U.S. made. Sizes 28–42 (no 35, 37, 39, 41).

Okay, if Nairobi can make an Aussie hat, Bombay trousers can be made in the United States. Hands, please: how many know what Bombay trousers are? How many know what color these are? Guess, please: did the copywriter know the photograph didn't show the pants?

Just what DO we say?

So, so many catalog writers struggle to write poetry, or to *over*describe, or to mask defects with rhetoric. When their copy does sell, returned merchandise comes back at a level higher than usual because the percentage of buyers who clearly understand what they're ordering is lower than usual.

Your turn: when you write a product description, do *you* still have unanswered questions in your own mind about what it is and what it does? If you do—and you're the writer—what chance do you have of convincing "those people" out there to order it?

Never-burn-down candles stay elegantly tall and never drip.

Add beauty to special occasions when you use these unique candles. They maintain their tall elegance all evening because each "candle" is actually a 12-inch metal case. Inside, there's a wax candle insert which, as it burns, is pushed up by a spring. The effect is a candle that never burns down...and won't ever leave melted wax on your table linens! Set includes two metal candle cases, 12 dripless wax candle inserts and two adapters to make them fit snugly in a candlestick. Each wax insert burns 3½ hours. White, ivory, green, crimson or gold cases; ¼" diameter.

Mamie Eisenhower discovered these candles in the 50s. Today, they still brighten White House functions, and dinners at luxury restaurants around the world.

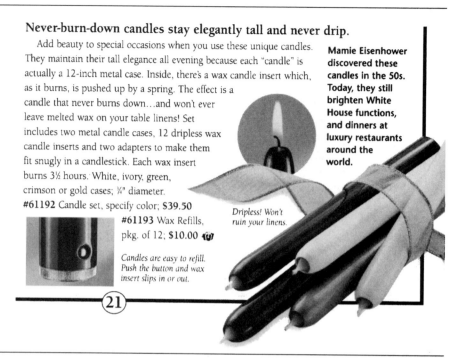

Dripless! Won't ruin your linens.

#61192 Candle set, specify color; $39.50

#61193 Wax Refills, pkg. of 12; $10.00

Candles are easy to refill. Push the button and wax insert slips in or out.

(21)

Fig. 19.2: How else, in a short headline, could a catalog copywriter give the reader a clear and compelling reason to buy these candles? Nice job.

A LOVING CUPS

Like lovers who respect each others' individual lives, these cups stand independently, and when joined, they create something even more beautiful. Each piece is handcrafted using heavy potter's clay, finished in a rich lapis blue, and fit together as one. An especially meaningful engagement or wedding gift—followed by mornings of coffee as a daily celebration of the couple's union. Approximately 7 oz. each. *Sold as a pair only.*

Couples Cups #56539......$56.00

Fig. 19.3: Read the first sentence of body copy. Does the simile—"Like lovers who respect each others' individual lives"—seem clear, or does it seem the writer is stringing words together? After several readings the point clarifies. Better: clarity on the first reading.

20

A Little Enthusiasm . . . and a Little More Clarity . . . Please!

First, *You* Try It!

Your assignment . . .

As copy chief, you puzzle over this description of an ornate purse-size mirror:

Exclusively from us, a pretty little purse mirror decorated with tiny mirrors and beading. Each $5\frac{7}{8}'' \times 3''$ mirror comes with a $7'' \times 3\frac{1}{2}''$ silk slip case embellished with antique Zari borders. The slip case could also hold eyeglasses or sunglasses. The mirror, handcrafted in India utilizing the lac technique, is of a specially treated and hardened wax. Six colors, please let us choose for you. From designs by Sudha.

You tell the writer: "I think we ought to make six changes." All right, name three of them. And decide: are your changes based on lack of enthusiasm in this copy or lack of clarity? Take thirty seconds. No longer than that.

Probably you quickly noted the more obvious suggested changes:

1. What's an antique Zari border? Tell us.

2. What's the lac technique? Lacquer? What?

3. How can a mirror be made of hardened wax? Obviously the mirror surface isn't wax. Something's wrong here, so clarify.

That gives you three out of six. How about the other three? If you didn't see them, read the description again before reading on to see suggested changes 4, 5, and 6. Find them? Right!

4. Telling the reader a mirror is decorated with tiny mirrors is peculiar copy. We need an adjective. "Tiny *diamond-shaped* mirrors"? Or instead of "decorated with," how about "glittering with more tiny mirrors inset into the decorative face and back"? The mirror-mirror reference needs separation.

5. "Is of" is technically correct, but it's awkward wording. Did you catch this one? If you did, you're a real pro.

6. Does everybody know what "designs by Sudha" are?

Did you attack lack of enthusiasm? I don't agree. "Pretty little purse mirror" and "please let us choose for you" give personality to this copy. But clarity? I'm on your side, although apparently the well-known cataloger-retailer that actually ran this description didn't share our puzzlement.

"What ABOUT This Suit?"

For one minute, let's pretend we aren't in the catalog business. We run a retail store and our image and sales volume both depend on our salespeople.

In comes a woman, shopping for a suit. She inspects the "deep discount" rack and asks your salesperson, "What about this one?"

The salesperson answers, "It's a three-piece navy-and-white suit with jacket and pull-on straight skirt in an acrylic-cotton-polyester knit. The blouse is polyester. The belt is leatherlike."

The customer sniffs. "I can see that much. But what *about* this suit?"

The department manager senses a lost sale and quickly intervenes. "This is a Chanel-inspired classic. The combination of acrylic, polyester, and cotton means it'll keep its shape. And you can see, it's right on target with this season's colors—crisp navy and white."

And the sale is saved.

All right: back to our real world.

Are we writers? Or dull salespeople?

This is the total copy block for the suit we just talked about:

3-Piece Navy and White Suit with jacket and pull-on straight skirt in acrylic/cotton/polyester knit. Polyester blouse. Leather-like belt. Sizes 6–16. #AC47A. Orig. *$455. Now $225.* [6.50]

Percentage of enthusiasm: zero.

Don't blind yourself to the problem by putting your "see-no-evil" paws over your eyes, covering the lack of enthusiasm by blaming tight space or the suggestion that heavy discounts are their own enthusiasm generators. If discounts stand alone, who needs a copywriter at all?

Would the copywriter's sweat glands have drenched the polyester blouse if, recognizing the copywriting function, copy had injected a little enthusiasm?

For example:

Chanel-Inspired Classic 3-Season Suit

Knit, of course. The jacket and pull-on straight skirt combine acrylic, polyester, and cotton for shape-retaining strength. Complete with matching polyester jacket and faux-leather belt. This season's colors—crisp navy and white. Sizes 6–16. #AC47A. Orig. *$455. A steal at $225.* [6.50]

Sure, we've used more words. But the catalog, as typeset, had plenty of open space at the bottom of the copy stack.

The Rule of Diminishing Enthusiasm

The Rule of Diminishing Enthusiasm justifies our existence as catalog copywriters:

✐ **Reader enthusiasm is geared to writer enthusiasm.**

Did the writer of the suit copy care about, or even know, the Rule of Diminishing Enthusiasm? More to the point: did the cataloger care about the rule . . . or instead, arrogate this assumption: being in our catalog bestows so much status enthusiasm isn't necessary.

Two exceptions to the Rule of Diminishing Enthusiasm:

1. When the catalog wants to project a stratospheric upper-crust image, bubbling enthusiasm parallels putting whipped cream atop a flute of Dom Perignon.

2. When a catalog has a hot list of closeout items, heavy enthusiasm is suspect because heavy salesmanship becomes overkill.

Have you tried Bartlett's unfamiliar quotations?

Getting tired of my pounding on the Clarity Commandment?

> ✏️ In force-communication, clarity is paramount. Don't let any other component of the communication mix interfere with it.

I guess I'm as familiar with Creative Desperation Syndrome as anybody in this business. We run out of superlatives. We run out of synonyms for *beautiful*. We run out of glorious ways to glorify what we're selling.

If you leave Roget's and hop over to Bartlett's, beware! The very act of having to look up an "apt" quotation suggests the reader may not have a working knowledge of that quotation.

A description of cotton separates has this overline:

"... AND I WILL MAKE THEE BEDS OF ROSES AND A THOUSAND FRAGRANT POSIES."

—Christopher Marlowe

Okay, what mood does this generate? What, in fact, does it have to do with this descriptive copy?

The mood is languid, your look romantic . . . in cool cotton separates from Cullinane. The button-front imported sweater has hand-made silk embroidered flowers on the sweetheart neckline. . . .

We begin to see what happened. The writer was looking for a touch-stone, seized on the silk-embroidered flowers, and searched out a floral quotation. Just one problem: literary though it is, it's a psychological mismatch for the "languid" mood (isn't this rhetoric a little sluggish?) and a descriptive misfit with the sweater this company is selling.

The Salesperson vs. the Robot Clerk

Once again, transport your imagination to the retail world. Two newcomers start work on the same day. One studies every stock bin, learns how to wrap packages perfectly, and can quote the printed product descriptions. The other studies principles of enthusiastic salesmanship.

Twenty years later, who's president of the company? If it's the robot clerk, you can bet this company hasn't achieved any market dominance or real corporate growth.

Let's project this same attitudinal disparity into catalogs. We establish the difference between a true marketer and someone who announces products for sale. Those companies with a dramatic growth pattern over the past ten years are those whose catalogs have *personality*—and personality is the single most necessary ingredient of enthusiasm.

Is it *creative* writing? Or fact regurgitation?

I'm looking at catalog copy for a phone-clock-radio. I just switched over from another catalog, where I read about the same manufacturer's "Print Phone Scanner/Facsimile/Copier." The scanner-facsimile-copier has timeliness going for it in today's marketplace but is described by seven bald bullets, none of which has any enthusiasm and one of which shouldn't be bullet copy at all: "Built to last."

In this second catalog, the writer's effervescence is contagious, even though the writing is only so-so:

Do you knock over the alarm clock every time you reach for the phone at night? Cobra's phone/clock/radio, in a clean, contemporary design, may be just what you need to clean up bedside clutter. . . .

(Why do I say the writing is only so-so? Because the copy block uses the word *clean* twice in one sentence and because the motivator—knocking over the alarm clock when you reach for the phone—is far-fetched.)

Enthusiasm has the power to add octane to nondescript copy. Imagine how it can help fact-regurgitating semi-writers. And imagine how it can add sparkle to copy, which, however professionally written, needs some bubbles.

A. Leather Jewel Box.
Combines Spanish leather with fine craftsmanship. 7¼" × 5¼" × 3¼" H.
4605. Orig. $159.00 Now $119.50 (9.00)

B. Black Leather Tote Bag.
Plush black leather with zip compartment on the outside, and comfortable 23" handles.
15½" × 4" × 12" H.
4721. Orig. $245.00. Now $122.50 (10.00)

C. Green Suede Jewel Box.
An elegant box in which to house jewels and accessories.
7¾" × 6" × 2 ½" H.
4746. Orig. $85.00 Now $42.50 (7.00)

D. Safari Scarf.
Light microfiber. 35" Sq.
4473. Orig. $22.50 Now $7.50 (5.00)

E. Clock Scarf.
Light microfiber. 35" Sq.
4474. Orig. $22.50. Now $7.50 (5.00)

F. Suede Travel Pack.
With zip closure, waterproof lining and zippered interior pocket.
10" × 4" × 7" H.
4728. Orig. $29.50 Now $19.50 (6.00)

G. Leather Cosmetic Case.
8" L × 1½" D × 5¼" H
4231. Orig. $54.50 Now $19.50 (5.75)

H. Scotty Dog Pin.
1¼" Dia. × 1½" H.
5680. Orig. $29.50 Now $14.50 (6.00)

I. Leather Gum Case.
⅞" × ¾" × 3¼" H.
4603. Orig. $26.50 Now $9.50 (5.00)

J. Currency Trio.
7" × 3" × 5" H.
4442. Orig. $59.00. Now $17.50 (6.00)

K. Ladies Attaché Case.
This attaché is elegantly crafted of faux suede, and secured with gilt side locks. 16½" × 12" × 3" D.
4504. Orig. $225.00 Now $115.00 (9.75)*

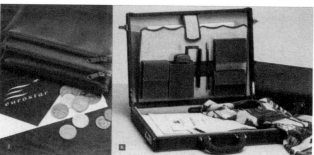

GIFT PRESENTATION. Our acclaimed gift presentation is available for an additional $5.00 per sale item. Exception, items marked with an asterisk*.

Fig. 20.1:   Enthusiasm isn't necessary, and may cause suspicion, when a catalog touts reduced prices with dignity. In this instance, the combination of minimal description and zero enthusiasm are less dignified than dull . . . and may leave some potential customers, who might react to enthusiasm, unmoved.

Stackable Rack Kits

Combine individual bottle access with very low cost. The **Stackable Racks** are made of solid unfinished pine, and are simple to assemble. Scalloped crossbars fit snugly into the end pieces. Available in two widths.

18-bottle Kit *(2 rows of 9)*
#1291A   **$39.95**   *(10.95)*
26-bottle Kit *(2 rows of 13)*
#1292A   **$49.95**   *(12.95)*

(9 bottles: 5⅝"H x 34" W x 12" D)   *(13 bottles: 5⅝"H x 46" W x 12" D)*

Fig. 20.2: Ho-hum. If the copywriter is bored, what happens to the reader's state of mind? The writer excretes facts without a hint of enthusiasm or salesmanship.

Smart Solutions

Black Tie Grids Offer Space-Saving Sophistication

Stylish, functional and affordable, **Black Tie Grids** make a wine storage statement. No other rack holds so many bottles so efficiently and effectively. Sleek, black, epoxyed steel grids that individually rack 152 bottles of wine. Their high tech appearance adds an air of sophistication to your living or dining room while their low cost per bottle makes them the ideal choice for any place in your home. Combinable side by side or double deep with optional braces to offer tremendous capacity and flexibility.

Black Tie Grid *(66"H x 30"W x 8"D)*
      #1270 $99.95   (17.95)

      SAVE 2–3 Grids
      $89.95/ea.   (17.95/ea.)

      SAVE 4 or more
      $84.95/ea.   (17.95/ea.)

      Wooden Braces *(combine 2 grids for double-depth)*
      #1338 $19.95/ea.   (3.95/ea.)

One Black Tie Grid

Fig. 20.3:   Compare this enthusiastic description of a wine rack with the unremarkable copy of figure 20.2. This is a more expensive rack . . . which suggests less need for heavy enthusiasm . . . but to a wine lover, either rack costs less than a single bottle of Chateaux Margaux.

21

The Negative Rule of Partial Disclosure: Don't Leave Them Hanging There!

First, *You* Try It!

Your assignment . . .

You're writing copy for an office supply catalog. You know as much about computer peripherals as the typical user, but you make no claims to expertise in this field. Your blood pressure goes up a couple of points when you see you're supposed to describe a "data switch."

Then it drops again when you see the art department already has prepared some line drawings showing the switchbox with a computer and what you assume to be "peripherals"—probably printers. To your relief, you also see the switch comes in two models, depending on whether the connection is twenty-five pin or thirty-six pin, so you don't have to explain this aspect. You write this description:

> *Two-position switches give one computer two choices for peripherals or let two PCs share one peripheral for sensible use of expensive equipment. Use DB25-style connector to connect parallel printers to IBM or clone PC 36-pin style for parallel data applications requiring centronics-style connectors.*

Your copy chief reads what you've written and says, "Okay, but you need more explanation of the 'what.'"

"Hey, hold it," you protest. "I'm no expert on computers."

"Maybe not," is your chief's squelch. "But you *are* supposed to be an expert in communication."

"But don't the drawings cover us?"

"Not in my lifetime," says your wise mentor. "Leave your copy block as is. Don't rewrite what you have, but clarify."

How do you clarify?

Take thirty seconds. No longer than that.

This challenge may have been unfair because the admonition "Leave your copy block as is" may seem to contradict the rest of the instruction. Not so.

How? A magical word: *subhead*.

Whenever you (or a critic) might suspect your description isn't adequate, lean on a wonderful crutch, these two words: *for example*.

This might be your missing, clarifying subhead:

> *For example, use one PC with a dot matrix printer and a laser printer; or two PCs with one printer, modem, or other attachment.*

Keep the notion of subheads and the words *for example* in your ditty bag of copywriting tricks. Edicts about format and style may prevent your using subheads, but nothing in any rule book can ever prevent you from knowing what many less-informed copywriters don't know: the advantage of those two marvelous lead-in words, *for example*.

One of Us Is Inept . . . and It Ain't Me!

Whoever said, "A picture is worth a thousand words," did a horrible disservice to the generation of catalog copywriters pounding their keyboards today.

I say this because we seem to be having an epidemic of copywriters depending on the illustration to say what they don't or can't say. We copywriters throw up a shield against criticism for lack of completeness: who has the gall to expect a writer to cover the photographer's ineptitude?

But let's reverse the problem. Do we expect the photographer to cover the copywriter's ineptitude?

In most cases, one of the differences between writing a solo mailing and writing catalog copy is *sequence*. The writer of a solo mailing gives the layout artist the proposed words and graphic treatment. The layout artist suggests illustrations. *Then* the job of taking or drawing pictures begins.

Not so in a catalog. The illustration comes with the assignment. The manufacturer or distributor supplies it, or the photo studio makes an extra print or transparency for the writer.

So the catalog writer has less excuse for blind dependence on illustration than the direct-mail writer. Evidence is on hand before the first word appears on the word-processing screen.

So why do they do this?

I'm looking at a catalog description for a limited-edition watch—the "Longines' commemorative watch designed by Charles A. Lindbergh."

At once I'm puzzled. Charles Lindbergh designed a watch? When did he ever demonstrate any talent in that direction?

Three photographs illustrate the copy. One shows the Lone Eagle himself, standing next to his airplane. His hands are in his pockets, so the relationship with the watch is assumptive, not evidentiary.

The second photograph shows a watch. It's a handsome watch with all kinds of numerals and bezel markings. But it's a watch.

The third illustration, placed too far from the copy block for immediate inclusion in the descriptive mix, is a picture of the backside of the watch, flipped open to show an engraving, in fine script. We can't read it all, but it says, "Longines Hour Angle something, Designed by Col. Charles A. Lindbergh, something Steel Waterresistant [sic], Swiss Made, 989-5215."

Now we're interested. How and when did Lindbergh design this watch? Did he wear it during his 1927 flight? And what's 989-5215? Lindbergh's phone number?

Copy tantalizes but doesn't explain:

To celebrate the 60th anniversary of Charles A. Lindbergh's historic solo flight across the Atlantic in the Spirit of St. Louis, Longines has produced a limited edition replica of the Hour Angle Watch designed by the renowned aviator. The replica at ⅕ size has the identical functions and features and is crafted in Switzerland for adventurers aloft and earthbound. . . .

The single paragraph of copy runs thirty-nine lines. Instead of answering the when and why, it adds another question: what?

This watch is a "⅕-size replica"? What does that mean? What's the rationale? Why couldn't it be a full-size replica? Even Mickey Mouse watches are the same size as the 1930s originals. Oh, and by the way: Why didn't the copy block mention it's water-resistant?

The Negative Rule of Partial Disclosure

An easy-to-understand rule of catalog copywriting, the Negative Rule of Partial Disclosure, helps explain my personal irritation at the hit-and-run "⅕"-size reference:

> ☞ The reader resents an unexplained variation from the anticipated description.

The Negative Rule of Partial Disclosure also jostles out of any reasonable position my appreciation of the relationship between Lindbergh and this watch. Exotic word puzzles in the remainder of this copy include "the equation of time, the constantly changing difference between mean and solar time." What do they have to do with Lindbergh? Or with me, for that matter? Explain, please: what is it? Relate the factual core to the reader if you want to sell a specialty.

One more carping point—the final sentence of body copy:

To receive the informational commemorative brochure call LFT 1-800-922-3545.

My question: what's that "LFT" doing there? With the abundance of vanity 800 numbers, the reader is as likely as not to dial LFT. If LFT is the company name, make it "Call LFT at. . . ."

Figure 21.1 was from a consumer catalog, not one dedicated to optical instruments. Take a look and decide whether, based on the description, you know how it works, what other equipment you might need, if any, and whether it's primitive or advanced.

Other guilty parties step forward.

Here's a catalog description of a cable channel converter. This catalog spells it "convertor," but that isn't my principal complaint.

This is every word of descriptive copy:

Enjoy cable programs on any TV set without additional cable box rental costs. Universal block convertor tunes in 47 cable channels and converts them to UHF. Permits VCR recording on one channel while watching another. Lets you use your current remote control on cable TV. Fine tuning control. FCC approved. UL listed.

Okay, what's missing? This:

Easy-to-Use Star Finder

This portable planetarium puts stars into the hands of star-gazers around the world. By aligning the month to the time of day, it teaches you the names of over 40 of the brightest stars and 70 constellations. Includes two computer drawn maps, four latitude adapters, and keychain flashlight. Comes in its own carrying case. 6" long and weighs only 10 ounces. France.

90-349 Stellarscope $35⁹⁵

Fig. 21.1:   Nothing in the description tells us how to use these pieces. Many who might be intrigued by a "Star Finder" will fear that this requires either assembly or a technical background: "What am I supposed to do?" is a sale killer.

(Of course, you have to be hooked up to a cable system.)

Yes, the line should be in parentheses. Truth in advertising doesn't mean we have to emphasize conditions that aren't part of what we're selling. But copy as written suggests the cable box is the key to cable reception. Without the disclaimer, this company shouldn't be surprised by a high rate of returned merchandise.

The assumption that readers know what you know is both arrogant and foolhardy. Those who have cable know, in general, how it works. Those who don't have it may think this will bring it to them, even if the cable company hasn't yet wired their street.

I had a parallel experience when I ordered a device whose catalog description told me it would bring in cable on every television set in the house. At the time, I had cable on one set but not on five other sets.

What the copy didn't tell me: the gadget requires hard wiring to each TV, and each can pick up only what's being watched on the master set. I sent it back and called the cable company to hook up two more sets. One descriptive line could have avoided my annoyance and the cataloger's shipping and restocking costs.

Here's another, from an office supply company: we see what appears to be a ream of copy paper and the legend "Save 61%." The price? $26.88.

Hey, wait a second. If this is $26.88 and I'm saving 61 percent, the regular price must be around $69. Can't be, even if this is one-hundred-pound paper. Let's see what kind of paper and how much we get for $26.88:

Top performing paper for use in both standard and high speed plain paper copiers. Also ideal for offset reproduction. All sheets are precision cut and lint free to assure quality reproduction and performance. Letter size, white. (#160966) LIST: $69.60.

I'm more confused than I was before. I not only don't know how many sheets I get, I still don't know the weight. It could be sixteen-pound paper. "All sheets are precision cut"? Does that mean they cut it one sheet at a time? And "lint free"? I never even considered lint. Does this mean the paper has cotton content?

How in the world can I—or anyone—order this paper? The Negative Rule of Partial Disclosure haunts response to this copy.

Have you told them enough for a comfortable "Yes"?

If you market an item that isn't drawing the response you think it should, ask yourself: have I fallen victim to the Negative Rule of Partial Disclosure?

What does the *reader* want to know? Mind readers don't need catalogs at all. They'll penetrate your brain to get the answers. The rest of us aren't mind readers, we're just catalog readers. We aren't so lucky, and when we read your partial disclosures, you won't be lucky either.

C. "REBECCA" FIGURE OF THE YEAR FROM ROYAL DOULTON. Rebecca is having some fun! Her hair sweeps to the side. She smiles with radiance. The yellow accents make this annual treasure even more appealing. She's 8½" tall. **New.** #394003 **$139.**

Fig. 21.2:   Not everyone who gets this catalog is a Royal Doulton collector. Descriptive copy is poor, and replacing it with a value statement might bring outsiders into the Royal Doulton orbit.

22

OVERfamiliarity: Is It the Cause of Your UNDERdescribed "Shadow Copy"?

First, *You* Try It!

Your assignment . . .

You're one of six writers generating a massive 116-page catalog of audio-video-stereo components. You already have written about sixty separate descriptions, many of which are for loudspeaker systems. Now, you're stuck. You have three models from the same manufacturer. Model 200SE is $319 a pair; model 250SE is $449 a pair; model 280SE is $529 a pair.

The only problem: all three have the same frequency response, 32 to 20,000 Hz. To audiophiles, frequency response is the bottom line on speakers.

So you've propped up model 200SE with "they let you hear the *power* of the music"; you've covered model 250SE with "if your speakers aren't up to the challenge, you should hear the 250SE"; you've puffed up model 280SE with "if your system can't capture the true excitement of a rock concert, we've discovered the cure."

Now you're looking over the copy. You're dissatisfied. Why?

Take thirty seconds. No longer than that.

This was an easy one, wasn't it? You're dissatisfied because you underdescribed each speaker, and you think—probably correctly—it's because you're too familiar with speakers.

Why is one more expensive than another? (You can't yet know because you don't have the spec sheets the original writer had.)

Okay, now take off your surrogate mantle. You're a sell*ee*, not a sell*er*. So you look, aggressively, for differences, without using one to damn another; after all, they're in the same catalog.

Ah! Model 200SE has 100 watts of power; 250SE has 125 watts; 280SE has 280 watts. Using the venerable Sears "Good, Better, Best" descriptions, move that element—now buried in tiny "Specifications" subdescriptions—to the prominent foreground. Then go ahead with your "power" surge for the 200SE; tack on a "Concert hall" overtone for the 250SE; and call the 280SE "Top of the line," which it is.

Your conclusion: underdescription can stem from overfamiliarity because the overfamiliar writer buries details the reader needs in order to decide.

What's Missing Here?

Since we're in an analytical posture: you're looking at a photograph of a colorful glass sculpture hanging in limbo, no props included in the picture. What would you add to this copy?

Illuminated illusions

Created exclusively for [NAME OF COMPANY] by artist Ross Waldberg, these ingeniously etched glass sculptures exquisitely demonstrate the mystical effect of colors, light, and glass. *Geometry in Motion* portrays an illusion of suspended forms, caused by the concealed neon lights reflecting through four differently shaped etched glass pieces. Each etched section (airbrushed with colors of red, blue, green and amber), when fitted into the lighted parallelogram base, appears to exhibit an apparition of a different dimension. Rearrange or turn the glass and the effect is entirely different.

[DRG751] Geometry in Motion $700.00 (9.75)

For the moment, don't think about word changes. That means you won't attack the evil "pieces," which, following "glass," suggests a sharp fragment. You won't suggest replacing it with "panel." You won't question the very questionable phrase "appears to exhibit an apparition" because "appears" and "apparition" become a redundancy in this use.

Instead, you take aim at two *omissions* in the copy.

1. The name of this glass sculpture is "Geometry in Motion."
   Where's the motion? What moves? Does the lighted parallelogram

base swivel? Apparently not, if we have to "rearrange or turn the glass" to generate a different effect. The reader hangs, unable to complete the visual image.

2. What size is this? The photograph shows the piece suspended in limbo and propless. Is it a tabletop miniature? A room-size display? What?

Would you as catalog reader know enough about this $700 curiosity to order it? Or would you pass, mildly annoyed because you're unable to decode the verbiage?

Me and My Shadow

"Shadow copy" *almost* tells us enough. Almost . . . but not quite. Frustration comes from inability to complete an equation: Illustration + Copy = What?

The paradox: as often as not, shadow copy results from a writer's *overfamiliarity* with an item. Overfamiliarity blanks out the *projected curiosity* the writer needs in order to take the posture of a casual catalog reader.

The claim "Everybody knows what this is" on the corporate level suggests arrogance, but for the catalog copywriter it more likely is the unconscious result of supersaturation with product knowledge.

This writer parallels a computer user who has mastered one word-processing program and writes with it every day for a year. Explaining it to a newcomer, the computer user invariably leaves out details—not because of lack of familiarity but because of take-it-for-granted overfamiliarity.

And we get copy such as this:

———————————

Experiment with Solar from Marklin

Marklin, the name synonymous with quality electric trains, has introduced a high—quality all metal solar construction kit for children. Designed for extended learning playtime, the child can spend hours building 5 different working models from this 215—piece kit. The child can further experiment in a variety of configurations only limited by his imagination. A complete series of additional parts, motors, control units can be added at anytime.

[DMS779] Solar Set $145.00 (6.90)

———————————

Many, many problems here. Grammar suffers from "Designed for extended learning playtime, the child can spend hours. . . ." The reference is absolute and wrong: it tells us the *child* has been designed for extended learning playtime. (Come to think of it, the statement is true for most kids.) But just incidentally, in the context used here, what *is* extended learning playtime?

Then we have the matter of using dashes instead of hyphens. We have "anytime" as one word, which is incorrect when used with "at." We have the neutral, nondescript "quality" repeated within the same sentence.

But okay, okay, this isn't Grammar Day. It's Shadow Copy Day. We want to know the significance of "Marklin, the name synonymous with quality electric trains." We aren't looking at an electric train.

The picture suggests it's some sort of construction kit. We see an electric wire stringing away, out of frame. What's *solar* about this kit? Is it the tiny, unexplained square panel at the bottom? Do motors operate the five working models? Models of what? Do they move? Copy doesn't give us a clue.

On the philosophical level, this copy has another problem. Our child can spend hours and our child can experiment. But how about enjoyment? "Extended learning playtime" parallels taking a piano lesson while the other kids are playing ball.

Do these harsh comments break a butterfly on the rack? I don't think so. This company wants $145 for the all-metal solar construction kit, and hasn't told us what it is.

On the other hand . . .

All golf clubs are pretty much the same, right?

Or—you have to swing a golf club before you'd ever buy it, right?

Not if you read a high-powered description in a sports equipment catalog.

I'm looking at a catalog loaded with golf clubs. It has AccuTech and Taylor and Wilson and Ping and Yamaha and Spalding and Callaway and Craig Stadler and a bunch of others.

Somehow this catalog writer gives each brand a unique selling proposition, so each has a buyer appeal that doesn't damn the other clubs around it.

AccuTech has "progressive weight placement"—explained. Yamaha has "a unique weighting ring around the circumference of the cavity"—explained. Callaway has a titanium insert that changes the center of gravity—explained. Craig Stadler clubs have "a wide sole to help you get under the ball from all types of lies, plus a deep cavity back"—explained.

Golfers are transported into a rhetorical golf pro shop, where, mentally, they swing and sample the various brands. Never does the writer use "unique" without telling us why. Never does the writer call any clubs "great" or "wonderful." Comparative benefit is specified . . . and readers think they understand what they're buying.

The Bullet Copy Solution

The catalog copywriter, sweating under space restraints the free-spirited writer of direct-mail packages doesn't have to endure, faces this ongoing problem: in a finite number of words (and sometimes even a finite number of characters) we have to describe well enough to sell.

A second problem: the catalog copywriter races from item to item, making the possibility of hit-and-run underdescription more likely.

Fewer catalogs allow bullet copy these days. We're in an era of high personalization, which means paragraphs instead of bullets. But for the catalog copywriter, bullet copy represents a writing discipline. It demands specifics.

(Figure 22.1 uses callouts to clarify superiority of five computers and bullets to clarify differences.)

A suggestion, if you reread your copy and think, "Uh-oh. I've left this out, and I haven't explained that, and I didn't tell the size of the other thing": make a list of bullets. Draw on that list for your copy, and you surely will see greater specificity in your descriptions. Since specifics outsell generalizations in *any* sales situation, the pulling power of your copy has only one direction to go—up.

Fig. 22.1: This page is *loaded* with copy, every word of which explains, sells, or clarifies. Note the callouts explaining components of the motherboard. The psychological effect is one of benefit projection, even if some of these callouts, on analysis, don't represent superiority. Bullets specify the relative value of each of the five computers, whose prices range from $639.99 to $1,469.99.

Fig. 22.2:   Suppose you're a golfer, trying to decide which brand of golf ball to buy. Price is the obvious difference among these various brands. But is a Pinnacle Bonus 15 Pack, at $15.95, worth a dollar more than the Dunlop TI Distance 15 Pack, at $14.95? The copywriter doesn't seem to think so.

23
___

"Hit-and-Run" Copy: Why Not Use Words That Turn the Reader ON?

Your assignment . . .

You're a freelance copywriter, and you want to show the superiority of a telephone answering machine over others on the market. This is your copy:

NEW! THE WHOLE FAMILY CAN TALK AT ONCE!

This full-featured telephone answering machine has everything you could want. Superior "pound" key is just the beginning. Desk- or wall-mountable, it's handy, convenient, and handsome. Remote is beeperless and you have four separate function buttons—one for on/off, one for "personal memo," one for "save," and one for "play messages." 12 one-touch auto-dial keys, speakerphone, hold button, and much more. $149.95

"What do you think of it?" you ask your client. He shakes his head. "You've missed the boat."

You look at it again . . . and you figure out why. Okay, why?

Take thirty seconds. No longer than that.

The lightbulb goes on. "Oh, I get it. I shouted 'New!' but didn't prove it. And the features I listed aren't unique at all."

Right. Suppose you go back over that copy. The headline is completely off target because you're describing a speakerphone. Even if this answering machine has a built-in speakerphone, you shouldn't lead off with it for two reasons: (1) the speakerphone capability is secondary, and (2) speakerphones themselves are too commonplace.

This *is* a point of superiority: "THE FIRST TELEPHONE ANSWERING MACHINE WITH HI-FI SPEAKERPHONE AND AUTODIALER BUILT IN." Or you might play up the "personal memo" key or the "save" feature.

But whatever you do, erase from your memory forever such nondescript openings as "This full-featured telephone answering machine has everything you could want." You'll never build excitement by grinding around in low gear.

What's Wrong with "Award-Winning Product"?

A catalog of gourmet specialties shows an attractive, stylized wine chiller. This is the descriptive copy:

B. & C. BYO CHILLER—When a picnic or party specifies "Bring Your Own," arrive in style with the insulated BYO Chiller. Freeze the BYO's removable chilling compartment and slip it into the carrying case with the wine, beer or soda and they will stay cold. The BYO's handle lifts up and locks the case's lid for traveling. Perfect for those occasions when you bring your own wine to a restaurant. On the table, the BYO sits inside its lid, making an attractive ice bucket. This product's award-winning design is displayed in New York's Museum of Modern Art. Gift-Boxed.

Two questions: (1) Which word in this copy block is the most jarring? (2) How would you have sequenced the sales argument, using the same informational core?

If your answer to the first question is "BYO," I can't argue . . . but we have to disqualify the low-class name from this consideration. It may have come from the manufacturer, which overrides any copy objection. My own choice for the most inappropriate word is *product*.

Follow my logic (and feel free to disagree with it): here we have an "award-winning design" (which award?), displayed in the Museum of Modern Art. Does calling it "product" do it justice?

Now the question more directly pertinent to *catalog* copywriting: the heading is "B. & C. BYO CHILLER"—how salesworthy is that?

Sure, the copywriter may be struggling inside a rhetorical straitjacket, unable to sway the immovable mind-set of whoever sets policy ("Every headline has to be the product name, damn it!"). But I don't think so because elsewhere in this same catalog we have "*NEW! KIR CARAFE*" and "FAMOUS BELLINI COCKTAIL SET."

Mild as they are, these variations suggest some latitude in headline copy. And anyway, even if an edict from above eliminates the possibility of selling in the headline, how about that deadly, not-quite-clever first sentence of body copy?

What are the strong points here? I see two: the smart design of the wine chiller and the honor of being displayed at the Museum of Modern Art. Is this the only wine chiller on display? Seems likely. Why not lead off with that?

Hit-and-run: will they take our word for it?

The catalog description of a punch bowl:

HOLLYWOOD PUNCH BOWL—Entertain in lavish style with this multi-purpose punch bowl set. This breathtaking service set is fully hand-made in of finest quality soda-lime glass. Comes complete with 13-quart punch bowl, a dozen 7-ounce glasses, and ladle. A stunning vessel certain to draw raves from your party guests.

Obviously a proofreader should have caught the double preposition— "in of." Too, the heading is "Punch Bowl," yet body copy says it's a whole set and explains, "Comes complete with 13-quart punch bowl, a dozen 7-ounce glasses, and ladle"; so a more logical headline is "Hollywood Punch Bowl *Set*."

Making those changes doesn't require the professional laying on of hands . . . or even professional analysis. But in our cold-blooded delight at dissecting somebody else's copy, let's probe a little deeper into the guts of this.

Do you see thoughtlessness here? I do, because I see hit-and-run copy. The writer throws out "multi-purpose" and never names another purpose. For that matter, I can't even think of another purpose. It's a punch bowl. If it *does* have other purposes (an apple-bobbing container? a fish bowl?), *name them*. Hit-and-run copy may slide past some readers, but others unconsciously subscribe to the Specifics Superiority Principle we discussed in several previous chapters:

> ✏️ Specifics sell; generalities don't sell.

The second problem here is an apparent assumption of familiarity with terminology. To the typical reader, unversed in glass manufacture, "finest quality soda-lime glass" is as powerful as saying "genuine imitation leath-erette." Why not use "crystal" instead of "glass"? And doesn't "vessel" make you a little uneasy? Instead, here's a good place to repeat "set."

The Rule of Information Saturation

Every one of us is infuriated when retail store clerks show less than perfect familiarity—not with what they are selling, but with *what we want to know* about what they are selling. As professionals, we shouldn't offer that same basis for criticism in our catalog copy.

Why? Because we have absolute control. If the information isn't complete, we can pick up the missing data before the reader ever has a chance to call our hand. That is, we can do it if we think the way the reader thinks.

It pains me to propose the Rule of Information Saturation:

> ✍ An information glut can lead the writer to play up details the catalog reader regards as trivial . . . and drop out details the reader needs to form a buying decision.

(I'm pained because in the twenty-first century this rule should be obsolete, instead of sprouting healthily.)

Really, the rule is a primitive example of a psychological truism: "ver-tical" education leads to loss of viewpoint. Haven't you had conversations with lawyers who were tongue-tied when they weren't talking about law and doctors who were lost when they weren't talking about medicine? What's more deadly than having as a dinner partner a professional, government official, or celebrity whose entire conversational gamut is introspective?

The catalog writer can be seduced or impelled by fear into quiet viola-tions of the Seller-Sellee Equivocation Equation:

> ✍ The seller's concern = what it is.
>   The sellee's concern = what it will do for me.

What do I mean by "impelled by fear"? Too many writers are at the mercy of overriding laws of economics. If they don't regurgitate what the owner or supervisor demands, they're in peril. So, even knowing better, they write what the seller wants to tell—what it is—instead of what the buyer wants to know—what it will do for me.

Verrrrry interesting . . . but . . .

A fascinating novelty idea caught my eye in a well-produced catalog. Total description:

Introducing the First Levitating World Globe.™ It Actually Suspends in Mid-Air!

How often have you searched high and low for a gift that's truly unique. Well, here's one for the person who has everything. A world globe that actually *levitates!*

It's simple to use. Just plug it in and the amazing magnetic forces cause the globe to levitate in the air. Go ahead . . . spin it! There's nothing holding the globe so it spins for the longest time because it's virtually friction-free! Truly an exceptional conversation piece.

#584500 $150

Gadget junkie that I am, I'd have been interested in this globe—except for a missing description component. Read the copy again if you didn't notice what's missing.

Precisely! The description starts in low gear but soon achieves a high plateau of lyrical enthusiasm. But the copy itself levitates. It never does come to land. And we never learn what size this globe is.

Will it fit on the desk? Is it toy-size? As so often is true of heavily art-directed illustration, the photograph doesn't even include a human hand to give us a means of judgment.

A Dedicated Picker of Nits

Do we become nitpickers by demanding the catalog copywriter think "I'm a buyer" instead of "I'm a seller"?

Heck, no. We become effective catalog-writing critics, the precursor to becoming effective catalog writers.

If we're always conscious of writing what the reader wants to see, instead of writing what we want to say, who knows? We just might move up to the next level *above* copywriters and become effective salespeople!

Fig. 23.1:   A guess: the other five audiocassette presentations on this page outpulled "The Secrets of Power Negotiating." Why? Because each of the other five had a turn-the-reader-on heading to generate acceptance.

A: toys for all the boys.

46A-C A collection of golf bags for all the members of your family. "My First Golf Bag" is perfect for young golfers (3-7 years of age); 6½"Dia. x 23"T. Comes with a 31" wood driver, 28" iron, and 26" putter and includes the lightweight cart. The junior bag and clubs are sized for ages 8-10 and include a 28"T bag, 33" wood driver, 30" iron, 28" putter, and cart. Carts fold and are made of lightweight steel alloy with rubber tires. All clubs have fiberglass shafts specially weighted for children.

And just so Dad doesn't feel left behind, we have designed a similar bag to use with his own clubs and cart. Imported. First Golf Bag and junior golf bag and equipment, also available in Children's World.
46A. My First Golf Bag, cart, and clubs, 200.00 (20.00).
46B. Junior golf bag, clubs, and cart, 225.00 (20.00).
46C. Adult golf bag, 225.00 (25.00).

Fig. 23.2: How friendly, how clear, how inviting! Someone who had no intention of buying even one golf bag might be persuaded to buy matching bags for the family.

"I can't think of anything more elegant, delicious and simple to serve my favorite guests."

Daniel Boulud
Owner/Chef of Restaurant Daniel
New York, NY

Serve fine caviar with bone or mother of pearl spoons. This prevents the delicate flavor of the caviar from being spoiled by metallic spoons. ▓

D. PRIVATE STOCK CAVIAR

Enjoy the freshest and highest quality Russian Beluga caviar available. Daniel Boulud's Private Stock Caviar is specially selected for New York's four-star Restaurant Daniel, and now can be sent to you overnight. Beluga caviar—prized for its soft, extremely large eggs—is the most refined taste in caviar and the ultimate indulgence. Available in 250 gram or 130 gram tins, with special protective liners to preserve the delicate flavor within. (Shipped chilled via express service.)

P1256A Boulud *"Private Stock" Beluga Caviar* (250g. tin) **$595**
P1257A Boulud *"Private Stock" Beluga Caviar* (130g. tin) **$355**

Fig. 23.3: When one asks $595 for a tin of caviar, what is that dreadful turnoff "Available" doing there?

24

At Last! A "Can't-Miss" Copywriting Instrument: The Benefit-Benefit-Benefit Principle

---

First, *You* Try It!

Your assignment . . .

You have to write copy for a dishwasher. What a tough assignment!

A dishwasher is a dishwasher, right? Oh, no, not if you're a dedicated catalog wordsmith. You dig for a unique selling proposition.

This one, it turns out, is easy. The manufacturer, whose shrewdness is exemplified by his ability to sell dishwashers to your company, has seen catalogs come and go. He gives you a tip: this dishwasher doesn't make so much noise it drowns out kitchen conversation. In fact, it's relatively quiet.

"Stress three escalating levels of benefit. You can't miss."

The caption over the product photograph is a strong hint: "The first truly silent dishwasher." You change it to:

Here at last is a truly silent dishwasher.

That's a statement of superiority, the first level of benefit. It should lead to two others. Can you think of *one* benefit to a homeowner, based on this first-level benefit?

Take thirty seconds. No longer than that.

I hope you didn't draw a blank. If you did, take another thirty seconds to think *how* a silent dishwasher benefits the user. That should do it.

Now: how does a silent dishwasher benefit the user? By not making noise. So the second-level benefit might be:

> *Clatter and noise in your kitchen are gone forever.*

To reach the exalted third level, we have to tell the reader how the second level improves life. So we might have:

> *For the first time you can play* soft *music in your kitchen . . . and actually hear it!*

The principle works every time, not only because adherence forces specificity but also because benefit and emotion are closely tied . . . and a sales argument appealing to the emotions outpulls a sales argument appealing to the intellect, every time.

The Height of the Art

The Benefit-Benefit-Benefit Principle, fittingly, is the subject of this, the last chapter.

Until a researcher or master practitioner discovers a more effective procedure, the Benefit-Benefit-Benefit Principle has to be the most powerful weapon catalog copywriters can aim at their targets.

For the on-line catalog, it's a double-indemnity insurance policy. Although a printed catalog would seem cloying and repetitive if many descriptions used this formula, an on-line catalog has a different ambience: no matter how it's structured, items not only appear one at a time but can be the cause of ongoing clicking or sudden disappearance.

Why is this such a potent weapon? Because it works every time. The specificity, forced by the absolute discipline of this principle, ties itself tightly to what the reader wants.

Not every writer can master the Benefit-Benefit-Benefit Principle. Huge pots of gold await those who can. And *you* can, because we'll analyze, dissect, and step-by-step it right here and right now.

The Three Stages of Benefit

These are the three stages of the Benefit-Benefit-Benefit Principle:

> 1. Make a statement specifying superiority over others.
> 2. Relate that superiority to your target readers.
> 3. Tell target readers how that superiority will bring dramatic improvement to their lives, careers, businesses, or images.

Here are the qualifiers:

1. The statement of superiority over others has to be within the experiential background of your target readers. The double admonition: when you compare what you're selling with directly competing products or services, (a) DON'T claim superiority without evidence because this smacks of chest-thumping arrogance, which kills rapport; and (b) BE SURE readers are familiar with your comparison victim and comprehend immediately what you mean.

That's the first level of benefit. Some business-to-business catalogs survive well using this level only.

2. When you move up to the second level you see why a statement of superiority ends in limbo if it doesn't connect with the reader's own background: you can't tie the first level to the second level. A simple mechanical trick, forcing out second-level copy: after stating the first-level benefit, say aloud, "Now you can . . ." and force yourself to finish the sentence. You'll have a second-level benefit.

If you can conquer the first two levels, you'll be writing copy whose force and effectiveness few other catalog copywriters can match. You're high up the force-communication ladder.

(Figure 24.1 is an example of totally acceptable professional copy that uses the first two levels well.)

3. Mastery of third-level description is the pinnacle of professionalism. So you'll be pleased to know the single easiest way to reach it: *practice*. You have up to four choices when telling target readers how that superiority will bring dramatic improvement:

    1. Does it improve lifestyle?
    2. Does it enhance career?
    3. Does it increase business?
    4. Does it build image, professionally or socially, or both?

A. TWICE THE ENJOYMENT

Perfect for entertaining, this Italian-style espresso maker has twin brewing systems so you can brew two cups at a time—and avoid keeping your guests waiting. By Briel, the professional quality machine is impeccably crafted of polished stainless steel with simulated woodgrain side panels. Its pump-driven system delivers perfectly brewed, evenly heated espresso at the touch of a button. Enjoy experimenting with espresso variations in your home.

P1125A *Briel Espresso/Cappuccino Maker* ... **$995**

Beverage Service

Fig. 24.1: As is true of many professionally written descriptions, this one easily covers the first two benefits. Benefit 1, a statement of superiority over others, is twin brewing systems. Benefit 2, relating the benefit to the reader, is that guests won't have to wait. Now, how about that third level? How will not having to wait for that second cup bring an improvement? If you link the ability to serve a loved one and yourself—or a business prospect and yourself—*together*, you're onto something.

If what you're selling has a single use, you may not have a choice; that's why you have *up to* four choices. But struggling to find all four is always worthwhile because you're forced into selling avenues you probably haven't considered before.

For example, can a silent dishwasher improve lifestyle? Sure: "You won't be a nervous wreck when you're cooking." Can it enhance career? Sure: "You can entertain in your kitchen, as high society does." Can it increase business? Sure: "When you're in the kitchen answering a business phone call, or even making one, you can concentrate on what you're saying instead of the mind-numbing racket." Can it build image, professionally or socially? Sure: "The quiet atmosphere is reassuring when a client or customer visits your home" or "You actually can invite guests to see . . . and *not* hear . . . your state-of-the-art dishwasher."

Are some of these stretching? Of course they are. This is an exercise, and what we're stretching are our salesmanship muscles. Unless we had a huge copy hole to fill, we'd never use them all; we'd pick the most dynamic one.

How About Short Copy Blocks?

Not every format lends itself to the Benefit-Benefit-Benefit Principle.

Tight little copy blocks may give you a choice: exhort or describe. If what you're selling is *competitively functional*, the principle may have to go out the window. Description comes first.

Can you apply the principle with bullet copy? Positively. In fact, as this text points out elsewhere, bullet copy is itself a discipline holding the sales argument on its proper rails.

Unquestionably the Benefit-Benefit-Benefit Principle is at its most forceful and most readable when it begins a long hunk of copy. Short copy may limit you to first level plus description, or first plus second, *or* third level plus description . . . or, once you've gained confidence using this method, second or third level *only* description. But incorporating all three levels into short copy *is* possible.

Small space tempts the writer to crash directly into the third level. Careful! Leaping directly into the third level may leave the reader out: overemphasis on third-level benefit, without the background of an earlier level, makes what you're selling secondary. When readers ask, "What is it?" they can be on their way to another page . . . or another catalog.

The Logical Sequence

Should you open with Benefit-Benefit-Benefit copy, stick it in the middle somewhere, or close with it?

If the illustration is at all competent, open with it. You're at point-blank range. After you've mortally wounded your target, *then* get down to nuts-and-bolts descriptions.

The easiest way, while you're testing this procedure, is to write a head-line of half a dozen words or so. This names the item:

OUR BEST TOASTER-OVEN BROILER

Follow with three subheads, each describing a higher level of benefit:

• Holds 40% more than most other models!

• One inexpensive toaster oven does it all—cooks, bakes, broils, defrosts, top-browns, even keeps the whole meal warm!

• At last, gourmet dinners with almost no cleanup!

From this point, copy writes itself. All you have to do is justify the claims you've made, add some manufacturing details, and name the price.

Opening with mechanical details ("The door to this half-cubic-foot model has an 'open/stop' setting . . .") is minor-league writing when you have the Benefit-Benefit-Benefit opportunity. But, fortunately for the mediocre writers among us, we don't always have that opportunity.

If you're blessed with a catalog whose format enables you to write long, proselike headings, you have naturally fertile ground on which to plant triple-benefit copy. It's best, at the fingertips of an accomplished wordsmith, when copy makes its telling points the way an accomplished debater would.

Can you fill a catalog with triple-benefit copy? Wow! I've never seen one, and as I pointed out earlier, one Benefit-Benefit-Benefit after another is logical primarily in Web catalogs. I suspect that in a printed catalog it would parallel serving a dinner with doughnuts as appetizer, heavily sugared fruit as salad, deeply frosted cake as main course, and rich ice cream as dessert. Too much! And what a challenge for the writer!

And in Conclusion, Ladies and Gentlemen . . .

Don't hide this book on a shelf somewhere until you've tried the Benefit-Benefit-Benefit Principle for yourself. Try it not just once, but three or four times or more.

You're in for an increasingly warm glow. Your first try will have sweat dripping onto the keyboard. Your second try will correct some of the sequential mistakes you made the first time, such as jumping from first level to third level so you can't ever find ammunition for what you think the third level should be. Your third attempt will be workmanlike. Your fourth will be printable.

By the time you've written half a dozen triple-benefit descriptions, the technique will come naturally, unforced, and your associates will wonder why your copy is so much stronger than theirs.

Solid Titanium Digital/Analog Watch

Combining the simplicity of analog with the versatility of digital is a stroke of genius from the quality watchmakers at St. Moritz. Each watch is waterproof tested to diving specifications, yet they are feather light on the wrist. The dial and hands use St. Moritz's Blackout Superluminous so you can read the time day or night without pushing any buttons. The Powerglo back light system illuminates both digital displays at the touch of a button. This high tech watch includes alarm, chronograph, countdown timer and dual time. The band is also solid lightweight titanium.

SMFC $235.00

Fig. 24.2:   As a mind-stretching exercise . . . perhaps while stuck in traffic . . . transform this well-written but benefit-buried description into a Benefit-Benefit-Benefit description. Which does a better sales job, their copy or yours?

4. CHRISTMAS ORNAMENTS
Basic geometric shapes come into play for this trio of updated tree ornaments. Pierced-metal pieces are designed by award-winning holiday card designer Susan Rooney. Made for the Museum of silver-plated brass in the USA. 3¼"h.
21559 Tree.
21557 Ball.
21558 Gift Box. $18.00 each.
21616 Set of three. $48.00.

Fig. 24.3: Here's a reasonably tough project: convert this colorless description into one incorporating at least two levels of benefit. A few hints: (1) The catalog is issued by one of America's most respected art museums; (2) Imagine how different from standard ornaments these will look; (3) Guests will admire your taste; (4) The ornaments look expensive; (5) You can enjoy them for years to come; (6) Your tree will look distinctive. None of these is exploited in the existing copy, which depends on design by a little-known holiday card designer.

Finally a Multi-Tool With a Comfortable Grip and *Real* Torque — So You Can *Use* It, Not Just *Play* With It!

We've found most other multi-tools suitable for light duty only. That's because those flat-steel handles gouge your flesh when you exert force. But the Swiss Mini Grip (from Wenger, makers of the Genuine Swiss Army Knife) tackles the toughest tasks with characteristic Swiss efficiency. To begin, the traditional arched Swiss Army grip conforms comfortably to your palm. The polished, full-size plier handle curves ergonomically for maximum leverage. A removable magnetic holder stores inside when folded, letting you carry 3 Phillips and 3 slotted bits in your pocket. Flip-out shank at one end converts Mini Grip into a full length (4⅝") screwdriver, letting you apply real torque to stubborn screws. Also includes a useful array of Swiss Army tools, including: large blade, double cut saw, metal saw and file, reamer/awl, can opener and bottle opener. Carry Mini Grip around the house on weekends, or as basic emergency equipment in your car, on your boat, or in the field — and you'll look for things to repair! *Select needle-nose or flat-head pliers.*

#TS185 Wenger Swiss Mini Grip — $89.95

Fig. 24.4:   This description is shot through with benefit and easily qualifies as Benefit-Benefit-Benefit copy. The headline may not be as specific as we'd like, but copy moves seamlessly through the three levels.

Conclusion

And in the Year 2010 . . .

As the catalog industry continues its march into the twenty-first century with increasing good health, three separate creative trends are becoming noticeable. What makes these trends worthy of comment and analysis is that they aren't in sync with one another:

1. increasing hyperspecialization of product within an already hyper-specialized catalog category
2. return to roots—catalog copy and layouts of the 1940s and 1950s; "feel good" and "Good Earth" concepts now are mainstream
3. reduction of lavish descriptions and two-page spreads for a single item (notable and logical exclusions: high-fashion and exotic-travel catalogs)

Mind you, now, I certainly am *not* claiming that all catalogs fall into one of these categories. Ours is a business that doesn't run on tracks, and we don't have a single mother lode . . . nor a limit of three mother lodes, for that matter.

What we do have is the two-edged sword of database: our best targets are the best targets of everybody else. That in itself is twenty-first-century justification for hyperspecialization, the catalog parallel of *positioning*.

Why the Internet Isn't a "Trend"

If this book had been published in 1996 or 1997, we could have called the Internet a trend. We're far past that point.

Internet cataloging isn't a trend. It's a permanent fact, and for some catalogers it's the medium that's keeping them in business. That so many practitioners misuse the Web, that so many believe Web surfers parallel recipients of their printed catalogs, that so many set up a website, tell no potential customers it's there, and wait in sublime confidence for a surge of on-line business—well, those circumstances are all to the benefit of the more astute marketers who tailor their offerings.

Therein lies the quandary for on-line catalogs. Is it worth the cost to custom create an on-line catalog presence for the relative handful of logical prospective buyers lurking in that neighborhood? The answer certainly is yes for computer-related products, sports equipment, travel, and entertainments such as CDs and videos. (Egghead Software closed all its stores and eliminated printed catalogs in favor of Web marketing only; as this book goes to press, the company says it's well in the black.) The answer is a cautious "Well, maybe . . ." for automotive items, books, gifts (including flowers), and on-line auctions. The answer is a dubious "We think it's working for us" for mass merchandise.

Technology seems to outpace creativity in Web design and execution. Already, we see a spate of awards for design, disregarding the ultimate way to keep score: did the phone and the cash register ring?

Ignoring the First Rule of Website Copy—Stop surfers in their tracks—is indicative of a creative infection that can become an epidemic, raging uncontrolled through a gorgeous but sterile website. Mouse becomes Mighty Mouse when the next click goes either way.

So recognition of what the person whose hand is on the mouse wants—speed and clear offer, not high definition after a protracted wait, nor elegance without benefit—symbolizes the site whose creators understand that first rule.

Actually, for the new site or one that seems to wallow in treacle, a simpler answer exists . . . a master key, although many regard it as the key to Pandora's box: big discounts plus heavy promotion in other media. Shallow pockets can start out in trouble because people won't come to your party if they don't know you're having a party.

From a marketing point of view, catalogs on the Web pose a challenge their printed cousins don't face: the inability to *aggressively* solicit speculative targets. The Web is passive, awaiting attention by anyone . . . and that can be a powerfully positive characteristic because serendipity can be at work. Mailed catalogs are active, singling out those the cataloger feels can and should buy.

That's unlikely to change, in 2001 . . . or 2010.

Forces at Work

Are we discussing the creative process or the broad aspects of marketing philosophy? In analyzing catalog trends, the two facets are scrambled. The effectiveness of hypertargeting is in direct ratio to convincing the target that uniqueness is beneficial—and this is the copywriter's function. The effectiveness of an old-time "feel good" catalog is in direct ratio to a yearning for the kinder, gentler times the Baby Boomers remember from their childhood. The diminution of lavish product descriptions? My guess is that this is the natural child of the laws of economics.

(No trend is universal. Upscale travel catalogs, such as those selling off-shore cycling trips, have picked up the mantle of multi-page descriptions.)

We can rationalize that a generation ago, neither lists nor databases were sophisticated enough to make possible the isolation of enough targets to make "product fragment" catalogs possible. But equally rational, if not more so, is that these catalogs reflect the fragmentation of society. Just as the general-circulation magazines have largely vanished—for example, *Collier's, Liberty, Look*—so have the general-merchandise catalogs largely vanished—Montgomery Ward, Sears & Roebuck, Alden's. That Sears survives in fragmented *specialty* catalogs underlines the trend.

Many forces have been at work here. First television, then cable, then the Internet established niche groups, rescuing as best they could a word that seldom applies in the heartless twenty-first-century marketing ambience: *loyalty*.

The word *loyalty* no longer means, in a marketing sense, what it traditionally has meant in interpersonal relationships. Airlines, restaurants, theatres, credit cards, even yogurt shops have loyalty programs. So do many catalogs. Are they really based on loyalty or are they based on greed—"What's in it for me?"

Loyalty to television programs isn't based on the program but on either how well the program reflects the viewer's own tastes, or what status the claim of viewership can bestow. This type of loyalty parallels the loyalty to the brand name sewn into the lining of a garment: the customer who carefully folds her coat so the Neiman Marcus or Valentino label shows is loyal to her own status, not to the source.

What's your specialty? We have a catalog catering to it.

A generation ago, who would have anticipated the presence of a catalog dedicated entirely to "world's hottest sounds" third-world CDs? Who would have envisioned *two* slick, colorful catalogs dedicated entirely to soccer apparel and gear? (I'm not a Soccer Dad but if I were I'd order from the one that numbers its pages. The other is frustrating because the text makes cross-references to specific pages . . . and the pages aren't numbered, damn it.) Who would have forecast a catalog dedicated entirely to gifts for grandchildren? Who would have backed a catalog whose pages are filled entirely with stuff such as a Mona Lisa pillow that giggles when you

GIGGLING MONA LISA
PILLOW
People have pondered her
expression for centuries and
now it's finally clear. She's
been laughing at us all along!
Squeeze this beautiful pillow
and Mona lets loose a peal of
laughter. 11" × 15". 100% cotton. Machine washable.
$26.00
Replaceable batteries included

Tee-hee!

THE WIND-UP
MICHELANGELO
PILLOW
Wind this beautiful pillow up
and an old-fashioned music
box plays "I Wanna Hold
Your Hand." Pretty & Witty.
15" × 11".
100% cotton.
$26.00

ORDER TOLL FREE: [800] 255-8371

Fig. 25.1:   Talk about a specialty catalog! This one has a Sigmund Freud fifty-minute watch, Albert Einstein slippers so you can walk "in the genius' footsteps," and these two pillows—the Giggling Mona Lisa Pillow that lets loose a wild peal of laughter and the Michelangelo pillow that plays "I Wanna Hold Your Hand." Catalogs that aren't for everybody demand careful list selection.

squeeze it and a pillow with Michelangelo's "Hand of God" Sistine Chapel ceiling painting that plays "I Wanna Hold Your Hand"?

The Incredible Shrinking Universe Rule

The Incredible Shrinking Universe Rule poses a twenty-first-century challenge to the writer of hyperspecialized catalog copy:

> Testing expands the universe of buyers. Inflexible repeats shrink the universe of buyers.

The rule was originally designed to prevent overdependence on databases for direct-response mailings. But it strikes home when the writer's job is to generate business from two disparate quarries—the solid base of aficionados or specialty-product owners without whom the catalog surely would fail, and likely prospects whose interests haven't been declared but might be parallel.

The perplexity and paradox are obvious: both terminology and demand are implicit in copy written for the in-group; use of proprietary terminology and assumption of demand can drive away those on the periphery. Yet a single copy block has to draw response from both.

Is a puzzlement.

Here is a catalog of puzzles. Jigsaw puzzles. "Kit" puzzles. Illusions and tricks.

The copy is bright and the illustrations are clear. So what is missing from this description, under the heading "3-D Jigsaws with Custom Wood Display Bases"?

Build Your Own Russian Cathedral. Our replica of Moscow's landmark, St. Basil's Cathedral, brilliantly captures the vibrant colors and intricate details of the original. From the spectacular designs of its soaring domes, to the graceful brickwork below, it's a stunning scale model of one of Moscow's most celebrated and enduring structures. Measuring $17'' \times 14\frac{5}{8}'' \times 18\frac{3}{4}''$ and made of 708, $\frac{1}{4}''$ thick foam-backed pieces with heavy-duty cardboard roofs. $39.95

Missing? Nothing is missing *if you already know the characteristics of a 3-D jigsaw puzzle*. The copy exemplifies the dilemma: how do we balance an appeal to preconditioned kindreds against an appeal to those who don't quite know what's involved in a 3-D construction offered under the jigsaw puzzle umbrella?

As hyperspecialization intensifies, the answer had better be there or the catalog succumbs to the Incredible Shrinking Universe Rule. One easy solution: include an extra copy block, a boxed enthusiastic description of what 3-D jigsaw puzzles are.

How hyper can you get?

Here are just a few of the subjects of hyperspecialized catalogs that never could have survived *as solo catalogs* in the days of less sophisticated database compilation:

Wall Street and financial collectibles
commercial matting
historical European reproductions
gifts for the dental professional (really!)
British videos and curiosities
lighting fixtures
Shaker furniture
specialties for enjoying wild birds
accessories for one model of automobile
pest-control products
home baking
Alaskan seafood

You get the idea.

The question is a shade more profound than "What will they think of next?" Oh, no . . . the question is "How many of these catalogs are in business five years after their launch?"

A generation ago every one of these catalogs could have represented a section within a more generalized catalog. What has changed is the type of appeal to the customer base. Specialty catalogs in no way pretend to be supermarkets; they say to their recipients, cover to cover, as twenty-first-century physicians say to their patients, "General practitioners can only refer. All problems are specialized, requiring specialized treatment."

And on the other hand . . .

Call this a countertrend. We're seeing catalogs whose copy and layout might have graced our mailboxes fifty years ago.

I have to admit, I'm a sucker for nostalgia. No, I'm not talking about first-person copy; that's the ongoing use of a 1970s development whose effectiveness is so elusive some catalogers wonder why their me-myself-I copy hasn't bowled over everybody exposed to it.

Nostalgia—or, more significantly, the desire to buy, based on nostalgia—comes from catalogs whose product mix includes lace dickies and toenail scissors, along with the mandatory cordless phone holders and "As seen on TV" icons that remind us we're well into a new century.

Except for the reference to "pvc," which probably was still experimental in those days, this description could have been from a 1940s catalog:

Easter Lawn Ornament Set

Delightful 3-piece set is the perfect decoration for your lawn or garden. Adorable bunnies are brightly colored in pastel hues, egg basket has space for you to personalize Easter greetings with your name. Weather-resistant pvc, each ornament approx. 13″ × 8″, with lawn stake for easy insertion.

How about this one, as an indication of the reaction against the constant pounding of New! New! New!?

PINE TAR SOAP

Grandpa's soap is the natural moisturizer. Called the "Wonder" soap, it's especially useful for removing scales of eczema, psoriasis, dandruff and dry skin. Thousands of testimonials and word-of-mouth are the only advertising this 100-year-old product has needed. No additives. Only pure soap and sweet-smelling pine tar oil. Lathers white.

In the same catalog with pine tar soap are throwbacks such as leather slippers, corn salve, nonbinding socks, a flexible shoehorn, magnetic bracelet and insoles, and a shoe stretcher . . . along with some contemporary sex aids that would have shocked Grandma, but we have to temper nostalgia with reality.

The catalog that most aptly demonstrates yesteryear's approach is the catalog of office products that labels its sealing tapes "Good, Better, Best," just as the Sears catalog did in bygone days.

Attention to Results-Per-Inch

The laws of economics too often bruise or even demolish the cataloger's desire for ego gratification.

Disclaimers: (1) Upscale fashions may demand a full page, if only to justify the retail price. (2) Travel demands long copy and multiple photographs to justify the price, and the number of such catalogs is increasing.

What seems to be vanishing is *arbitrary* dedication of more space than an item can justify. Candidates for space reduction are exercise equipment, utilitarian furniture, consumer electronics, and automotive equipment.

The rationale is obvious enough. For example, in the early days of personal computers or fax machines or cellular phones or DVD/Divx disc players, the catalog's educational job was dual—first, to convince the reader of the *generic* value of what was being sold, and second, to convince the reader of the *comparative* value of what was being sold.

As a product category matures, the need for generic education diminishes. Telling the reader what a computer or fax machine or phone or DVD player does isn't at all parallel to telling the reader of a puzzle magazine how to assemble a three-dimensional jigsaw puzzle. Every logical prospect of 2001+ knows what computers and fax machines and cell phones do. We don't need the common exposition. We sell comparatively and competitively. Eliminating that basic education also eliminates the need for the extra space that once was required.

But yet another factor enters into the mix: turn-of-the-century impatience.

Our grandparents looked forward to the Sears and Ward's catalogs as entertainment. Many an evening, sprawled comfortably near the fireplace, they would marvel over the latest catalog, savoring its pages one by one.

Compare that with today: will tonight be *NYPD Blue* reruns or what's on HBO3 or maybe a couple of hours in chat rooms? What are others in the family doing? Their own thing.

So if we're going to grab and shake the casual prospect, we do it inside that prospect's experiential background and obvious or hidden desires. Courtship is competitive. Compete fast or get out.

All of which means what?

We're in danger of drowning.

But then, argue those who mistake pure history for sociological trends, we always were. What's the difference between getting three catalogs of 1,000 pages each or thirty catalogs of 32 pages each?

Simplistic answer: the difference is in the number of catalogs.

More complex answer: Norman Rockwell is dead and no single picture of Americana exists . . . so each of us is a boiling cauldron of multiple interests. And those interests change with the wind.

For the alert cataloger of the twenty-first century this means refining the siren song . . . drawing enough of the right people into the specialized orbit to counteract defections . . . and staking out an unassailable position, the way a gold miner stakes out a claim.

Not easy? Of course not. If it were, anybody could do it.

Appendix A

The Catalog Copywriter's Profitable Game of Twenty Questions

The catalog writer who bangs out "blind" product descriptions, not considering why people buy, is costing the company some money.

Why? Because the three great twenty-first-century communication weapons (with no end in sight . . . and no end wanted) are *clarity*, *benefit*, and *verisimilitude*. No one needs a massive talent to write clearly.

But . . .

Injecting reader benefit, within the experiential background of the catalog's selected readership, requires some talent in salesmanship. Validating benefit, by varnishing the copy with verisimilitude (the appearance of truth), requires at least a seat-of-the-pants talent in human psychology.

Can any journeyman writer superimpose those elements on his or her copy? I say yes. How? By playing and winning the Catalog Copywriter's Game of Twenty Questions before casting each product description in bronze.

In my opinion the game should be valid for at least the next ten years. Why? Because more and more companies are jumping into the swirling catalog-waters, stirring up mud and snakes. Because the typical recipient gets more and more catalogs, sophisticating the inevitable skepticism attending a competitive situation. And because on-line catalogs, skyrocketing in significance, demand these three qualifications even more than printed catalogs do.

So, here, for use at least until the year 2010, are the questions to ask as you wearily pound the keyboard:

1. Do you know who reads your catalog?

One quick example: a toy catalog could have three distinct levels of readership:

1. prime buyers—those who look for toys because of a direct parental or grandparental relationship

2. users—children who respond to visuals and described excitement

3. possibles—catalog recipients who have no immediate reason to buy

Who reads your catalog? Who seeks it out on the Web? Probably all three groups, but not in equal numbers.

2. Is your copy pitched specifically toward the biggest target group?

As I said a few paragraphs back, professionalism in catalog copywriting includes a working knowledge of salesmanship. A good salesperson at a store selling expensive toys knows how to sell to the parents without alienating the child. A good catalog copywriter knows how to sell to the biggest target group without killing off the less-knowledgeable or less-motivated casual readers.

3. Do you tell the catalog recipients or on-line visitors repeatedly why they should buy from you?

Developing a competitive edge is a management decision. The copywriter is only the hired Hessian, the implementer of selling notions handed down from above.

The writer's job is to convince the reader; if *no* selling notion comes down from above, the writer gets, by default, not only the job of telling the readers why they should buy but also the job of creating the competitive edge in the first place. That's professionalism!

4. What about your product descriptions motivates the reader to buy?

An inventory clerk can describe an item. A supersalesperson can make a customer want it. That's why a supersalesperson makes more money than an inventory clerk. I suggest catalog copywriters emulate the salesperson and not the clerk; you don't need a professional copywriter to repeat a laundry list.

5. Do you repeatedly use sentences longer than twelve words?

Long sentences slow down the reader's comprehension, especially in narrow copy blocks. We aren't writing textbooks, and even if we were, we're supposed to be communicators, not puzzlemakers.

An easy way to improve comprehension is to limit the number of words in each descriptive sentence. Don't worry; readers won't think you're a refugee from *McGuffey's Reader*.

6. Does your description match the illustration?

If you say, "I never see the illustration," I suggest a change in production procedures.

A mismatch, or mutual avoidance by photographer and copywriter, can generate confusion. Worse, when the illustration emphasizes one aspect and the copy emphasizes another, the reader may disbelieve both. That costs you.

7. Does your description cover deficiencies in the illustration such as (if a "limbo" shot) relative size, (if a black-and-white shot) colors, or (if the product has multiple uses) descriptions of each possible use?

Here's another reason for the copywriter to see the illustration. Sure, the photographer could have shown the size of that platter by putting a rose on it. But he didn't. Now what? Sure, the two models should have worn different-colored sweaters. But they didn't. Sure, that chemical could have been shown working on a motor as well as on a cement floor. But it wasn't. Your job, writer.

8. If you have a "welcome" letter is it just a bunch of words or is it genuine salesmanship?

Look at the catalogs on your own coffee table. Inside the front cover of most of them is a "personal" note from the head of the company. How many of those letters have any sincerity at all? How many climb above the cliché-ridden "We're pleased to serve you" and "Your satisfaction is our dedication"? How many project a genuine personalized image?

You'll find, I fear, that too many waste the one logical use of space allocated to creating an aura of uniqueness.

9. Is your copy peppered with in-talk the average reader might find incomprehensible?

This is a fault too common with on-line catalogs. Too many of them aim themselves at a coterie rather than at the broadest group of potential visitors. Readers resent an in-group of which they aren't part. You can assure this reaction by showing off technical terms and insider jargon.

Talking down to readers and suggesting they are nincompoops because they don't share our specialized terminology are short roads to reader rejection. (An easy solution: if you need that terminology, include a short glossary of terms.)

10. Can someone unfamiliar with a new product visualize a reason to buy it, from your description?

You have an "elbow-arm" that holds a computer monitor. Okay, so what? Why should I spend $95 to move my monitor from its comfortable perch atop my desk to an uneasy midair hammock?

If your copy just tells me what the elbow-arm does, I'm half-sold, unsold, or product-antagonistic. So you don't just tell me what it does, you tell me what it does *for me*, because *benefit* is one of the three golden pedestals supporting powerful catalog copy.

11. Is your order form simplified, easy to fill out?

At the moment of truth, we want no obstacles. The customer should be able to breeze through the order form without a single crease in the forehead. On the Web, it should be simplified, resimplified, and then once again resimplified.

A good order form does most of the work for the customer. Does yours? Or do you challenge the customer? (In a duel, you'll lose.)

12. Does the catalog cover excite the reader?

The cover sets the mood. The cover sets the image. The cover sets the reader's state of mind. The cover sets your catalog apart from the competition.

Excitement doesn't depend on whether you show merchandise on the cover or not. It does depend on how well you fight your way inside the reader's experiential background. You don't scream at the winds, "This is exciting!" You point at the reader and declare, "This is exciting—to *you*!"

13. Have you cleansed your copy of egomania and megalomania?

Once again, the writer is a practical psychologist. Part of the job is to avoid dislocating the corporate arm by using it to pat the company on its own back. Another job, which requires a steady hand and uncommon restraint, is creating a climate of acceptance in which the person getting the catalog does the backslapping for you.

"We have this for you" is better copy than "We have this" because action ostensibly aimed at the reader's welfare has implicit verisimilitude; self-aggrandizement breeds skepticism.

14. Do you pepper your copy with "spot" testimonials, bonus gifts, toll-free number reminders, or early-bird discounts?

Excitement doesn't end with the front cover. Any catalog has holes. Fill those holes with inducements; who knows when the urge to order something will strike?

A solid page of testimonials is puffery; a sprinkling of testimonials, here and there, suggests a bandwagon movement.

15. Does your copy stroke the reader by saying, "Only you . . ."?

You can't always answer yes to this question because some catalogs, especially business-to-business, don't lend themselves to personalization.

Still, exclusivity isn't that hard to suggest. An "issue price" on the cover (which the recipient hasn't paid), some copy about the exclusivity of catalog distribution, a "private club" overtone, a "Member's Daily (or Weekly) Special" on the Internet—these help transmit the flavor of those two lovely rapport-building words, *Only you. . . .*

16. Does your catalog project an image, and does your copy match that image?

Who are you? The cheapest source? The fastest source? The most comprehensive source? The avant-garde source? The snootiest source? The good-folk source? The kindly-uncle-and-aunt source? The no-nonsense all-business source?

Whoever you are, your copy should match. Trying to combine two images muddies both those images and damages buyer confidence. If you do wear two hats, separate your catalog into sections ("This is the *bargain* section"; "Park Avenue Exclusives"; "Billy-Joe's Personal Choices") and you create a magical world in which unlike elements can coexist.

17. Is your copy timely, tied to the season or period of issue?

Considering seasonality will keep you from heavily art-directed page after page of copy reversed through four colors. Why? Because changing copy becomes a major operation if it's more than a black-plate change.

Here's an easy trick to keep copy seasonal: on a separate sheet of paper, list every word you can think of that reflects the time of year. (Example: for Christmas, *Yule, Noel, caroling,* a thousand more; for spring, *crocus, robin, young man's fancy,* a thousand more.) Sprinkle these through the copy. As casual references, they're the Butter Buds of catalog copy, adding nuggets of flavor.

18. Do you write in active rather than passive tense?

If a cynical reader might ask, "By whom?" some of your copy is too quiescently passive.

"These were brought to us . . ." By whom? "It was decided . . ." By whom? "Your order will be shipped . . ." By whom? Take responsibility and assign responsibility and you've written dynamic copy. "We'll ship your order" re-cements the relationship with the customer; "Your order will be shipped" keeps that relationship at arm's length. (Some circumstances call for deliberate avoidance of relationship. In such cases, passive voice comes into its own.)

19. Are you sure you've selected the key selling point for each item?

To do this, you have to go all the way back to the second question. Is your copy pitched directly at the reader?

You may be fascinated by a peculiarity of an item—solid wood buttons, or automatic justification of the right margin, or never add water, or never needs oiling, or one size fits all. But is that what the reader regards as the key selling point? The copywriter's job is to write for the reader, not the writer.

20. Are you positive your catalog has no product descriptions you could have written more vividly if you'd had more time or more information?

If you dismiss the question with "*Every* catalog has this problem with some items," go to the foot of the class. If you say, "Yes, but . . ." then okay, you have another chance: your next catalog. Not enough time? Your problem to solve. Not enough information? That's your problem, too. Get the time and get the information. Sluggish indolence is for others, not the creative department.

And that's the current list. But please, don't stop here. Make up your own list, based on the deficiencies your steely, unflinching eye discovers in the copy you and your associates are grinding out.

Catalog copy, with its impossible deadlines, impossible space limitations, unlimited on-line competition, and impossible demands on the writer's prior product knowledge, is a challenge unlike any other facet of professional copywriting. Facing and occasionally conquering that challenge is the most exhilarating aspect of an exhilarating job—*professional* catalog copywriting.

Appendix B

Compendium: The Rules This Book Has Explained

The Rule of Absolute Communication Connection:

> Simplifying the description won't alienate those who have the same background you do; showing off your product knowledge with terminology and "Level II" description positively does alienate those who don't have the same background you do.

The Law of Absolute Confusion:

> Buying interest decreases in exact ratio to an increase in confusion.

The Anti-B.S. Procedure:

> It's more logical to throw selling facts at the reader than to mask lack of facts in lavish production.

The Benefit-Benefit-Benefit Principle:

> 1. Make a statement specifying superiority over others.
> 2. Relate that superiority to your target readers.

3. Tell target readers how that superiority will bring dramatic improvement to their lives, careers, businesses, or images.

The Incredible Shrinking Universe Rule:

✐ Testing expands the universe of buyers. Inflexible repeats shrink the universe of buyers.

The Boilerplate Avoidance Proposition:

✐ The possibility of depersonalized, interchangeable, nondescriptive copy decreases in exact ratio to an increase of usable fact presented to the writer.

The Catalog Copywriter's First Charge:

✐ The purpose of catalog copy is to sell the item you're describing. *Every* other facet of creative copywriting is subordinate to this, except maybe the Clarity Commandment, without which copy isn't copy.

The Clarity Commandment:

✐ In force-communication, clarity is paramount. Don't let any other component of the communication mix interfere with it.

The Law of Competitive Selectivity:

✐ Select only the vulnerable targets, and attack.

The Deception Perception:

✐ When a reader penetrates a statement whose intention is to mislead, getting an order drops to a likelihood of near zero or less.

The Rule of Diminishing Enthusiasm:

✐ Reader enthusiasm is geared to writer enthusiasm.

Two exceptions to the Rule of Diminishing Enthusiasm:

1. When the catalog wants to project a stratospheric upper-crust image, bubbling enthusiasm parallels putting whipped cream atop a flute of Dom Perignon.
2. When a catalog has a hot list of closeout items, heavy enthusiasm is suspect because heavy salesmanship becomes overkill.

The Rule of Effective Communication:

✏ The target reader's comfort is the paramount consideration in word choice.

The Evidential Superiority Principle:

✏ Declaration isn't as convincing as evidence.

The Imperative Exception Rule:

✏ When the desired action implies work, or difficulty, or the need for capabilities the reader may not possess, an imperative can cause unease.

The Five-Word Nail Admonition:

✏ Catalog copy nails readers within the first five words or loses them forever.

The Top-End Catalog Five-Word Nail Exemption:

✏ The top-end catalog, which may allocate a whole page to one item, is exempt from the Five-Word Nail Admonition. The reader knows from its *format* this isn't a direct, condensed description.

The Rule of Implied Importance:

✏ Importance should relate to the state of mind of the reader, not the writer.

The Rule of Importance Determination:

✏ If you claim importance, prove it.

The Rule of Information Saturation:

✏ An information glut can lead the writer to play up details the catalog reader regards as trivial . . . and drop out details the reader needs to form a buying decision.

The "Its-It's" Law:

✏ Never say anything positive about copy which misuses the words *its* and *it's*.

The Live Encomium Rule:

✏ A generic description becomes dead puffery unless ongoing copy justifies it.

The Rule of Preestablished Attitude:

✏ A product is what it is, plus what the buyer thinks it is.

The Negative Rule of Partial Disclosure:

✏ The reader resents an unexplained variation from the anticipated description.

The Puffery-Defeat Inevitability:

✏ No amount of puffery or self-applause can sell as effectively as a listing of specific benefits.

The Seller-Sellee Equivocation Equation:

✏ The seller's concern = what it is.
The sellee's concern = what it will do for me.

The Seven Basic Reactions of Catalog Recipients

1. disgust
2. annoyance
3. neutrality
4. faint interest
5. moderate interest
6. strong interest
7. rapport

The Rule of Spartan Avoidance:

⇨ When illustrations don't clarify the difference between similar items, copy must clarify the difference between similar items.

The Specifics Superiority Principle:

⇨ Specifics sell; generalities don't sell.

The First Rule of Weaseling:

⇨ An effective weaseled claim is written so the reader slides past the weasel without realizing it.

The First Rule of Website Copy

⇨ Stop surfers in their tracks.

The Web Exploitation Rule:

⇨ Make a deal. Make visitors feel rewarded for having tapped and clicked and paid for the time.

The Law of Web Romance:

⇨ The smart website says to a visitor: "You love me . . . and this is why."

The Whose Message Is It Anyway? Rule:

✏️ Your message should operate within the experiential background of the message recipient, not within your own experiential background.

The Rule of Word Re-Use:

✏️ If you have to re-use a word, emphasize the key word before its second use to show the reader the repeat is intentional.

The Yell-Out-Bargain Rule:

✏️ When you're shouting "Bargain!" play up price. The very act of shouting implies a price lower than competitors charge, even when it may not be true.